.

THEATRE
IN THE FACE
OF WAR

PIOTR
HORBATOWSKI

THEATRE
IN THE FACE
OF WAR

POLISH-UKRAINIAN
THEATRICAL TIES
AFTER THE RUSSIAN
INVASION IN 2014

JAGIELLONIAN
UNIVERSITY PRESS

REVIEW
Prof. Paul Allain, University of Kent

COVER DESIGN
Marta Jaszczuk

On the cover: Chad Nagle, The Donetsk Regional Russian Theater of Drama

The publication has been supported by a grant from the Faculty of Polish Studies under the Strategic Programme Excellence Initiative at Jagiellonian University.

Niniejsza publikacja została sfinansowana ze środków Wydziału Polonistyki w ramach Programu Strategicznego Inicjatywa Doskonałości w Uniwersytecie Jagiellońskim.

ISBN 978-83-233-5474-1 (print)
ISBN 978-83-233-7646-0 (PDF)
ISBN 978-83-233-7647-7 (epub)

JAGIELLONIAN
UNIVERSITY
PRESS

www.wuj.pl

Jagiellonian University Press
Editorial Offices: Michałowskiego 9/2, 31-126 Kraków, Poland
Phone: +48 12 663 23 80
Distribution: Phone: +48 12 631 01 97
Cell Phone: +48 506 006 674
Bank: PEKAO SA, IBAN PL 80 1240 4722 1111 0000 4856 3325

TABLE OF CONTENTS

INTRODUCTION

This book aims to commemorate and honour the people and events in Polish and Ukrainian theatre during a time when human solidarity is especially crucial and should rise above nationalistic biases, historical resentments or political interests. For Polish and Ukrainian theatre creators, the year 2014 and the beginning of the Russian military intervention in Ukraine marked a unique period in which very distant theatrical poetics and traditions, as well as artists who were not creatively or socially connected, began to work together. They started to discover each other and their theatre in the face of an enemy that was, for some, a real and present threat in their country, and for others, a potential danger.

The year 2014 will also serve as the foundation for the discussions in this monograph. The choice of 2023 as the closing date is not because a specific phase has ended. The war is ongoing, and the stance of Polish and Ukrainian theatre towards the war and their cooperation are variable and dynamic, with new performances and initiatives emerging. Nonetheless, it is important to document these events now rather than wait for the war to end. There is a pressing need to record the human emotions, fears, courage, solidarity and decency that have emerged during this transformative time.

The ambition of this book is to present artistic activities within a broader social and political context, which significantly influenced the shape of Polish-Ukrainian theatrical cooperation. It is important to remember that the war led to a rising number of refugees from Ukraine after 2014 (not only theatre professionals, who constitute, as expected, a small minority) arriving in or seeking refuge in our country. On one hand, these refugees were part of the European migration crisis, which also, and perhaps primarily, involved people from the Middle East and African countries. On the other hand, they faced the local situation and the Polish government's migration policies. It is worth noting that after 2015, the Polish government held extremely anti-refugee views. This context will be outlined at the beginning of the book. Attention will also be given to how prepared Polish theatre was for subsequent waves of refugees and whether it had developed mechanisms for integrating migrants into its life. This context seems necessary for a better and fuller understanding of the phenomenon of Polish and Ukrainian creators' collaboration in the face of war.

I. THE NONEXISTENT THREAT – POLAND IN THE CONTEXT OF THE EUROPEAN MIGRATION CRISIS

In Poland challenges linked to a large influx of refugees arose significantly later than in other European countries. These challenges didn't involve refugees from the Middle East and Africa, but rather stemmed from war refugees from Ukraine after the full-scale Russian invasion in February 2024. However, this situation didn't lead to significant social problems, largely because these individuals adapted easily to life in Poland.

To a large extent Poland was spared from the impact of the migration crisis that peaked in 2015–2016, and which was caused by uncontrolled migration to Europe due to conflicts, persecution and extreme poverty mainly in the Middle East and Africa. Despite being ethnically monolithic since 1945 and protected from external influences during the communist era, Poland was not a major destination for migration after the political transformation in 1989, leading to the absence of significant issues related to refugee matters. Before 2014, when a gradual influx of people from Ukraine to Poland started, individuals from other nationalities and ethnic groups made up only 1 to 3% of the population, with just 0.2% having non-Polish citizenship (GUS, 2011). The estimated number of Muslims was around 5,000, many of whom had long settled in the country, and their presence did not generally cause social unrest. The overall positive attitude of Poles toward foreigners was rooted in the communist era when Western countries supported Poles and the anti-communist opposition, creating widespread sympathy for foreign countries and citizens. The critical sentiment was primarily directed towards Russians, seen as representatives of an oppressive regime. After 1989, especially following terrorist attacks by extremist groups from Muslim countries, attitudes toward refugees became more ambivalent, particularly towards those from different cultural backgrounds. Religion played a significant role in this shift, with over 90% of the Polish population identifying as Catholics, leading to a wary view of newcomers practising a different faith.

After Poland joined the European Union in 2004, there was a shift in the process of Poles becoming more open to those with different cultural and religious backgrounds. Surveys conducted around that time revealed that when asked if they would invite someone of a different skin colour and religion to their home for dinner, a positive response was given by as many as 89% of respondents (CBOS, 2014). Data from before the migration crisis suggests that Poles' views on immigrants were, on the European scale, at least moderately positive. This positive attitude towards migrants was significantly influenced by the fact that around this time several million Poles, benefiting from European Union rights, had migrated to various EU countries in search of employment and improved living conditions.

The 2015 refugee crisis brought challenging relocation tasks for the European Union, primarily from regions in Greece and Italy. The liberal coalition led by Civic Platform (Platforma Obywatelska), governing Poland at the time, agreed to accept nearly 5,000 refugees. Despite sparking heated political discussions, 72% of Poles supported the project, expressing their willingness to welcome refugees from conflict-affected countries, while only 21% opposed. However, 2015 became a turning point for Poland with the victory of the ultra-right, nationalist Law and Justice (Prawo i Sprawiedliwość) party. This resulted in adverse changes affecting civil rights, relations with the European Union and the stance on refugees. The ruling camp instrumentalised refugee issues for propaganda and political purposes, particularly evident during election campaigns. Fear management strategies and the creation of a false image portraying refugees as a threat to Polish culture and citizens' safety were cynically exploited. An explicit example was Law and Justice leader Jarosław Kaczyński's statement at an election rally, citing various dangers in Europe, including diseases (such as cholera and dysentery) supposedly brought by refugees, alongside various types of parasites and protozoa:

> These are issues related to various dangers in this sphere. There are already symptoms of the appearance of very dangerous and long-unseen diseases in Europe: cholera in the Greek islands, dysentery in Vienna, various parasites, protozoa, which are not harmful in the bodies of these people, but can be dangerous here (sk, mc, 2015).

The new Prime Minister, Beata Szydło, swiftly rejected the previously accepted relocation law, closing Poland to refugees from that region. The negative campaign, backed by subservient public media controlled by the ruling party, led to a radical shift in societal attitudes. By February 2016, only 39% of Poles declared their willingness to help refugees, while 57% believed that they should not be accepted at all (Wiśniewski et al., 2016).

The narrative of Polish right-wing politicians aligned with similar trends in some other European Union countries. In those places, a fundamental human right was challenged – the freedom to choose where one wants to live:

> Our new era of borders and hyper-legal immigration and deportation superstructures has criminalised one of the most basic human yearnings, one of the most basic ways in which human beings complete themselves, one of the most basic worlds open, eyes open, and hearts open. We are living in a period of shame in which human beings are referred to as 'aliens' and deportations are discussed as 'removals', as if a person is a piece of furniture or a can of garbage. This the humanisation of nomads, travellers, searchers who are equipped with the courage and tenacity to leave everything that is comfortable behind and to venture against all odds into the unknown looking for change and willing to sacrifice everything for it – the dehumanisation of the very flower of humanity demeans the species. It lowers all of our sights, blunts and tempers the courage of all of us, and shrinks generosity into a sad space of selfishness, fear, and mistrust (Cox, 2014, p. IX).

Having said that, refugee issues were not a significant societal problem in Poland until 2021. Migrants from the Middle East and Africa were mostly there legally, often holding work visas and employed by various corporations, integrating relatively well into their new surroundings. However, in the summer of 2021, Poland faced its first major crisis, a result of intentional actions by Belarusian President Alexander Lukashenko, likely orchestrated by Russia. He supported the illegal cross-border smuggling of migrants into Lithuania, Latvia and Poland. Hundreds, later thousands, of unsuspecting refugees from Iraq, Afghanistan and other countries in the Middle East and Africa, enticed by the promise of easy entry into the European Union, found themselves in a deadly trap. Belarusian military and special services unlawfully (and often violently) moved refugee groups beyond the Belarusian border, where they would fall into the hands of Polish border guards who didn't always apply the procedures afforded to illegal refugees under global humanitarian conventions. Instead, what was often used was the method of 'pushing back' these individuals beyond Poland's border. Belarusian authorities would detain them, only to throw them back onto the Polish side under the cover of night. The refugees were trapped, spending weeks, then months, camping in the forests between Belarus and Poland. Among them were many women and children. Initially, they could count on medical assistance, food and warm clothing provided by volunteers. The actions of the border guards triggered protests from independent media and cultural institutions, including theatres, which aimed to expose abuses and convince the authorities to find a humanitarian solution to the problem. In response, the government declared a state of emergency in border regions, enforcing hefty fines and, in some cases, arrests for breaching a protective zone extending several kilometres along the border. This way, the public had no choice but to depend exclusively on untrustworthy reports from media supportive of the government, and the refugees were left without any support. The number of people who died from exhaustion and exposure during that time remains unknown.

The anti-refugee campaign intensified again during the electoral campaign for the Polish Parliament in October 2023. Previously, the Polish government, along with Hungary, was the only one to vote against the EU solidarity pact on refugee relocation. Subsequently, propagandistic media consistently presented drastic scenes of destruction and crimes allegedly committed by refugees in various Western European countries. Seeking to legitimise their methods and hoping for additional votes, parliamentary elections were combined with a referendum, where two out of four questions specifically concerned refugees. Interestingly, these questions were formulated in a highly biassed and aggressive manner towards the European Union. One of these questions read: 'Do you support the admission of thousands of illegal immigrants from the Middle East and Africa, in accordance with the forced relocation mechanism imposed by European bureaucracy?', while the second question was: 'Do you support the removal of the barrier on the border between the Republic of Poland and the Republic of Belarus?' (DS, 2023).

The negative stance of Polish society toward the government's methods at the Belarusian border may be indicated by the fact that, despite over a 70% turnout in parliamentary elections, only 40% obtained referendum ballots, rendering the referendum invalid. It is possible that the inhumane approach of the ruling party towards refugees from the Belarusian border contributed, to some extent, to the Law and Justice party losing the elections and having to relinquish power in October 2023 after eight years of governance.

In Poland the situation of migrants from Ukraine looks completely differently, however. Even before the 2014 conflict with Russia, many Ukrainians had migrated to Poland, primarily for employment opportunities. Since the political transformation in 1989, Ukrainians have consistently formed the largest group of foreign nationals in Poland, coming for both temporary and permanent stays, numbering in the hundreds of thousands. The outbreak of the war and Russia's annexation of Crimea notably amplified the influx of Ukrainian citizens, driven not only by economic factors but also, even more importantly, by political considerations. By the close of 2015, Poland was home to over 1.2 million Ukrainians. The full-scale Russian invasion in February 2022 triggered a substantial increase in Ukrainian arrivals. Since then, over 12 million individuals have crossed into Poland, with 10.5 million opting to continue to other EU countries or return to Ukraine. As of July 2023, it is estimated that approximately 1.5 million Ukrainians are residing in Poland, comprising over 80% of all foreign nationals in the country.

In practice, one might assume that it is indeed migrants from Ukraine that pose a real challenge for Poland, involving all the issues associated with hosting refugees on a very large scale. However, this is not the case, and it is not possible to compare this situation with the refugee crisis in other European Union countries. Above all, Ukrainian migrants in Poland exhibit high adaptability in their new country. A significant portion of them has been able to find employment and legal work in Poland. Ukrainians are also perceived quite favourably, at worst neutrally, by Poles. If in the 1990s Poles viewed Ukrainians mainly as individuals selling goods in street markets, today cases of Ukrainian companies, such as construction firms, effectively competing with Polish counterparts, are not uncommon, not only in terms of prices but also in the quality of work performed. Particularly visible are young individuals who have opted to pursue studies in Poland. After 2014, during a period of significant recruitment challenges for Polish universities, the influx of Ukrainian students saved many higher education programmes from being closed. The perception of Ukrainians' national distinctiveness has also changed among Poles. In the 1990s, they were quite commonly referred to as 'Ruski', which, even during the communist era, was a pejorative term for Russians. This stemmed from Poles' lack of knowledge about Ukrainians' and Ukraine's cultural and national distinctiveness and categorising them instead as within the sphere of Russian influence. However, awareness gradually grew, and after 2022, there is no longer any doubt about Ukraine's national and cultural distinctiveness, perceived as a nation that, like the Poles, has been grappling with the same adversary, Russia, for centuries. The presence of migrants from Ukraine generated notably fewer controversies in Poland compared to refugees from the Middle East and Africa. Research conducted before 2015 showed that over 80% of Poles had no issue working with or having Ukrainian neighbours. During this time, there was a relatively positive perception of Ukrainians in Poland. This is despite the fact that, especially among the older borderland population and within nationalist circles, memories of the complicated and bloody events from the past of both nations, were meticulously maintained, often translating into strong hostility towards Ukrainians and Ukraine. However, these negative sentiments were not widespread. The relatively favourable atmosphere related to Ukrainian citizens in Poland was also tied to religious considerations, as in a predominantly Catholic country fellow Christians were not seen as culturally alien. Notably, among European Union countries, only Greece places higher importance on the religious faith of foreigners settling for an extended stay. The skin colour of migrants is also a significant criterion in these considerations, with Poland ranking fourth in the European Union based on such criteria. Linguistic proximity undoubtedly aids individuals from Ukraine in the assimilation process, too. Ukrainian, part of the common Slavic language family along with Polish, is similar enough to facilitate relatively easy communication with Poles. After a brief learning period, newcomers can express themselves quite fluently in the language.

In addition, the presence of migrants from Ukraine in Poland was marked by notably fewer political tensions. With the exception of the highly nationalist Confederation party, all other political parties, including Law and Justice, regard Ukraine's membership in the European Union and NATO as a priority in Polish foreign policy. This perspective has been prevalent since Ukraine gained independence in 1991. In 2013, when the pro-Russian Prime Minister of Ukraine, Viktor Yanukovych, influenced by Russian authorities, withdrew from the Association Agreement between Ukraine and the European Union, sparking widespread protests and clashes between Ukrainian society and pro-Russian authorities, the Ukrainian Revolution of Dignity garnered support from all Polish political parties in parliament. Leaders from nearly all Polish political parties, including the former president and representative of left-wing forces, Aleksander Kwaśniewski, the prime minister of the liberal government at that time, Donald Tusk, and also Jarosław Kaczyński, the leader of Law and Justice, appeared on Kyiv's central Independence Square, known as Maidan, the focal point of protests and the site of violent clashes between the population and the police and military. The last of the aforementioned politicians even conveyed significant assurances to the protesters, stating that his party would steadfastly pursue policies aimed at Ukraine swiftly becoming a full member of the European Union.

The initiation of the Russo-Ukrainian war, the occupation of Donbas and the subsequent annexation of Crimea were all met with unanimous criticism and expressions of solidarity from Polish politicians. However, after coming to power in 2015, Law and Justice initiated a form of a political game. While the right-wing nationalist government continued to diplomatically and internationally support Ukraine (and condemned Russian aggression), at home it made attempts to consolidate the most radical and nationalist electorate. To that effect, it emphasised events from the history of Polish-Ukrainian relations where the Ukrainian side was deemed responsible for the deaths of

Poles, for example. Before February 2022, Polish-Ukrainian relations could therefore be considered correct but still falling short of complete trust.

The day of February 24th, 2022, was a profound shock for Poland and its people, akin to that experienced by the entire Europe and the democratic world. The unexpected scale of the Russian invasion was particularly startling for Poland, given its proximity just beyond the eastern border. Almost immediately after the outbreak of war, Poles witnessed refugees, mainly women and children, crossing the state border *en masse*. The depth of support and empathy towards the Ukrainian people appeared to surprise even the Poles themselves. It's noteworthy that, before the government could formalise support for refugees, the civilian population and tens of thousands of volunteers organised various forms of assistance, offering their homes to those arriving. Direct accounts suggest that refugees from Ukraine received kindness and voluntary aid even from individuals who had been critical of Ukrainians before. This included the older generation, which remembered the events of 1943 and the Ukrainian pogroms against Poles in Volhynia.

In this situation Polish politicians across nearly all political groups, including the Law and Justice government, offered clear support to Ukraine. This support was evident through arms shipments to Ukraine, visits by high-ranking officials to Kyiv, Poland's active engagement in Ukrainian matters at various international forums and spontaneous expressions of sympathy between the presidents of both countries. As far as the political groups that entered the Polish parliament in October 2023, the only deviation from the aforementioned stance came from the nationalists, specifically the Confederation party. Voices from this party called for halting aid to Ukraine and expressed concerns about the alleged and ongoing process of Ukrainianisation in Poland. While not dominant, the support gained by this party in the recent elections – 7.2% of the votes – indicates that it is not entirely negligible.

The situation underwent some changes just before the October 2023 parliamentary elections in Poland. Once again, the ruling Law and Justice party, prioritising its own political calculations over national interests, a sense of solidarity and decency, chose to shift its stance toward Ukraine. In an effort to secure votes from the nationalist electorate, the party significantly altered its tone, voting against EU resolutions that would have facilitated Ukraine's grain imports to Poland. This shift contributed to a substantial cooling of Polish-Ukrainian relations. The defeat of Law and Justice in the elections, and the democratic opposition's assumption of power, offer hope for a reversal of this situation.

At the time of writing this text, it has been 2 years since the outbreak of the war in February 2022. In Poland, there is a noticeable sense of 'war fatigue' and weariness concerning the issue of refugees from Ukraine. Questions are being raised about whether state support for this group in various aspects of their lives in Poland should continue. Despite this, the attitude of Poles toward Ukrainians residing in Poland remains generally favourable. Two weeks after the invasion, 94% of the population strongly supported the necessity of receiving and assisting refugees from Ukraine. A year later, in March 2023, this figure remained at 83%, and by July of the same year, it had decreased to 76%. For comparison, only 33% of respondents expressed positive opinions about the need to support refugees from the Middle East and Africa who found themselves on the Belarusian-Polish border during the same period.

II. POLISH THEATRE'S STANCE ON MIGRATION ISSUES BEFORE 2022

⌒

Very limited was the extent to which the Polish theatre addressed migrant issues, let alone created mechanisms to involve migrants in artistic activities. Instead, it maintained a monoethnic and linguistically uniform character, primarily because migratory problems, which at the time posed significant challenges to Western European societies, were essentially absent in Poland. Several institutions established to carry out artistic work with migrants and refugees who arrived in Poland were not the result of state-supported, coordinated, far-reaching programmes, but rather individual projects initiated by individuals or theatre institutions. Political factors and societal resistance to the far-right, nationalist government's anti-refugee, xenophobic policies had a significant influence on the emergence of such initiatives.

In Western European countries, addressing migration issues has long been a central social, political, and ethical task for theatres. However, in Poland, this topic largely remained on the outskirts of mainstream theatrical discussions (Prykowska-Michalak, Szymańska, 2020, p. 87). This was primarily due to the marginal nature of migration itself. What's more, post-1989, during the political, social, and cultural transformation, Polish theatre focused on themes present on Western stages, while also navigating the contemporary and tumultuous changes within its own country. It was predominantly a monoethnic and monolingual theatre, with ensembles comprising mainly Poles in artistic and technical roles. Even after 2014, as the numbers of migrants and war refugees from Ukraine and Belarus increased in Poland, there were no coordinated government or local initiatives recognising the need to support these groups and engage in integrative actions through theatre. Occasionally, artistic institutions showed interest in grassroots initiatives, but they couldn't rely on consistent support from local or nationwide programmes. For example, in Germany,

> the massive influx of refugees posed a significant social challenge. One response was adopting a policy of cultural participation involving local authorities, cultural institutions, and independent artists. Artistic activism promoted practices of cultural participation. Cities like Dresden, Göttingen, Hamburg, Mülheim, Berlin, and Munich implemented diverse artistic and sociocultural projects, whether associative or institutional, to bridge people from different backgrounds and encourage interaction through art and cultural practices for newcomers (Martiniello, 2019, p. 3).

In Poland artistic projects involving collaboration with migrant and refugee communities were rare to say the least and emerged from the enthusiasm and determination of individuals. Often, during artistic internships or private trips abroad, these individuals familiarised themselves with European theatres addressing socio-political issues and integration processes for migrants and refugees, attempting to implement similar solutions in Poland. It's crucial to note that these projects remained on the fringes of the artistic mainstream. Notably, such initiatives were usually found on independent stages rather than in large, state-funded institutional theatres. These stages were dedicated to realising non-conventional, progressive artistic projects strongly linked to the social mission of theatre. One noteworthy example is the Strefa WolnoSłowa (Free Word Zone), operating for over a decade at the Teatr Powszechny (Public Theatre) in Warsaw.

Everyday work – Strefa WolnoSłowa (Free Word Zone)

The individual who initially brought attention to the needs of migrants in Poland was Alicja Borkowska, a director and cultural animator specialising in creative work with multicultural groups. Her education at the Department of Theatre Studies at the Academy of Theatre in Warsaw provided her with both theoretical and practical knowledge related to artistic pursuits. A crucial element of her future theatrical ventures was Borkowska's involvement in the Erasmus programme that enabled her to undertake the Data Management for Data Science Laboratory programme at the University of Bologna. During her time in Italy, she also initiated collaboration with Teatro dell'Argine, an urban ensemble based in the small town of San Lazzaro near Bologna, dedicated to artistic work within the local community, including migrants and refugees. Additionally, she undertook a postgraduate course in multicultural event management organised by ATER Formazione and pursued a master's degree in Ethno-Systemic-Narrative in Rome. Borkowska reiterates that it was in Italy where she witnessed 'theatre being conceptualised as a tool for change, dialogue, and the convergence of individuals with diverse backgrounds, education, and origins' (Borkowska, 2020).

She brought to Poland extensive knowledge of artistic strategies employed by leading teams working with migrants across various European countries. She was also aware that she would be a pioneer in the country, in which, at least as of 2012, none of the artistic institutions had implemented programmes focused on and/or in collaboration with the migrant community. In the same year, she established the Strefa WolnoSłowa Foundation in Warsaw. The name was crafted through a linguistic play, associating its sound with the Polish version of 'free-trade zone', replacing 'trade' with 'word'; literally, it translates to 'free-word zone'. This name, while evoking cross-border movements, emphasises freedom of speech, the democratic nature of the association, and its independence in actions and judgments. The Strefa programme placed a strong emphasis on a plan for consistent, daily engagement with migrant communities, highlighting the extensive scope of the institution's activities:

[Strefa WolnoSłowa – P.H.] is an initiative comprising individuals involved in theatre, literature, dance, music, and various cultural and artistic activities. Our goal is to organise artistic, cultural, and educational activities that focus on intercultural and intergenerational dialogue. By involving male and female refugees and migrants residing in Poland, we conduct actions at the intersection of art and social intervention, addressing current issues in the country, Europe, and the world. We provide support to individuals who are excluded or at risk of marginalisation. Our projects aim to engage refugees and migrants in creative activities, promote multicultural education, unveil and narrate refugee stories, and enhance social awareness of migration, refugee issues, human rights, and their violations. In the fight against exclusion, Strefa WolnoSłowa is highly attuned to all forms of discrimination and violence, including verbal, not only based on cultural and religious backgrounds but also on sexual orientation, gender, and social origin. Inspired by and collaborating on numerous projects with Teatr Powszechny and Gorki Theatre in Berlin, Strefa is committed not only to addressing the challenges faced by migrants and local communities but also to tackling pressing global issues related to ecology, minority rights, feminism, and violations of democratic principles and civil rights (Strefa WolnoSłowa's Manifesto, 2023).

Close to Strefa's philosophy are also the views formulated by Milo Rau in the Manifesto of NTGent. One of the key principles of operation is not to limit oneself to merely portraying the world as it is but to strive to change it: 'One: It's not just about portraying the world anymore. It's about changing it. The aim is not to depict the real, but to make the representation itself real' (The Ghent Manifesto, 2018). As a result, projects of Strefa WolnoSłowa often extend beyond the theatre building. Contact with the local community, residents of Warsaw not associated with Strefa and its activities, is essential. On one hand, this broadens the possibilities for mutual communication between these groups. It enables migrants to develop visibility strategies, to be noticeable (Damery, Mescoli, 2019, pp. 46–62). This gained particular significance after the rise to power in Poland after 2015 of a nationalist authority that frightened society with migrants and refugees. The strategy of visibility, showing oneself in creative action, was meant to illustrate that these 'foreigners', deemed a threat by the authorities, are neither strangers nor a cause for fear and concern. In turn, by venturing into society within the framework of implemented projects, operating in various urban spaces, participants find it easier to assimilate into a new environment: 'art offers opportunities for migrants to actively participate in the socio-cultural and political environment in the host country and to claim various forms of official and unofficial belonging and local citizenship' (Martiniello, 2019, p. 2). Strefa WolnoSłowa also extended its projects beyond the borders of Poland. In this regard, it was not as radical as Milo Rau, who prepared or performed at least one of his productions each season in a conflict zone or war zone (The Ghent Manifesto, 2018). Nevertheless, Strefa conducted theatre-reportage workshops in Iran, Uruguay, and Palestine. Moreover, it implemented numerous international artistic-research initiatives such as *The City Ghettos of Today*, *Migrating Theatre*, *The History Atlas Under Construction*, or *Beyond Theatre*, collaborating with over 20 theatres and cultural institutions and numerous artists in dozens of countries worldwide, including Italy, Belgium, France, Germany, Greece, Sweden, Albania, Egypt, India, Iran and Palestine.

The team's work organisation, akin to NTGent and other theatres collaborating with migrants, is rooted in fully democratic and non-hierarchical principles. Authorship of artistic and project activities is shared among all involved individuals, including both professionals and amateurs. In numerous projects, the participants' stories, encompassing their fears, traumas, experiences from their home country, challenges of the journey, and their new life, serve as the starting point. This fundamental aspect positions them as the central figures in all ensuing endeavours.

A fundamental aspect of Strefa's initiatives is the belief that the main objective of transcultural projects should not be solely the artistic value of the final outcome but rather the creative process and collaborative efforts that foster changes in attitudes, behaviours, and the self-discovery of individuals involved in these activities. In this context, the concept of artistic work shares similarities with practices such as 'Community dance' organised in England or the principles of Theater der Migranten in Berlin (Prykowska-Michalak, Szymańska, 2020, pp. 95–96).

The range of activities undertaken by Strefa WolnoSłowa, supported by modest city grants and acquired funds, is extensive. The theatrical endeavours encompass performances, performative actions, festivals, and creative workshops. A pivotal year for Strefa was 2015, marked by its collaboration with Warsaw's Teatr Powszechny. The organisation relocated its headquarters to spaces in and around the theatre intentionally. Teatr Powszechny, named after Zygmunt Hübner, and, since 2014, led by Paweł Łysak, stands out as one of the more, if not the most, progressive institutional urban theatres in Poland. Notable productions, labelled scandalous by nationalist-Catholic circles and the Law and Justice government, unfolded here, including *Klątwa* (*The Curse*) based on Stanisław Wyspiański's work and directed by Oliver Frljić. The guiding motto of the institution is *Teatr, który się wtrąca* (*Theatre that gets in the way*), signifying its active and even forthright engagement in social, political and local affairs. Additionally, Teatr Powszechny made history in 2018 by becoming the first institutional theatre in Poland to employ an actor from outside Europe, namely Mamadou Góo Bâ from Senegal. His journey began in Senegal, continued with a move to France as a member of the international artistic group LaFabriks Jean Michel Bruyère, and eventually led him to Teatr Powszechny from Strefa WolnoSłowa, where he commenced collaboration upon arriving in Poland.

In collaboration with Teatr Powszechny Strefa undertakes a variety of extratheatrical initiatives. One notable project is the *Ogród Powszechny* (*Community Garden*), situated in close proximity to the theatre, serving as a hub for meetings, discussions, debates, workshops, and concerts. The Garden caters to both migrants and the local community, providing a space like the *Stół Powszechny* (*Community/Communal Table*), a café that serves as an open platform for intercultural creative activities, conversations and storytelling – facilitated over coffee and through art. Regular events include book club meetings, performative readings, concerts featuring migrant musicians, film screenings, and workshops for children. Simultaneously, the Open Institute targets creators, cultural animators, social activists and individuals with diverse cultural backgrounds. It offers workshops, training and collaborative artistic endeavours, with a primary focus on creative methodologies tailored to culturally and nationally diverse communities, particularly migrant and refugee groups. As described by the project initiators, the core objective is to use art as an experience that erases divisions between 'us' and 'them' where foreign communities are concerned, and fosters a shared social identity. An innovative programme within the institute is the 'Międzypokoleniowy Chór Ruchowy' (Intergenerational Movement Choir), designed for individuals spanning a wide age range, bringing different generations together through movement, gymnastics, choreography and dance. Programmes are developed based on movement tasks and choreographic exercises refined during a several-month workshop, culminating in an open performance for the public. Overseeing the musical aspects of all Strefa's activities is its in-house musical ensemble, featuring both migrant and Polish musicians, under the leadership of saxophonist, composer and educator Ray Dickaty.

The partnership with Teatr Powszechny not only allowed Strefa to stage performances with migrant amateurs but also facilitated collaborations with professional artists. This collaboration gave rise to new extra theatrical programmes: the School of Social Dramaturgs and Social Dramaturgies. The first one provides migrants and the local community with a several-month cycle of creative-training sessions, catering to individuals interested in writing for socially engaged theatre. The project centres around the creation of texts addressing social, racial, local and international issues, drawing inspiration from the real stories of participants in artistic activities and the biographies of those involved in creative processes. The starting point is real stories, interviews, narratives and biographies. Texts developed during the workshops are then published and some are brought to the stage. At the same time, the core concept of Social Dramaturgies is to produce artistic events resulting from the collaborative efforts of artists, including individuals from migrant and refugee communities, and the local community – individuals not professionally connected to the arts, varying in age and cultural background.

The core team at Strefa WolnoSłowa comprises only a few dozen individuals, encompassing directors, cultural animators, workshop and performative training experts, performance producers, cultural promotion specialists, book designers and publishers as well as playwrights. Notably, there is no fixed artistic team, as each project is open to everyone. However, a consistent group of several dozen individuals actively participates in the programmes. Initially, a majority hailed from Ukraine and Belarus, with later additions including migrants from the Middle East, Africa, Vietnam, India and Turkey. Over Strefa's 11-year existence, several hundred foreigners have engaged in its activities, resulting in the realisation of numerous performances and performative projects. A prominent event on Warsaw's landscape is the annual *Refugee Fest*, organised cyclically on June 20th in celebration of World

Refugee Day. The guiding ethos of the festival, which includes performances, performative actions, and workshops, is to facilitate meetings between refugees and permanent residents of Warsaw, fostering the creation of a collective 'safe haven', a city welcoming to all. The festival gained particular significance amidst the refugee crisis at the Polish-Belarusian border. In 2022, the organisers expressed on their Facebook profile:

> The search for safety, asylum, and refuge has become our shared experience in recent months. More intensely than ever before. We shared stories, memories, moments of despair, hope, and small joys. We sought answers and solutions, improvised, and tried to do everything in our power. We learned how to give space, share it, and build together from scratch (Strefa WolnoSłowa's Facebook, 2022).

A notable performative event during the festival was the cycling performance *Bicycle Thieves*, serving as a manifestation of diversity and multicultural poetry. Drawing inspiration from Vittorio De Sica's film of the same name, the performance incorporated choreography, monologues, texts, narratives, stage actions, videos and sounds. The dramaturgy seamlessly blended De Sica's narrative with stories and materials gathered during workshops, the biographies of participants and the narratives of refugees. The performance served as a reflection on Warsaw's identity and its openness to newcomers, addressing themes such as work, its absence and its pursuit, dissent in adapting to overarching rules, a sense of responsibility for one's life and offering support for the experience of alienation.

Performances featuring the direct narratives of migrants and refugees stand out as key elements in Strefa's artistic pursuits. This approach was also employed by Alicja Borkowska, the director of the 2019 production *Uchodź! Kurs uciekania dla początkujących* (*Run! Escaping course for beginners*). The performance was a collaborative effort between migrants associated with Strefa and professional artists from Teatr Powszechny. It offered a somewhat ironic perspective on the shortcomings of Poles – their national megalomania and a reluctance, even fear, of 'aliens'. At the start of the show, one of the Iranian actors would rush onto the stage, provocatively shouting to the audience: *Attention! There are Muslims in the room. There are refugees!*. This referenced official messages from government propaganda encouraging the public to view this group as a mortal threat, without providing any concrete evidence of its existence.

The performance emerged from a multi-year project conducted in Warsaw and Tehran. Artur Pałyga, a prominent Polish playwright and director, crafted the script based on authentic biographies and stories of Polish refugees in Iran during World War II and contemporary Iranian refugees in Poland. These narratives served as a lens to depict the collision of two cultures –

23

the historical Iranian hospitality juxtaposed with the contemporary state and religious oppression in Poland. Set in a private apartment in Warsaw during a celebration commemorating Poland's 100th independence anniversary, the event, organised for Poles by a group of Iranians in Poland, provided a platform to reminisce about wartime experiences, contemplate national identity and religion, celebrate Iranian hospitality extended to 120,000 Polish refugees in Iran in the 1940s and engage in discussions about the meaning and significance of the phenomenon of displacement.

In 2013 Strefa developed another performance using a similar approach. The improvisations of foreigners led to a unique reflection on Polish contemporary life and history, presenting a narrative about social and political events that are significant for Poles. Foreign residents in Poland grappled with the perceptions Poles had about migrants and the stereotypes that had developed towards anyone 'not from here'. The creation of the performance was preceded by multicultural workshops attended by individuals from Ukraine, Belarus, Macedonia, Cuba, Russia, Armenia, and Belgium. The participants' improvisations, combined with stories about their experiences in Poland, were woven together with literary fiction, shaping the essence of the drama. The performance was also influenced by Raymond Carver's collection of short stories, *Cathedral*.

Numerous projects by Strefa addressed not only Polish issues but also delved into refugee problems on a broader European scale. A notable example is the 2015 production *To jest Europa* (*This is Europe*). The creators drew inspiration from South American models of community theatre, shaping the performance as a dinner-theatre experience involving professional performers, amateur actors, and the audience. The central character, Jan Nawazi, an Afghan refugee fleeing from war and an amateur actor, became the focus of a series of interviews conducted by Strefa WolnoSłowa. Forced to leave his country in 2000, Nawazi, helped by people smugglers, embarked on a seven-year odyssey, travelling on foot through mountains, hiding in truck trailers, crossing the sea, and taking up various jobs to fund his journey. Eventually arriving in Europe, he found employment in Bologna, Italy. In this dinner-theatre production, Nawazi's firsthand accounts of refugee experiences interweave with excerpts from Voltaire's *Candide, or Optimism*, providing a theatrical narrative framework.

After 2021, Strefa WolnoSłowa actively participated in humanitarian efforts for refugees stranded at the Polish-Belarusian border. They supported volunteer groups, organised drives for clothing and medicine and engaged in protests and appeals directed at Polish authorities. Additionally, artistic projects were developed. A notable production that won awards at national festivals was the performance-installation *Imperium* (*Empire*). Describing the spectacle, the creators explained that

> *Empire* is a performative installation inspired by the image of the walking for-est from *Macbeth* and the experiences of individuals migrating and assisting at the Polish-Belarusian border. The work draws inspiration from Shakespeare's text and images of the humanitarian crisis at the border to reflect on survival strategies during escape, the role of nature in crises, ways to assist refugees, and how acts of solidarity are criminalised by authorities. Finally, it delves into the question of how much wrongdoing can be tolerated by an unaccountable authority (Website of the 27th International Shakespeare Festival, 2023).

Empire portrays a contemporary situation that unfolds realistically and in-timately close to the audience, yet within a space seemingly untouched by their daily lives. The audience, safe in their roles as citizens of the state and participants in a societal system, of which this situation constitutes an inher-ent part, is confronted with an uncomfortable truth. Reluctantly acknowl-edged, this truth is pushed aside as it's disrupting their so-called comfort zone. Throughout the performance, a narrator guides the audience through the events unfolding on stage. Her identity is somewhat ambiguous, serving as both a caretaker of the forest and someone who hides within it. Viewers navigate between these perspectives, simultaneously immersed in the world of Shakespeare's *Macbeth*. Consequently, the performance weaves a narra-tive about illusory hope, fear, and oppression, combining realistic portrayals and immediate descriptions with metaphor. It prompts contemplation about an individual's position in the web of social connections, particularly in a world facing significant disruptions to fundamental values.

Strefa WolnoSłowa stands as the singular theatre institution in Poland committed to the ongoing, systematic engagement with migrant and refugee communities. Its unique and comprehensive action plan aims at supporting these groups in their integration journey while seeking acknowledgment and acceptance within the local community. Notably, Strefa's base and primary project locations are situated in Praga, a Warsaw district predominantly in-habited by a working-class community. This community is characterised by lower education levels and tends to hold somewhat conservative, less wel-coming views toward outsiders. Despite these initial challenges, the persis-tent efforts of Strefa bore fruit, with participants in its programmes becom-ing increasingly visible within the local community over time. Strefa played a pivotal role in facilitating the mutual integration of migrants and refugees hailing from geographically and culturally distant parts of the world. It is cru-cial to underscore that Strefa, as a practice, generally refrained from making explicit political declarations, placing a primary focus on the social mission embedded in its activities. Another institution contributing to this realm is Scena Prezentacje, also based in Warsaw.

Theatre and politics – Scena Prezentacje and Biennale Warszawa

The rise of the Law and Justice party to power in Poland in 2015 marked a pivotal moment for the country's theatrical landscape. Even during the communist era, a great majority of Polish artists strongly aligned themselves with democratic values, opposing the prevailing authority and championing civil rights and freedom. These principles persisted and remained significant even after the political changes of 1989. Consequently, when the Law and Justice government brought back the way of governing that challenges the principles of the rule of law, artists collectively responded with a resistance, often described as 'cultural resistance'. The latter is a term defined by Polish researcher Jacek Drozda as 'emerging in lieu of revolution and encompassing elements of class struggles, identity formation, and social debates with varying scopes and degrees of influence on reality' (Drozda, 2015, p. 23). Other researchers describe this phenomenon as 'countless, non-heroic acts, more of a moral than political nature' (Bleiker, 2000, p. 178), aimed at 'emancipatory struggle' (Barnard, 2019, p. 119).

In Poland, cultural resistance found expression in the artistic works of creators who criticised the government on both domestic and foreign policy fronts as well as social issues. Their actions aimed to raise awareness about the society manipulated and divided by those in power, including the manipulation surrounding the portrayal of incoming migrants and refugees as a false threat to Poland. Cultural resistance, in this context, became a form of opposition against the methods employed by the right-wing authorities. Unlike the activities of Strefa WolnoSłowa, where the focus was on regular work with migrants and refugees, in this case, political opposition played a more prominent role. In this context,

> pro-refugee art, considered a manifestation of cultural resistance, [was – P.H.] expressed through various media, spanning theatrical performances, squats, the entertainment industry, and the seclusion of prose, each contributing to a distinctly political significance. It [served – P.H.] as an expression of values and attitudes held by minorities and marginalised groups, providing them with

a platform to articulate and communicate counter-discourse (Kuligowski, 2019, p. 51).

The Warsaw-based Scena Prezentacje, particularly through its flagship project, Biennale Warszawa, stood out as a leading advocate for political theatre opposing anti-refugee government policies. In 2017 Paweł Wodziński and Bartosz Frąckowiak took charge of this theatre after four years at the helm of Teatr Polski in Bydgoszcz. Under their leadership, the Bydgoszcz theatre earned a reputation as the most politically conscious theatre in the country, championing contemporary, socially engaged repertoire that amplified the voices of young, uncompromising creators. It was precisely this uncompromising attitude and the desire to create theatre on a European scale that led the authorities of Bydgoszcz, who were expecting a less ambitious and more local approach, to terminate their contract.

In Warsaw, their goal was to implement a somewhat similar programme and entirely reshape the artistic profile of Scena Prezentacje, which had previously focused on light, comedic repertoire. They faced exceptionally challenging conditions, however, as the city allocated them a budget equivalent to only 25% of the average funding received by small municipal theatres. Furthermore, at the time that Wodziński and Frąckowiak took the reins, Scena Prezentacje also lost their theatre building. Faced with these challenges, the directors decided to create an entirely new type of institution – 'a hybrid that wasn't strictly a theatre, museum of modern art, research institution, or activist watchdog organisation. Instead, it encompassed elements of each' (Majmurek, 2017). In their artistic programme, they emphasised:

> We will actively participate in the artistic, discursive-research, and activist domains simultaneously. Our goal is to intersect these three fields by executing specific projects. We aspire to implement genuinely transdisciplinary initiatives, breaking away from strict divisions between theatre and visual arts, as well as artistic practice and research activities. The aim is for a research project to simultaneously inspire a documentary theatre performance (Majmurek, 2017).

Departing from the typical Polish theatre formula, Scena Prezentacje, now Biennale Warszawa, shifted its focus from repertoires and consecutive performances. Instead, it prioritised fostering discussions, bringing people together, and implementing artistic, social, and political projects. The institution invested in ideas and organised residencies for artists from other countries. It operated without a permanent ensemble. The adopted action plan included a two-year period of artistic-research-project work, culminating in a major event summarising the two years of efforts and comprising performances of Scena Prezentacje as well as guest theatres from Poland and abroad, alongside exhibitions, projects and performative actions. Over time, the institution also changed its name from Scena Prezentacje to Biennale Warszawa.

From its inception, the institution has been dedicated to engaging with current social and political events. According to Wodziński, the years leading up to 2017 witnessed

> significant global and Polish events that reshaped both international and domestic landscapes. During this time, real and symbolic violence escalated, and the prevalent political approach shifted towards fear management, finding fertile ground in the European migration policy crisis. The institution's programme was crafted with a keen awareness of these situations, challenges, and phenomena, aiming not only to comment on current events but also to generate alternative visions, project the future, and stimulate imagination. Art, being exceptionally suited to this purpose, became a focal point (Majmurek, 2017).

The programmatic principles emphasised that the cultural activities undertaken by the institution were crucial in constructing a modern, tolerant, and critical society that not only upholds democracy and civil liberties, but also embraces diverse perspectives, religions, sexual orientations, and backgrounds. The issue of migrants was given a prominent focus within Biennale Warszawa. Wodziński aspired not only to curate an appealing artistic programme for this group but also to conduct activities that would integrate migrants into the social fabric of the city and its residents:

> We are particularly interested in the lives of immigrants and refugees in Warsaw. The city is home to a substantial number of Ukrainians, Belarusians, Turks, Vietnamese, and Indians. Yet, we have limited knowledge about their cultural practices. Reportedly, three Ukrainian theatres are operating in Warsaw – yet we have no awareness of the existence of such places. Our goal is to connect with these communities, understand their cultural practices, ways of life, thoughts, and challenges. We want to explore how cultural institutions in Warsaw can address their needs. This extends beyond programming; it involves reshaping institutions to be spaces capable of inclusivity. It requires altering institutional practices and organisational forms, incorporating migrants, and fostering communities of foreigners around the institution. Our vision encompasses an institution with an open nature and a commitment to community development, among other considerations (Majmurek, 2017).

The theatre's interests extended beyond domestic matters, emphasising the importance of a global perspective, especially towards Southern Europe and the Middle East – regions typically overlooked by Polish artistic institutions:

This global focus was driven by political considerations. The Middle East, in particular, stands as a hub for various political conflicts and a wellspring of migration flows towards Europe. Although these migrations might not directly affect Poland, they instil anxiety in a considerable portion of society, influencing right-wing policies. Consequently, it becomes crucial for Poles to possess authentic knowledge about the Middle East, equipping them with tools to understand the ongoing processes in the region (Majmurek, 2017).

Biennale Warszawa's operation came to an unexpected halt after six years, in 2022, when the authorities in Warsaw decided to rename the institution as Warszawskie Obserwatorium Kultury (Warsaw Cultural Observatory). Despite City Hall's assurance that this move didn't imply the institution's closure, there are substantial doubts about its future. Throughout its existence, the institution faced criticism and fierce attacks from the right-wing government and pro-government media. They went so far as to accuse Biennale Warszawa of training street 'troublemakers' in workshops designed to organise subversive demonstrations that posed a threat to the capital's security. The Deputy Minister of Justice expressed his views on Biennale on the radio, questioning 'whether the institution's activities were not simply unlawful, possibly not of a terrorist nature, but at least characterised by actions that violated legal order' (Mrozek, 2021, p. 5).

The impact of Biennale Warszawa is evident in its organisation of 217 events with over 11,000 participants within its first three years. The main event, Biennale, held twice in 2019 and 2022, featured performances, exhibitions, performative and audio-visual activities, along with panel discussions. The 2019 edition, themed *Organise Your Future*, was particularly significant for migration-related matters discussed here. It delved into issues related to new political projects, economic, social, ecological and educational alternatives, structured into four thematic blocks: direct democracy, democratic education, transnational metropolis, and transnational solidarity, with a focus on migration and refugees in the latter two. Among the 14 performances showcased, four addressed these themes. One of them, world-renowned *Orestes in Mosul*, directed by Milo Rau, was presented as a guest performance for the first time in Poland. A notable Polish production was *Refugees* (*Uchodźczynie*) from the Powszechny Theatre in Warsaw, directed by the young, very talented Katarzyna Szyngiera, winner of numerous festival awards. The play featured female refugees from Iraq, Dagestan and Tajikistan, a Chechen socio-political activist and Polish artists. Over several months Szyngiera utilised workshops, discussions and improvisations to encourage migrant women to share their challenging stories, emphasising the central theme of trust within the narratives. Beyond immigration, the focus extended to identifying common ground despite cultural differences. The stories of refugees encompassed fears, anxieties, lived traumas, hopes, dreams and the belief that encounters and dialogue with the 'other' can dismantle walls and prejudices.

At the same time, Katarzyna Kalwat's performative project *Staff Only* aimed to shed light on the societal transformations occurring in Poland due to the increasing influx of economic migrants. The project's creators called for a redefinition of the understanding of national culture, urging a departure from xenophobia and an openness to multicultural influences. This challenge was directed at the outdated 19th-century concept of the nation prevalent during Poland's partition era. The performance primarily delved into the understanding and functioning of national culture within theatrical activities, emphasising the consequences of archaic views, such as the mono-ethnic and monolingual nature of Polish stages and a reluctance to embrace migrant artists. The project raised questions about why theatre in Poland couldn't evolve into a new Tower of Babel. Criticisms centred on the 'glass ceiling' hindering individuals of foreign origin from securing employment in the artistic industry. Artistic institutions faced accusations of hypocrisy, ostensibly championing commitment to social spaces, freedom, and civil rights on one hand, while becoming instruments that reinforce social divisions and exclusion. This interdisciplinary project, combining elements of theatre, performance and lecture, prominently featured artists who were migrants. The final performance was the culmination of months of project activities, encompassing sociological research, analysis, and, ultimately, dedicated theatrical rehearsals.

The multicultural project, culminating in a performance described as a performative lecture titled *The Suits We Own...*, entailed extensive research spanning months to explore the connections between Central-Eastern Europe and Africa and the Middle East. The final performance featured two intertwined narratives. The first one drew from ethnographic interviews conducted in Lebanon in 2018 and 2019, gathering stories of Palestinians and Lebanese who lived in Poland during the 1970s, 80s, and 90s and later chose to return to Lebanon. Their experiences blended memories from Poland's period of political transformation with the Lebanese civil war, offering a comparative view of life in both countries. The second narrative involved archival research conducted in collaboration with journalist and writer Max Cegielski. Visual materials and texts from various Polish and Lebanese newspapers and magazines were incorporated and presented on stage, utilising resources from archives, including those of the Polish Committee of Solidarity with the Peoples of Asia and Africa. The performance revisits the era of socialist globalisation on one hand and brings to light the forgotten contemporary social solidarity that has been obscured behind the scenes of global politics, trade exchanges, and the dominance of national culture.

In addition to staging performances, Biennale Warszawa organised a wide array of events centred around refugee themes, including exhibitions, film screenings, concerts, debates, conferences, lectures, and seminars. A particularly notable exhibition featured the works of foreign artists living in Poland. Through their art, these artists aimed to explore the impact of their stay in Poland on their creativity as well as the challenges and opportunities they faced as assimilating artists seeking to sustain their careers in a new country. The exhibition showcased pieces by several creators who arrived in Poland by chance, through personal events, or for political reasons, such as the migrations from Vietnam in the 1990s or recent escapes from the war in Ukraine and repression in Belarus. These artists spanned different generations and engaged with art institutions in diverse ways. However, they shared a common experience of relative invisibility and limited interest in their work from mainstream Polish cultural institutions, largely due to the absence of supportive structures. The exhibition, complemented by an accompanying research project, aimed to bring attention to this situation, challenge the self-satisfaction of Poles and Polish cultural institutions in claiming openness to multiculturalism and raise awareness about the unequal opportunities afforded to artists.

The artistic project *Immigrant, take a vote!* addressed the problem of unequal opportunities and exclusion by shedding light on Poland's reliance on outdated, stigmatising categories and processes that divide people into citizens and non-citizens across various social activities. Non-citizens faced significant bureaucratic obstacles and limitations on social rights, impeding their integration and resulting in discrimination and exclusion. Marta Romankiv, the Ukrainian creator of the project and a doctoral student at the Academy of Fine Arts in Gdańsk, directly confronted the exclusion of non-Polish citizens from political participation. Key questions raised were: How is citizenship defined in Poland? Are current democratic forms suitable for today's globalised society? Why do antiquated divisions persist in shaping perceptions of the 'other' amidst ongoing changes? The year-long project culminated in a provocative happening aimed to depict the discriminatory position of an immigrant in the nation-state, which was strategically timed before the first round of presidential elections in Poland. It involved collecting votes from migrants and submitting them to the State Electoral Commission. This marked the first instance where individuals without Polish citizenship but residing in the country 'voted' for president. The action unfolded in six Polish cities: Białystok, Gdańsk, Lublin, Poznań, Szczecin, and Warsaw. The votes, while not valid or counted in the official results, aimed to bring attention to a broader issue beyond the elections themselves.

The closure of Biennale Warszawa significantly limited opportunities for artists from other countries residing in Poland and left a void in advocacy for the rights of migrants and refugees to engage in artistic pursuits.

Other theatre centres engaging with refugee themes in their activities

In other Polish theatre centres, projects addressing migration and refugee themes as well as those involving migrants and refugees, were infrequent and sporadic. These initiatives were often tied to tumultuous events in Poland or other European countries, such as the events in Ukraine in 2014, the peak of the refugee crisis in Europe in 2015–2016 or the protests in Belarus in 2020 and 2021, brutally suppressed by the Lukashenko regime. The decision to engage in long-term collaborations with foreign nationals residing in Poland and prioritise refugee issues in artistic activities was a rarity among theatres, especially beyond the ones previously mentioned. Interestingly, these specific projects tended to emerge in smaller, non-state theatre groups, on alternative stages, and in institutions that placed significant emphasis on multicultural creative endeavours.

One notable project outcome was the performance *Tolerated Stay*, a collaboration between the Independent Culture Centre Teatr Szwalnia in Łódź and the Theatre Centre Kana in Szczecin. The production's development involved extensive research into the plight of refugees in Poland, direct interactions with them, workshops in migrant centres, and ongoing engagement with a Chechen family (parents with five underage children) residing in Poland under tolerated stay status[1]. Defying easy categorisation into a specific theatrical genre, it can be best described as a performative act. The project's initiator welcomed anyone interested into her private apartment for discussions about their experiences with working and interacting with refugees. Guests were treated to Chechen cuisine and narratives about the project's main characters were shared. Over time, these gatherings evolved to incorporate more sophisticated performative elements and visual effects illustrating the discussed events. The project commenced in 2013, with the first 'home gatherings' occurring in 2014.

---

[1] Tolerated stay – (legal term) a form of protection through which a foreigner, who has been denied refugee status, can legally stay on the territory of a foreign country.

The Zar Theatre in Wrocław creatively utilised the presence of artists with refugee status in Poland, too. Zar, an experimental theatre, embarks on artistic projects through source-based explorations and the development of a new theatrical language rooted in music from diverse cultural traditions. The ensemble includes actors from various countries, predominantly Italy, Armenia, Ukraine, and Poland. Its name is derived from funeral songs performed by the ethnic group of the Svans, residing in the high regions of the Caucasus in northwestern Georgia. In 2016 the theatre staged the performance *Medeas. On Getting Across*, using the ancient myth of Medea as a pretext for symbolically portraying the world of refugees at the gates of Europe. The impact of the performance went beyond exposing the audience to the horrors

> faced by those fleeing to Europe from war, hunger, and death; it gradually placed us, the calm and secure, at its cruel and centerless core, where Medea's quest for understanding proves futile. In the culmination of the performance, […] darkness descends, accompanied by a choir singing a Georgian zar – a mourning song facilitating the peaceful departure of souls from this world. […] This is the zar for us, for a Europe that has forsaken its own cradle, closing its gates to newcomers from the lands that once gave it life and vitality for centuries (Kosiński, 2017, p. 67).

The performance centred around multicultural songs performed by actresses from Iran, Egypt and Turkey. It featured multiple languages, with translations into Polish displayed on screens.

> The protagonist of the Medea narrative is the female character, Simona Sala, accompanied by the singing of two songstresses, Marjan Vahtat from Iran (whose sister was sentenced to five years in prison in Iran for anti-government activities, including… singing) and Fatma Amary from Cairo. In the premiere shows, Selda Öztürk, a singer from Turkey, also participated. Their voices intertwined with Catholic hymns echoing from the semi-darkness, where the male singers remained. Yet their powerful singing – which played a prominent role in earlier Zar Theatre performances – has now assumed a more subdued role, delicately supporting the musical narrative of songs in languages we do not understand and increasingly fear: Arabic, Persian, Kurdish (Kosiński, 2017, p. 67).

In a context where the European refugee crisis largely passed Poland by, theatres embraced refugee themes to scrutinise traits of Polish society by leveraging the populace's apprehensions about a nonexistent threat. The productions sought to disabuse Poles of their deeply ingrained belief in openness, solidarity, and empathy. As early as 2003, Teatr Ósmego Dnia[2], a prominent Polish

---

[2] The Teatr Ósmego Dnia (The Eighth Day Theatre) group was formed in 1964 as an alternative, independent, politically engaged, anti-system student theatre. It is considered a legend of Polish alternative theatre, staging significant productions with a spirit of opposition during

independent theatre, delved into such themes with *Portiernia* (*The Porter's Lodge*). In 2019, amid heightened anti-refugee political rhetoric in Poland, the ensemble chose to revisit the *Portiernia* project, crafting a second, altered version to align with new political realities. This emotionally charged performance addressed issues of Polish xenophobia, intolerance, forgetfulness and disdain for the impoverished and marginalised. In the programme, the creators stressed:

> Once, as a society (including us as a group), we experienced life in a poorer, 'worse' part of the world. We thought this experience would make us all more sensitive to the issues of immigrants, whom we were also, and that it would open our hearts to those who now live behind the 'iron' curtain. But that didn't happen then, and today it's even more difficult… The world is shaped by the idea of division – through barriers, selection, the porter's lodge. We are already on the other side, within the circle of the good civilisation. Even a clergyman in a red cassock rushes to the lodge to bless the barrier and cross to the other side. But what about those left behind, suffering and starving? If we forget about them, we lose eternity. Life without memory is an escape. Without memory, we lose our humanity (*Portiernia wersja druga/ The Porter's Lodge. Second Version*, 2022).

In this visually compelling performance, rich in metaphors and symbols, the ensemble explores the unyielding nature of the new moral-economic order. In this reality, there is no room for insecurities, reflections on the past, hesitations, or doubts. The weak, the ugly, the disabled, and the foreign are given no opportunities. The performance, often engaging in direct discourse with the audience, underscores the potential deafness of viewers to others' suffering, driven by the reprehensible joy of finally encountering 'those worse than us who evoke memories of our former inferiority'.

The 2016 play *Refugee Conversations* (*Rozmowy uchodźców*) by the independent theatre group Korporacja Teatralna in Poznań brings attention to the emergence of xenophobia, intolerance, and aggression in people's minds when there is no real refugee problem in Poland. Director Andrzej Pakuła clarified his motivations, stating:

---

the communist era. The theatre's political involvement led to repression from authorities, and the group was disbanded in 1985. Artists could only resume their activities after 1989. Following the political transformation and the fall of communism, Teatr Ósmego Dnia retained its sensitivity to social and political issues, respect for human dignity and civil rights as well as principles of equality. The theatre gained immense recognition internationally, performing in Mexico, Colombia, Brazil, Venezuela, Singapore and South Korea, among other places. It received numerous awards, including the prestigious Fringe First at the Edinburgh Festival.

This is not a play about the refugee experience; we do not portray their stories on stage. The issue of refugees – except for immigrants from Ukraine, mainly in the east – does not really concern us in Poland. Those refugees who cross the seas and go through barbed wires simply do not exist here [...]. What we aimed to address in this play is a specific refugee figure that functions in public discourse – in politics, journalism. And only there. We wanted to capture what this figure has done to us over the last two years. Because it has done a lot. Mostly bad. It brought out a few 'skeletons from the closet'[3], triggering a wave of nationalism and aggression in language (Kaźmierska, 2016).

Pakuła's play drew inspiration from two different sources. The first was Bertolt Brecht's *Refugee Conversations*, written when he himself was a political refugee in Scandinavia. The second part of the play incorporated contemporary press reports, derogatory comments about refugees on social media, and authentic statements from politicians such as Angela Merkel, Viktor Orban, Jarosław Kaczyński and Donald Trump.

In the prestigious dance performance *Intro* by the renowned Gdańsk-based dance theatre group Teatr Dada von Bzdülöw, the company humorously tackled the issues of Poles' attitudes toward migrants. Premiered in 2015, during the early stages of the Law and Justice party's nationalist programme implementation, the ensemble boldly incorporated the adjective 'Narodowy' (National) into its name, branding itself as the Narodowy Teatr Dada von Bzdülöw (National Dada von Bzdülöw Theatre). The performance centred on xenophobia and the perceived fears of Poles regarding the alleged arrival of other nationalities *en masse* in their country. In a provocative manner, the ensemble crafted an ironic narrative about foreigners who had developed an affection for Poland and aimed to contribute their best to the country. Employing various artistic conventions, the artists adeptly tapped into the emotions linked to national identity issues in Poland within the context of the immigration crisis facing Europe.

In the performance, each dancer delivered a 'foreigner's monologue'. Despite hailing from different parts of the world, the main characters' destinies were intertwined with Poland. The first character portrayed herself as a devoted admirer of Poland, while the second claimed divine inspiration to support the country along the Vistula, where a mononational Tower of Babel was emerging. The third character pledged to share the best of what he had with the Poles, including Arab fundamentalism and sweet nuts. Driven by love for Poland, the fourth character made a poignant decision to sacrifice himself for the country, becoming the first to detonate.

---

[3] It's important to note that these words were spoken in 2016 when refugees from the Middle East and Africa were hardly arriving in Poland at all.

The performance seamlessly blended elements of horror, grotesque and comedy, incorporating playful themes and surprising ideas. It featured collective music video dances to lively, rhythmic songs revolving around the theme of death. The show employed provocative satire, ridiculing the absurdity of fears that haunt Poles regarding 'foreigners' flooding their country, including the remarkable, unique, and exceptional aspects of Polish culture.

In 2021 there was a notable surge in theatrical responses to the refugee crisis, coinciding with the situation at the Polish-Belarusian border. The majority of theatres across Poland showed support through symbolic gestures, including appeals, protest letters to authorities, fundraisers and providing assistance to refugees in forests alongside the border. Profits from performances were also allocated to these efforts. Renowned Polish actors, such as Maja Ostaszewska and Maciej Stuhr, personally visited border areas to support volunteers. Importantly, these initiatives were predominantly led by independent and alternative theatre scenes. One such project took place in Krosno, a city in southeastern Poland, close to the Ukrainian border, without significant theatrical traditions. Supported by the Bureau of Art Exhibitions in the city, the project was created by Nihad Jami, a playwright and theatre director born in Iraqi Kurdistan. Previously working in Kirkuk with the Experimental Theatre Ensemble, Jami, a former lecturer at the Theatre Institute and editor-in-chief of the quarterly *Szanokar* dedicated to contemporary theatre art, faced death threats for staging a play on Islamic terrorism, leading him to emigrate in 2019. Despite having the right to political refugee status in Poland, he struggled for over three years to obtain a permanent residence card. In the end Jami received support from artistic circles, and the Bureau of Art Exhibitions in Krosno granted him a one-year residency, offering temporary legal stay, living expenses, and the opportunity to pursue artistic endeavours. This allowed him to realise, in 2022, the project *Panahanda, Let This Night Finally End* (*Panahanda. niech ta noc wreszcie się skończy*). The word 'Panahanda' means 'refugee' in Sorani, the language of Iraqi Kurds, and the experiences of displacement and the refugee perspective were the central themes of the project, consisting of two parts. The first part, a monodrama titled *Refugee*, drew from Jami's own experiences, with him serving as the director. It unfolded in an open space under a tree in Krosno's market square, featuring a tent covered in tape symbolising decay. A Polish actress collaborated with Jami, sitting inside and narrating a poignant story of uprooting and longing for home. She portrayed the main character, a refugee facing a foreign and hostile world, becoming vulnerable and experiencing a psychological crisis with escape found only in memories. The story lacked a happy ending, and the repeated question by the protagonist, 'Will this night finally end? Tomorrow, surely, I will get my permanent residence card and be able to live like a human'[4], remained unanswered. In the second part, the performer led the audience into a building where everyone participated in a Kurdish agrarian ritual called Kaunara, focused on life and death. Whilst the first part was presented in Polish, all ceremonies in the second part were accompanied by songs and rituals in Sorani. At the heart of the event was a woman chanting invocations to deities, performing symbolic gestures, pouring grains of cereals and mixing them with earth and water. Her hands were wrapped in white fabric symbolising the sea through which people seeking freedom and a secure life traverse, often perishing in its depths. The ritual served as a prayer and a plea for support to the deity who gives life but also takes it away.

The 2023 dance performance *Homesick / Sick Home* by the B'cause Dance Company delves into the theme of venturing into an unfamiliar and unwelcoming world, once idealised as the 'promised land'. Established in 2018, the company actively engages in social dialogue, creating performances that tackle crucial societal issues and stimulate debates and reflections among the audience. In this performance, the actors' focus centres on the beacon of a lighthouse, a symbol of hope for shipwreck survivors that often saves lives. The choreography, characterised by restlessness, neuroticism, and a perfect balance, guides the audience through the narratives of individuals who risk everything for a better future. However, the journey to a new world compels refugees to let go of their values and culture, which do not align with the new reality. Maintaining their uniqueness there is met with a lack of acceptance, driven by the principle: If you want to live among us, you must live as we do. In today's world, there is no room for 'non-conforming values. The performance raises significant questions for the audience: Are we providing others with the opportunity to find their place in a foreign culture while preserving their identity? Does our world offer such opportunities for others?

The play *Dworzec – rezygnacja* (*Resignation Station*), performed by artists from the Kupala Theatre in Minsk who themselves were political refugees in Poland, vividly illustrates the harsh reality faced by refugees escaping political repression under Belarusian President Alexander Lukashenko. The performance does not carry any sense of hope or contemplation about the possibility of a new life; rather, access to this world is portrayed as tightly closed. The drama unfolds at the Polish-Belarusian border, exposing the challenges and hardships experienced by refugees. The narrative centres around a Kurdish family that, once content in their homeland, is forced to flee due to war, eventually finding themselves in the forests of Podlasie (Podlachia). As Border Guard officers make their appearance, the refugees undergo humiliation and inhumane treatment, with their acceptance or rejection determined by

---

[4]   The quote is from the play: *Panahanda, Let This Night Finally End.*

the colour of their skin. The actresses portraying the guards adopt a look and acting style that makes them terrifying figures, accentuated by the fact that they walk on stilts, consistently looking down on people and wielding absolute authority over them. In stark contrast to this world filled with cruelty and animosity, a volunteer character endeavours to save the teenage daughter of the Kurdish family, who has succumbed to hypothermia due to the harsh conditions. Despite facing severe consequences from the guards, this female volunteer attempts to defy the oppressive system. *Dworzec rezygnacja* therefore serves as a poignant reflection of the situation in Poland at that time – an environment marked by an inhumane and empathy-devoid authority represented by the guards, and societal groups striving to address the injustices and extend assistance, albeit often finding themselves powerless against the prevailing brutality, oppression, and force.

The play *Odpowiedzialność* (*Responsibility*), directed by the esteemed Polish director Michał Zadara at the Teatr Powszechny in Warsaw, stands out as one of the most critical productions addressing the authorities' treatment of refugees at the Polish-Belarusian border[5]. The narrative unfolds around the authentic story of Issa Jerjos, a Syrian refugee who tragically lost his life in a forest by the border due to exhaustion and exposure to the elements. Issa sought in Poland what Syria could not provide: peace, the rule of law, respect for human rights, work opportunities, and the chance to rebuild his life. Unfortunately, what he encountered instead was an exceptionally militarised zone under a state of emergency, where armed soldiers searched for defenceless individuals in the forest, compelling them to return to Belarus without any inquiry into their circumstances. Issa Jerjos passed away on the Polish side, within the emergency zone. He sought refuge from state officials in a country whose constitution underscores unwavering commitment to action based on the respect for inherent human dignity, the right to freedom, and the duty of solidarity with others. Notably significant in the context of the religious importance in Poland is the fact that the name Issa translates to Jesus in Polish, adding a poignant layer to the social drama.

The performance took on the essence of documentary theatre, devoid of any theatrical fiction. The trio of actors[6] had the explicit task of presenting the audience with raw facts, devoid of interpretation or commentary, by recounting the contents of retrieved accounts and referencing legal documents, including the Polish constitution. The overarching aim, akin to a courtroom

---

[5] It premiered on June 26th, 2022.

[6] Three esteemed Polish actors appeared in the performance: Piotr Głowacki, Maja Ostaszewska, and Barbara Wysocka. The presence of Ostaszewska is particularly significant, as she herself was a volunteer and activist, assisting refugees for several months at the Polish-Belarusian border.

trial, was to determine responsibility for the depicted death. The staging was minimalist, featuring a black stage, a table, music and visuals such as photos and short films projected on the screen. Actors read all the texts from prompters, not due to a lack of familiarity with their roles but to ensure accuracy, much like the precision required in a courtroom setting. *Odpowiedzialność* encompassed three main elements: the narrative of Issa's fate, an analysis of documents related to legal responsibility, and musical segments from Johann Sebastian Bach's *Passion According to St. Matthew*. The script for the performance evolved during university classes, where director Michał Zadara, alongside a group of students, delved into Greek tragedy, followed by the works of Polish romantic playwright Juliusz Słowacki, and finally, contemporary issues. Zadara emphasised

> the fundamental continuity between Greek tragedy and 'Responsibility', asserting that theatre has always grappled with the consequences of politics on humanity. Tragedy, born 2500 years ago, remains a compelling narrative that explores the unsettling space between life and death. The core formula of tragedy revolves around the scenario where heroes are alive, yet in a moment, they cease to be. This echoes the stories of Hamlet, Iphigenia, Medea, Agamemnon, and Lady Macbeth – and, in the context of the performance, it reflects the stories of several hundred people at our border. Tragedy serves as the narrative of death that we need to comprehend our fate and, perhaps, effect a bit of change (*Teatr wobec kryzysu*, 2022).

Towards the conclusion of the performance, photos of specific Polish politicians, including the Minister of Internal Affairs, Mariusz Kamiński, and the Chairman of Law and Justice, Jarosław Kaczyński, emerge on the board. Throughout the show they are identified as bearing direct responsibility for this death and numerous others.

III. CONTEMPORARY POLISH AND UKRAINIAN THEATRE – THE INITIAL PHASE OF MUTUAL ACQUAINTANCE

In Poland there was little familiarity with contemporary Ukrainian theatre. The beginning of Polish-Ukrainian theatrical relations was primarily driven by political factors, linked to the 'dignity revolution' in Ukraine and the protests in Kiev's central square, Maidan Nezalezhnosti, in 2014. Joanna Wichowska played a crucial role in fostering these relations. The laboratories, workshops, and theatre festivals she organised in Ukraine and later in Poland facilitated initial contacts between Ukrainian and Polish creators, especially those from independent theatre scenes. These contacts allowed them to see that they were connected not only by geographical and linguistic proximity, and partially by cultural aspects, but also by the themes and aesthetics of their creative pursuits.

Polish theatre's response to the political protests in Ukraine and the Russian aggression in 2014

The events on Kiev's Maidan in 2014 spurred action from individuals also in the cultural and artistic communities. Theatres throughout Poland strongly protested against the oppressive policies of Ukrainian leader Viktor Yanukovych, his decision to withdraw from the association agreement with the European Union, and most importantly, the brutal and bloody crackdown by the police and military on the Ukrainian protesters. As Russia's so-called hybrid war began, followed by the occupation of Donbas and the annexation of Crimea, symbolic gestures of support grew stronger. Theatres showed solidarity with the Ukrainian people, also by including Ukrainian migrants in protests they organised. Various forms of artistic activity, like singing songs or reading excerpts from Ukrainian works, were often paired with fundraising efforts for money, medicine and food to aid the population in Ukraine. Shortly after, Polish creative communities also responded to the appeal from Ukrainian playwrights to theatre activists worldwide in March 2014, urging for support and solidarity. In an open letter to the Polish Prime Minister they requested the allocation of one billion euros to an international emergency aid fund for the new Ukraine. Individual artists, particularly those with prior professional connections to Russia, also showed gestures of support for Ukraine and condemnation of Russia. Krystian Lupa's decision received the most significant social attention. His trips to St. Petersburg and Moscow were already scheduled for March 2014. In that first city, at the Alexandrinsky Theatre, he was scheduled to stage Leonid Andreyev's *Anathema*, while in Moscow, at the Bolshoi Drama Theatre (Большой драматический театр), a project related to Thomas Bernhard was planned. Lupa cancelled both trips, explaining that given the escalation of the Ukrainian-Russian conflict and the Russian military intervention in Crimea, he sees no possibility of travelling to Russia and will not undertake work there until the country's policies undergo a radical change. Daniel Olbrychski, a well-known actor in Poland, is also highly popular in Russia for his roles in numerous Russian films, TV series, and theatrical performances, primarily in Moscow theatres. However, he has also cut off all artistic contacts with Russia. Andrzej Seweryn was one of the most active advocates for the Ukrainian cause, openly opposing Russia's actions. Following the onset of protests against Yanukovych's government in Kiev, he personally went to Maidan Square to support the demonstrators. From there, he travelled directly to Kharkiv, where he performed his monodrama *Shakespeare Forever* as a guest at the Arabesky Theatre. He delivered it in Ukrainian for the audience, which included war refugees from Donetsk, Crimea and Luhansk. Since then, he has consistently raised awareness about Ukraine's situation, even during his international guest performances[7]. In 2015, he invited the Arabesky ensemble to perform at his theatre.

The interest of theatres in Poland in the war in Ukraine, except for a few exceptions, soon disappeared. According to Olha Matsiupa[8], a Ukrainian playwright who has been permanently residing in Poland since 2011, the topic of Ukraine began to appear in Polish theatres in 2014 as part of political circumstances, only to quickly be overshadowed by other global crises, such as the war in Syria. Since 2015, there have been significantly fewer artistic initiatives focused on Ukraine in theatres in Poland[9]. One of the more notable texts staged at that time was *The Maidan Diaries* by Natalia Vorozhbyt[10]. The play was a collaborative effort involving a group of artists associated with the New Ukrainian Drama movement. They all participated in the protests during the Kiev Maidan, conducting interviews, gathering testimonies, and materials about the people and events taking place there. They spoke with students who had been beaten during the initial attempts to suppress the demonstrations, with the Cossacks who formed the protective force of Maidan and adhered to the principles of the Zaporozhian Sich, and with young boys who constructed catapults and threw bottles with flammable substances at the regime's Berkut police. However, *The Maidan Diaries* also includes accounts and opinions from opponents of the protests. Based on this, Vorozhbyt created a dramatic text, which she herself described as a documentary play. The author deliberately did not write any ending, explaining that there is also no end to the Ukrainian fight for freedom and justice.

The Wybrzeże Theatre in Gdańsk, one of Poland's most prominent institutional theatre companies, was the first to stage Vorozhbyt's text. In March 2014 they presented the play, with the participation of Ukrainian actors, as a performative reading directed by Andrej May-Malahov, a Ukrainian director who was then working at the Ivan Franko National Academic Drama Theatre in Kiev. In October of the same year, *The Maidan Diaries* were already staged as a performance at the Teatr Powszechny in Warsaw, directed by the Polish director Wojciech Klemm and featuring Polish actors. The play

---

[7] He was among the first individuals who, already at that time, wore a pin featuring the Ukrainian flag on the lapel of his jacket or coat. This information comes from Svitlana Oleshko, the director of the Arabesky Theatre, who is currently employed at the Polish Theatre in Warsaw as a playwright.

[8] More information about Olha Matsiupa in the appendix.

[9] Information obtained in an interview conducted by the author with Olha Matsiupa on September 10th, 2023.

[10] More information about Natalia Vorozhbyt in the appendix.

was part of a larger project organised by the theatre titled *What are we killing each other for? War. Peace. Ukraine* (*O co się zabijać? Wojna. Pokój. Ukraina*). Theatre director Paweł Łysak announced it in the following way:

> For three months, the Teatr Powszechny stage will host a variety of events, including screenings of films about Euromaidan, concerts featuring old Ukrainian songs in modern arrangements, exhibitions, premieres, drama readings, and live broadcasts of radio plays. In total, there will be dozens of events complemented by debates and discussions. The project will kick off with a unique artistic referendum on October 19th, 2014. Can we alter the course of history this time? Who needs politics in the theatre? – We aim to engage the audience in an intellectual response to the recent events in Ukraine (*Teatr Powszechny...*, 2023).

As part of the significant Theatre and Maidan project dedicated to Ukraine, there was also a performance reading of *Glory to the Heroes*, a play by Ukrainian playwright Pavlo Arie[11], hosted at the Cultural Centre in Lublin. The project was organised in Lublin by the East European Performing Arts Platform and the International Festival Konfrontacje Teatralne. The premiere was preceded by a panel discussion, during which Ukrainian and Polish theatre experts, artistic curators, critics and playwrights, including Pavlo Arie, discussed the role of protest in the Kiev Maidan in strengthening Ukraine's national identity as well as the impact on the changes that occurred in Ukrainian theatre and drama as a result. Arie's work aligns with the topics discussed during that conversation. Primarily it references the differing historical experiences of Ukrainians living in the east and west of the country, which leads to challenging societal divisions in modern times. Meanwhile, instead of consolidating people and tackling economic issues, the authorities exploit and further fuel existing conflicts. The protagonists of the drama are two war veterans, hailing from western and eastern Ukraine. The first was a soldier of the pro-nationalist Ukrainian Insurgent Army, while the second served in the Soviet Red Army. They now find themselves sharing a hospital room. Despite a lengthy discussion, they cannot reach an agreement because reconciliation seems impossible. Former enemies also try to pass on hatred to their descendants. However, the younger generation evaluates things using entirely different criteria. The granddaughter and grandson of the two veterans meet and fall in love. Their romance echoes the story of Romeo and Juliet, but in this case, both Hania and Petro aim to lead ordinary lives. The performative reading was prepared by actors from the Juliusz Osterwa Theatre in Lublin, with Pavlo Arie serving as a consultant.

---

[11] More information about Pavlo Arie in the appendix.

For Polish theatre the war in Ukraine and the resulting increase in Ukrainian refugees in Poland have become a pretext for a critical examination of the Polish society's response to this entirely new situation. It points out to Poles their national flaws such as xenophobia, colonialism and lack of tolerance. Such diagnoses are found in the works of prominent Polish directors, such as Jan Klata's play *Polish Thermopylae* (*Termopile polskie*), based on Tadeusz Miciński's work, performed at the Polish Theatre in Wrocław; Marcin Liber's adaptation of Leo Tolstoy's *War and Peace*, presented at the Teatr Powszechny in Warsaw; and Remigiusz Brzyk's play *Mordor Will Come and Devour Us, or the Secret History of the Slavs* (*Przyjdzie Mordor i nas zje, czyli tajna historia Słowian*) staged at the Juliusz Osterwa Theatre in Lublin. Particularly, this latter production offers a harsh diagnosis of Polish sentiments of national superiority and lack of empathy towards 'others', whose culture is perceived as significantly less valuable and worthy of respect. The play is based on a book by contemporary Polish writer Ziemowit Szczerek. It tells the story of Polish tourists travelling to Lviv to visit the grave of a young boy who defended the Polish identity of the city in 1918. The trip lacks deeper patriotic motivations, however. Instead, it simply reflects a characteristic aspect of Polish 'nationalistic folklore' and serves as an opportunity to take a 'selfie' to share later on Facebook. The declared solidarity of Poles with Ukraine also turns out to be fiction, as historical disputes and memories of past grievances remain relevant. Polish tourists, while travelling across Ukraine, display a rude sense of superiority towards its inhabitants. They treat Ukrainians according to the stereotypical image prevalent in Poland, viewing them as descendants of serfs who worked in Polish estates in Ukraine in the past, serving the Polish nobility. Consequently, Poles travel to Ukraine with a sense of colonial, aristocratic superiority. In this scenario, it's difficult to talk about any solidarity.

Furthermore, Polish theatre has offered critical commentary not only on Poles but also on the broader European community. An example of this is the performance in the form of a performative reading titled *The Birds That I Eat*, based on the play by Polish playwright Marzena Sadocha. The production was staged at the Polish Theatre in Wrocław and directed by one of the prominent contemporary Polish theatre directors, Marcin Liber The play was a strong protest against Europe's inability to respond to the dramatic events in Ukraine. The author described her work as a poem about the powerlessness of those who fight and those who watch them on TV. About Europe's helplessness and the war dance we arrange for ourselves from time to time, probably because, just as we fear war, we also desire victory. Ukraine is a replay of history and the theatre is a place to protest against such repetitions.

The involvement of Joanna Wichowska and the Theatre Institute in establishing ongoing collaboration between Ukrainian and Polish theatres

The artistic situation of Ukrainian theatre in the context of the political events of 2014

The events on the Maidan in Kyiv in 2014 had a tremendous impact not only on the changes that began to occur in Ukrainian society, the strengthening of the sense of identity and national unity, but also on Ukrainian culture, including theatre. The situation in which the Ukrainian theatre found itself at the time Ukraine gained independence was not easy. The Soviet Union strongly opposed the development of independent national cultures, which is why Ukrainian theatre was overwhelmingly dominated by Russian influences. This persisted for decades, and in 2014, it was challenging to identify any distinct national characteristics in Ukrainian theatre scenes. Joanna Wichowska, a director and theatre animator well-versed in Ukrainian theatre, highlighted that during this period, Ukrainian theatre operated in complete isolation from societal influences (Wichowska, 2014). State theatres primarily showcased classics, including numerous Russian plays. The main criterion for selecting repertoire was the success achieved by a particular work in Russia, preferably in Moscow. Ukrainian dramaturgy was solely presented in a rigid, 'museum-like and folkloric' manner, relying on texts that overlooked topics relevant to contemporary society. The paradox of Ukrainian theatre was that the first to demand change were Ukrainian creators who had received their education and recognition in Moscow, such as Natalia Vorozhbyt, Oleksandra (Sasha) Denisova[12] and Maxim Kurochkin[13]. Many of them collaborated with theatres that, by Russian standards, were independent, staying outside the circle of artistic activities aligned with the government's favourable propaganda.

Artists like Vorozhbyt and Kurochkin also played a key role in initiating the first changes in Ukrainian theatre. The escalating authoritarian policies of Vladimir Putin, coupled with increasingly harsh anti-Ukrainian rhetoric from Russian authorities, led them to leave Russia even before 2014 and return to Ukraine. There, they attempted to establish their own independent

---

[12] More information about Sasha Denisova in the appendix.
[13] More information about Maxim Kurochkin in the appendix.

theatre scenes. An example of this is the Theatre of the Displaced[14], founded by Vorozhbyt, Kurochkin, along with the German director Georg Genoux and war psychologist Aleksiej Karachynskyi. Their performances take on a documentary style. The artists collaborate with displaced individuals from Crimea and Donbas, sharing their stories on stage. Another similar initiative

---

[14] The Theatre of the Displaced is one of the prominent Ukrainian independent theatres, recognised beyond Ukraine's borders, and collaborating with numerous groups across Western and Eastern Europe. Founded in October 2015 at the Centre for Science and Art 'DIYA' in Kyiv, it was established by German theatre director Georg Genoux, psychotherapist Aleksiej Karachynskyi and Ukrainian playwrights Natalia Vorozhbyt and Maxim Kurochkin. The theatre aimed to bring to life, through real-life stories, the experiences of numerous internally and externally displaced persons who had moved around or indeed arrived in Ukraine from (other) war-torn countries. Additionally, it served as a means for these individuals to work through trauma and find new perspectives on life in their changed reality. The Theatre of the Displaced is thus not only a documentary theatre, but also a witness theatre. The protagonists of the performances are migrants from Donbas, volunteers and soldiers who have returned from the conflict zone. On stage, they depict real-life situations they have experienced. The idea of establishing the theatre emerged when Ukrainian society faced the first armed conflict on the eastern border in the history of independent Ukraine. In the theatre's first premiere (*Where is the East?*) real migrants from Donbas performed. The play was written by Georg Genoux, Natalia Vorozhbyt and Aleksiej Karachynskyi. Since then, it has been shown several times in Kyiv with different groups of immigrants. Participants often share very personal stories, which is why a psychotherapist and one of the founders of the Immigrant Theatre, Aleksiej Karachynskyi, collaborates with them. At the end of 2015 the popular online portal *Gazeta.ua*, relying on a survey among theatre critics, named the Theatre of the Displaced as Ukraine's theatrical project of the year. The theatre has been a frequent participant in events such as the *GOGOLfest* theatre festival, the *DONKULT forum* in Lviv, the *Docuday.ua* documentary film festival and others. In March 2016, a tour took place in Berlin at the Maxim Gorki Theater, where performances of *Goods* and *Where is the East: Monologue 1*, written by Natalia Vorozhbyt and directed by Georg Genoux, were presented. In the same month, in Konstanz (Germany), the play *Nikolayevka* was staged. It featured students from Nikolayevka, which is a small town in the Donetsk Oblast, where active military operations were underway during the summer of 2014. At the Dreiländerspiel festival in Zittau (Germany) in 2016, the premiere of the documentary play *Enslaved* took place, a project by the renowned young Ukrainian documentarian Alisa Kovalenko and director Georg Genoux. In the same year the theatre also participated in organising the international project *Class-Akt*, during which children from both eastern and western regions of Ukraine collaborated to write plays. Subsequently, these plays were staged by top young Ukrainian directors alongside the best Ukrainian artists at the Scena festival of the Kyiv Youth Theatre. The Theatre of the Displaced also participated in the international project *Undernational.affairs*, initiated by the Maxim Gorki Theater in Berlin. Several leading theatres from Western and Eastern Europe, with a focus on political and documentary theatre, took part in the project.

is PostPlay[15], established by writers Den Humennyi and Jana Humenna, in collaboration with Crimean directors and actors.

The protests of 2014 have intensified such actions. Wichowska highlighted 'the remarkable energy of Maidan, which, overall, also entails the realisation among many people that they can effect change. This awareness wasn't handed to them; they discovered it through their own experiences' (Wichowska, 2014). At that time, a significant number of Ukrainian artists emerged: playwrights, directors, and actors, who had previously attempted unsuccessfully to effect change within the stagnant state theatre scene. Now, they decided to take matters into their own hands. According to Wichowska (2014), 'these are artists with an incredible readiness to act, to cross boundaries, to take risks. This potential stunned me'. Ukrainian theatre expert Nadia Sokolenko[16] emphasised that Maidan became an opportunity for the previously entirely absent independent Ukrainian culture to have a chance to emerge in the public sphere. The Maidan protest was not only a political manifestation of Ukraine's independence but also an opportunity for cultural expressions, including theatrical performances. One of the leading advocates for the reform of Ukrainian theatre, Roza Sarkisian, argues that there emerged what's known as the 'Maidan Generation' in the artistic community, a group advocating for a breakthrough in Ukrainian art, the emergence of contemporary theatre and dramaturgy engaged in current political and social issues, including the ongoing war in the country.

> Theatre must pose new, fundamental questions: who are we? What do we want? And we want to speak a new language, our language, not the one previously imposed by propaganda and cultural traditions emanating from Russia. This new generation is trying to break away from the Russian narrative, which

---

[15] PostPlay Theatre is an independent Ukrainian theatre created in Kyiv in 2015 by playwrights Den Humennyi and Jana Humenna and directors Galina Dzhikaeva and Anton Romanov. Other independent theatres and performers often appear on its stage as well. It is a typical underground venue for contemporary art, located in the premises of a former factory. It addresses current topics related to painful, controversial and socially and politically 'uncomfortable' issues, including matters concerning gender, sexual orientation, migrants and refugees as well as groups discriminated against in cultural and national contexts. Its most notable performances address the issues of war in Ukraine and internal refugees (*Gray Zone*, *The First 50 Days of War*), separatists (*Mercenaries*), as well as the war on a universal scale (*Black Snow*), where the creators focus on four symbolic cities: Nagasaki, Sarajevo, Donetsk and Aleppo. PostPlay Theatre is inherently rebellious and often speaks out against the commonly accepted narrative or even says what the audience doesn't want to hear to the extent that Den Humennyi, its founder, has reported serious threats from individuals who disagreed with the theatre's repertoire.

[16] Nadia Sokolenko – theatreologist, theatre critic, editor-in-chief of the magazine *Ukrainian Theatre*, co-founder of the independent organisation Theatre Platform.

viewed Ukraine and its culture solely through the Russian prism and failed to recognise its distinctiveness. The Maidan Generation is also a quest for our own identity, not in contrast to the West, but rather challenging stereotypes in Western perceptions of Ukraine and Ukrainian-ness. It's an ongoing process, one that's clearly reflected in Ukrainian theatre[17].

Following this, numerous non-state, independent scenes began to emerge in Ukraine. Teams like Arabesky[18], PostPlay, Beautiful Flowers Theatre)[19],

---

[17] Author's interview with Roza Sarkisian, October 18th, 2023. More information about Roza Sarkisian in the appendix

[18] The theatre studio Arabesky was established in 1993 by students from the theatre department of the Kharkiv Institute of Arts. Initially, the focus was on experimental work, with occasional presentations of their findings to the public. However, by 1997, the theatre's concept had evolved. Alongside workshops covering vocal, dance, stage movement and speech, the group aimed to establish a repertory theatre and embarked on active touring. Arabesky is renowned as a leading advocate for reform in Ukrainian theatre. Svitlana Oleshko serves as its founder and director.

[19] The Beautiful Flowers Theatre (Театр Прекрасні Квіти) is an independent, professional theatre founded in 2011 by graduates of Kharkiv Art University. It is one of the most renowned and respected independent stages in Ukraine. The creators themselves pioneered a distinctive genre known as Funk-Futurism, which continues to define the theatre's essence today. According to the team, the fundamental principles of this genre include:
· A state of consciousness that is liberated and imperceptible to the human eye.
· Blending the mood of funk music with the revolutionary fervour of early 20th-century futurists.
· Embracing a youthful mindset and carefree awareness.
· Challenging established norms and aspiring to create art for the future.
· Preferring expression through one's essence over words.
· Rejecting the traditional author's role in favour of collaborative art creation by the team.
· Maintaining a sense of discretion.
· Offering an exclusive experience tailored for connoisseurs. After sampling, one may experience either disgust or pleasure, prompting a desire for more.
The stage's creative endeavours are directed towards advancing theatrical art, aiming to elevate it to new heights by seamlessly blending traditional and contemporary theatrical forms and techniques. The initial premiere of *Szczur* (*Rat*), described by the creators as an absurd play without words, set in the comedic crime genre, caused a certain contrast with other non-state theatres in Kharkiv. However, the performance received significant acclaim from both audiences and critics at Ukrainian theatre festivals. Successive premieres further establish the theatre's presence within the realm of Ukrainian independent stages. A notable production was *DPYU*, which drew upon real-life accounts from the combat zone, featuring war veterans from Donbas. Playwright Dmytro Levytskyi helped create it. In 2014, Oksana Cherkashyna, one of the most prominent actresses of the independent scene, joined the ensemble.

The Dykiy Theatre[20], Maj Busz[21], The Theatre of the Displaced, The Play-wrights' Theatre (Teatr Dramaturgów), and others spearheaded the imple-mentation of various changes. In a Ukrainian theatre magazine, these dy-namic transformations were described as follows:

> At last, theatre became more active in Ukraine. In the years 2014–15, there was
> a surge in the opening of new venues, renovation of existing theatrical facilities,
> and the organisation of independent projects and festivals. During this time,
> several theatres were established, including the Dykiy Theatre, PostPlay Theatre,
> Practicum, Immigrant Theatre, the Pic Pic Association, Do or Die Theatre,
> Misanthrope Theatre, Tata Art Project, Roof Theatre, and others. And that's just
> in Kyiv. In Lviv, the 'Drama.UA' festival underwent reorganisation, evolving into
> a permanent venue known as the First Stage of Contemporary Drama. In Zapor-
> izhzhya, the Zaporizhzhya New Drama Theatre was established, and in Poltava,
> the Contemporary Dialogue Theatre emerged. And this is just the beginning.
> Performances in such projects vary greatly, which sometimes leaves the audience
> unsure of what to expect. Last year, during the production 'Love/Sex' (directed
> by Andrij Mai) at the Franko Theatre, the organisers underestimated this factor
> to such an extent that the audience demanded refunds for their tickets. However,
> by correctly labelling the poster with designations such as '18+', 'strong language',
> 'possible scenes of violence' (etc.), conflicts could have been avoided. At least, suc-
> cessful experiences from the Dykiy [Wild – J.L.] Theatre confirm this. Regardless
> of how shocking its performances may have been to the audience, the majority of
> them remained satisfied (Hołownienko, 2017).

Each of these theatres had its own programme and unique artistic strategies.
However, it was precisely in these relatively small, self-financed institutions
with limited staff and technical support where a search for a new theatrical
language in Ukraine, open to current and contemporary themes, and a departure from rigid artistic forms, was pursued. The aim was to establish a new
national theatre, rooted in the traditions of Ukraine's theatrical reform. One

---

[20]   The Dykiy Theatre is one of the most popular independent theatres in Ukraine, found-ed in February 2016. It creates sharp social performances based on plays by contemporary playwrights as well as various independent theatre projects, musicals, etc. Provocation, spec-tacle and shock constitute the main tools of interaction with the audience. The theatre has al-ready delivered over 20 projects, bringing together over 120 actors from various theatres into its team and reaching over 60,000 audience members. Performances take place in various plac-es, not only within the premises of the theatre, but also in zoos or nightclubs, the theatre does not have a permanent ensemble.

[21]   The Maj Busz Theatre was founded by Natalia Blok in Kherson as the theatre of the current drama, reaching primarily for contemporary Ukrainian repertoire. The founder her-self wrote that it is a theatre of the young, brave, modern people who are not afraid of experiments.

of the key figures referenced by artists was Les Kurbas (1887–1937), a prominent Ukrainian reformer, theatre creator, actor and director. He founded
three theatres: The Young Theatre, Kyjdramte (The Kyiv Drama Theatre) and
Berezil. Kurbas was a leading figure of the so-called Executed Renaissance –
a generation of Ukrainian artists and scholars active in the 1920s and early
1930s within the Ukrainian Soviet Socialist Republic. They advocated for
the revival of a modern, autonomous Ukrainian culture[22].

One of the strategies used by the reformers, known as the 'occupation
strategy', involved attempting to take control of state-funded theatres from
within. Young creators would apply for managerial positions there in order
to subsequently implement necessary changes. In several instances, this approach proved effective. Lubov Ilnytska[23] was appointed as the literary director of the Lviv Academic Kurbas Theatre, Olha Puzhanovska won the competition for the artistic directorship of the Lesya Ukrainka Academic Theatre
in Lviv, Olena Apchel[24] was named as the artistic director of the Zoloti Vorota
Theatre in Kyiv, and Roza Sarkisian became a full-time director at the National Academic Drama and Music Theatre in Ivano-Frankivsk. The most active centres of progressive Ukrainian theatre were four cities: Kharkiv, Odesa,
Kyiv and Lviv. However, over time, this map gradually expanded. Wichowska
expressed her thoughts on the matter in this way:

> At one point, I wrote that in Ukraine, especially state theatre, is engulfed in
> a post-Soviet way of thinking and aesthetics. For many years I have been regularly
> travelling to Ukraine and in 2012 I observed mainly small islands that tried to
> resist this trend. However, for about the past two years I have been witnessing
> an eruption of projects that attempt to make up for this lost time. Without a doubt,
> this is linked to a devastating, painful crisis – war, to put it plainly. The current
> situation that Ukraine finds itself in demands a response from artists. However,
> within institutional theatre, such responses are rare: there is little room for bold
> statements directly confronting reality. In these institutions, Ukrainians are
> troubled by the rigid adherence to outdated thinking, particularly concerning
> theatrical aesthetics. Performances often feature beautiful and significant texts
> from the canon, typically concluding with a comforting moral. State theatres
> resemble half-dead remnants inherited from the Soviet Union, lacking the nervous
> system that once transmitted impulses from Moscow. Now they are kept in such
> a lethargic state (Wichowska, 2014).

---

[22] The overwhelming majority of individuals from this generation were arrested and executed by the NKVD in the 1930s. See: https://openkurbas.org/en/, last accessed: 08/09/2023.

[23] More information about Lubov Ilnytska in the appendix.

[24] More information about Olena Apchel in the appendix.

The Maidan generation aimed for a thorough overhaul of the culture management system. Sokolenko remembered a gathering of cultural figures during this time initiating discussions on necessary reforms. Calls were made for a complete revolutionising of the Ministry of Culture. The proposal for a Committee for Humanitarian Strategy and Security emerged, tasked with crafting a holistic cultural development strategy for Ukraine. In her analyses, Joanna Wichowska highlighted finances as the primary challenge confronting Ukrainian culture:

> A more comprehensive strategy is needed, involving discussions and the implementation of appropriate, well-considered cultural policy. This won't be resolved in a matter of months, especially that this issue has not been competently addressed thus far. The core problem for theatres, whether national, academic, regional, or municipal, isn't cultural policy but rather a struggle for survival, for financial support. These theatres receive funding mainly for actor salaries and, perhaps, for one new production or premiere per season. To cover other expenses, they must either generate revenue through ticket sales or venue rentals or secure sponsorship. This dynamic shapes the theatres we see today. If a playwright has financial backing from a businessperson, the play gets staged. However, a young author lacking funds may struggle to get their work produced (Wichowska, 2014).

However, the ambitious plans for change were not fulfilled. As of 2022, the situation remained largely unchanged. Institutional theatres absorbed the majority of funds from the state budget, leaving little for institutions striving to rejuvenate Ukrainian theatre, which often operated in small clubs or partially renovated basements. These establishments frequently lacked adequate resources for artistic endeavours, let alone salaries for their staff. In this respect, the Kyiv Maidan fell short of expectations. Sokolenko summarised its achievements with a sense of defeat, saying: 'For young people, there is no room in this system – they have to wait until the older generation retires. They create their independent art in makeshift spaces like basements – until they eventually begin searching for other jobs to sustain themselves' (Wichowska, 2014). In this context, the words spoken by Lena Liahushonkova[25], one of the leading young Ukrainian playwrights currently residing at the Polish Theatre in Bydgoszcz, were also significant:

> To find a good play, I had to wander from theatre to theatre in Ukraine like a cat chasing after a golden ring. It's like exploring fifty shades of colonialism: from Russian classics and Little Russian dances to romantic comedies set in Paris. That's why I started writing myself – so that there would finally be something worth watching. It didn't matter, however, as established theatres didn't want to stage my

---

[25] More information about Lena Liahushonkova in the appendix.

plays. Instead, I had to mainly write scripts for children's morning shows, jubilees, and adaptations of classics. Success had to be achieved first in Moscow. State theatres ignore Ukrainian playwrights. Yet, they receive the most funding. Social-political statements, contemporary themes and revisiting historical traumas are not of interest to them (I can't even recall a Ukrainian play about World War II written in the last 30 years). Their repertoire isn't aligned with contemporary context but rather with some Moscow standards from the 1970s. But what can the 1970s be without censorship and socialist realism? Various initiatives that started appearing after the Maidan were either stifled by quarantine or by the inconsistent policies of the Ministry of Culture[26].

Joanna Wichowska – the opening of the Polish-Ukrainian theatre collaboration

Despite their proximity, Poland and Ukraine did not sustain vibrant theatrical connections. Ukrainian theatre remained relatively unknown in Poland, with sporadic visits by Ukrainian groups, usually during international theatre festivals, failing to alter this perception. One notable exception was the Arabesky Theatre from Kharkiv. In their case, the interest in Polish theatre largely arose from a profound passion for Polish contemporary drama, particularly the works of the Polish avant-garde playwright Witkacy, driven by one of Arabesky's actors and privately, by the husband of the theatre's director Svitlana Oleshko[27], Mykhailo 'Miśko' Barbara[28]. He translated several plays by Witkacy into Ukrainian, which were subsequently staged at the Arabesky Theatre. In the mid-90s, Arabesky invited Polish composer Mikołaj Trzaska to create music for one of their productions based on Witkacy's works. Additionally, Arabesky collaborated with various smaller, independent theatres in Poland, including the Travel Agency Theatre in Poznań and the In Vitro Stage in Lublin. The theatre made its debut in Poland in 2011, performing one of Witkacy's plays, *The Madman and the Nun* in Warsaw. It returned to Poland 4 years later, in 2015, collaborating with the Polish Theatre in Warsaw, where it showcased productions including *Chernobyl (Czarnobyl)*™, *Letters from Kharkiv (Listy z Charkowa)* and *Decalogue: Local World War (Dekalog: Lokalna wojna światowa)*. Arabesky Theatre was effectively the sole Ukrainian theatre planning a permanent, long-term collaboration with Polish theatre teams. In 2015, Svitlana Oleshko and Mykhailo Barbara revisited Poland,

---

[26] Lena Liahushonkova, information gathered from an interview conducted by the author of the text on September 10th, 2023.

[27] More information about Svitlana Oleshko in the appendix.

[28] More information about Mykhailo Barbara in the appendix.

this time through a several-month *Gaude Polonia* scholarship aimed at deepening their understanding of contemporary Polish theatre and, as they themselves hoped, 'fostering long-term Polish-Ukrainian theatrical cooperation. We are seeking projects that would captivate Polish audiences and that we could collectively bring to life here, alongside the Polish theatre community' (Charków–Warszawa, 2015).

An important role in promoting Ukrainian theatre in Poland could have been played by the inaugural International Ukrainian Theatre Festival *East-West*, held for the first time in 2014. This yearly event takes place in Krakow and is organised by the Mass Spectacle Foundation in partnership with the Youth Centre and the independent KTO Theatre. While the organisers highlight the participation of over 100 professional and amateur theatres from Ukraine, Poland, Germany, Austria, Latvia, Georgia, Finland, Hungary and Armenia over the ten editions of the Festival, and emphasise its unique position as the sole European showcase for Ukrainian theatre, its influence, particularly in Poland, remains relatively modest. Although diverse Ukrainian theatres, occasionally esteemed ones, are welcomed in Krakow, where they present contemporary Ukrainian drama, this has only marginally contributed to forging stronger connections with the theatre community in Poland.

The familiarity with Polish theatre in Ukraine mirrored a similar situation. Roza Sarkisian asserted that during her artistic education, she acquainted herself with the profiles of significant Polish theatre artists like Jerzy Grotowski, Tadeusz Kantor, avant-garde groups such as Teatr Gardzienice, and contemporary creators like Krystian Lupa and Krzysztof Warlikowski. However, this knowledge was sporadic, especially since it was very difficult to see performances by these creators in Ukraine[29]. Ukrainian artists had minimal familiarity with the most contemporary Polish theatre, including its interests, issues and challenges. Few had this knowledge, mainly those who had previously collaborated with Polish creators, such as Svitlana Oleshko, as well as Ukrainian playwrights and directors working in Russia, primarily in Moscow. This is because the theatre connections between Poland and Russia were much stronger despite the political differences between the two countries.

Theatre workshops and laboratories

The mutual introduction of a larger group of Polish and Ukrainian artists, the initiation of genuine collaboration and the comprehension of shared artistic objectives were made possible thanks to the passion and immense

---

[29] Statement obtained during an interview with Roza Sarkisian, conducted by the author of the text, on October 18th, 2023.

dedication of Joanna Wichowska – a practitioner and theorist of thea-tre, playwright, theatre scholar, curator of numerous theatre festivals and projects, critic, actress and performer. Since her days as a student, Wichow-ska has been fascinated by experimental, multicultural theatre that pushes be-yond the confines of traditional institutional theatre, all while staying deeply rooted and engaged in social issues. While studying theatre at the Jagiel-lonian University in Krakow, she began her collaboration with one of Po-land's leading experimental theatres, the Centre for Theatrical Practices 'Gardzienice', renowned for its experimental anthropological approach. Sub-sequently, in roles as a playwright and literary manager across various Polish theatres, she contributed to the creation of highly praised, often controver-sial productions that critiqued social pathologies. Notable examples include *The Death of the Squirrel-Man* (*Śmierć Człowieka-Wiewiórki*), directed by Natalia Korczakowska at the Cyprian Kamil Norwid Theatre in Jelenia Góra and *Non-Divine Comedy: Remnants* directed by Oliver Frljić. The premiere of the latter at the National Old Theatre in Krakow was cancelled by the manage-ment. Additionally, she was involved in *The Curse*, also directed by Oliver Frljić, and *Radio Mariia*, directed by Roza Sarkisian, both staged at the Powszechny Theatre in Warsaw. Wichowska's unwavering character drove her to fight for issues she considered important, regardless of the personal cost. An illustra-tion of this can be found in her tenure as the literary manager at the Norwid Theatre in Jelenia Góra from 2006 to 2009. Collaborating with the director, Wojciech Klemm, and talented young directors Monika Strzępka, Natalia Korczakowska and Michał Zadara, they successfully transformed a weak, pro-vincial theatre into one of the most prominent and socially engaged theatres with a modern, critical agenda. However, this radical transformation clashed with the local authorities, resulting in the dismissal of both Wichowska and Klemm.

Ukraine, its culture, and theatre were among Wichowska's greatest pas-sions. Her proficiency in Ukrainian enabled her to forge connections within the theatre community there. Much like in Poland, her interests did not cen-tre on mainstream or institutional state theatres but rather on independent theatre, which faced significant challenges in Ukraine's post-2014 landscape. Wichowska was often seen during the protests on Kyiv's Maidan, where she connected with independent theatre artists from Kyiv, Kharkiv, Odesa, Lviv and other smaller Ukrainian cities. Her goal was to support their ini-tiatives, particularly in securing assistance from Polish theatre. Since 2013 Wichowska has had the support of the Raszewski Theatre Institute in War-saw. Under its leadership, initially with Maciej Nowak and later with Dorota Buchwald from 2014, the Institute prioritised finding new artistically vibrant locations worldwide where Polish and international artists could collaborate in multicultural settings. Notably, the Theatre Institute had funding to execute projects, offering Wichowska an opportunity to secure financing for her programmes.

The plans involved long-term, coordinated cooperation and the exchange of ideas and experiences. A crucial aspect of Wichowska's approach was that the Polish side should not adopt the role of all-knowing teachers or masters, if only because they themselves could learn a lot from their Ukrainian counterparts. As such, the collaboration between Polish and Ukrainian creators aimed to foster intercultural exchange, seeking common ground for dialogue beyond language barriers and creating a form of theatrical expression accessible to both parties (Sting, 2010). The artistic objectives were deeply intertwined with social and political issues, addressing critical concerns in both societies. Wichowska saw artistic workshops and laboratories as the most effective means to achieve these goals. While a performance or specific performative action, accompanied by a public presentation, often marked the culmination of the work, it was not the sole focus. What truly mattered was the collaborative process preceding it: the collective effort, the exploration of innovative solutions, and the impact of artistic endeavours on the participants. Much like the concept of the Free Word Zone, the essence of theatrical work was to instigate a shift in the mindset of the artists engaged in the aforementioned laboratories and workshops.

The initial laboratories, orchestrated by Wichowska in 2014 and 2015, were directly connected to the Maidan events. Spread over 2 years, these sessions occurred in five different cities across Ukraine: Lviv, Kherson, Kyiv, Kharkiv and Odesa. The Polish contingent consisted of artists and theatre theorists actively involved in contemporary, socially critical theatre. Conversely, the Ukrainian side was characterised by a prevalence of young creators hailing from various regions of the country. As Sarkisian notes, the most valuable aspect was that the 'rebels' and reformers of the stagnant Ukrainian theatre could gather in one place, converse, exchange views on their artistic concepts, discuss the theatre models in which they operate, and, above all, realise that they are not alone in their endeavours, that there are others like them[30].

Each laboratory had a specific theme. In the theoretical segment, alongside an introductory lecture, discussions explored how the raised issues could be applied to stage practice. The practical segment diverged from pre-written dramatic texts, emphasising collaborative performative actions culminating

---

[30] A comment obtained during an interview with Roza Sarkisian, conducted by the author of the text, on October 18th, 2023.

in a final performance. For instance, one laboratory theme was 'artistic viruses', as recalled by Sarkisian:

> We explored the concept of acting as a virus that could penetrate the antiquated, ailing structures of Ukrainian theatre, fully dismantle them, and destabilise the rigid system to pave the way for a new, reformist approach. This new approach would be dedicated to addressing contemporary issues, deeply rooted in Ukrainian concerns, while remaining open to intercultural exchange and global perspectives. The outcome was a performance that arose from collaborative efforts[31].

Sarkisian also pointed out another effect of the laboratories:

> Interestingly, in 2015, following these 5 or 6 laboratories, it became apparent that many participants assumed roles as artistic directors and managing directors of numerous theatres, including state-run ones. Thus, these 'viruses' began to take effect and spread throughout Ukraine. The laboratories occurred at a crucial juncture for Ukrainian artists as they embarked on a quest for their identity and creative direction post-2014. These workshops provided guidance, on one hand, while helping participants better understand their goals and the shared pursuit among fellow artists in Ukraine[32].

The ongoing war in Ukraine at the time significantly influenced the agenda of subsequent meetings. Several workshops and their concluding performances were centred around this theme. They also delved into questions of individual identity within the context of Ukraine's multi-ethnic and multilingual landscape. Additionally, discussions related to Polish theatre arose during the laboratories. During one of the workshops, Marcin Kościelniak, a theatre critic and author specialising in contemporary performative and visual arts, led lectures on Polish theatre and visual arts in the context of societal identity formation. Kościelniak, who also teaches at the Faculty of Theatre and Drama at the Jagiellonian University, provided insights into these topics through his extensive expertise. Additionally, Dariusz Kosiński, the Deputy Director of the Theatre Institute, delved into the issues surrounding contemporary Polish theatrical avant-garde. The discussions also delved into the shared Polish-Ukrainian perspective on researching phenomena, as evidenced by the open discussion titled *Artists in times of political upheaval: Experiences of Poland and Ukraine*.

---

[31] *Ibid.*
[32] *Ibid.*

The project Maps of *Fear/Maps of Identity*

The achievements of the projects carried out in 2014 and 2015 encouraged Wichowska to extend the Polish-Ukrainian laboratories into the subsequent year. She received content-related and organisational support from Sarkisian on the Ukrainian side. Once again, the Theatre Institute in Warsaw provided conceptual and financial backing. This time, it was decided to centre each subsequent session around a single overarching theme titled:

> *Maps of Fear/Maps of Identity*. The project's website described it as follows: This Polish-Ukrainian performative project will try to study and define the cultural and social state of the Eastern part of Europe by means of metaphorical '*maps of fear*'/'*maps of identity*'. What is the difference between individual and public 'maps of fear' and how do they correlate with the official cartography? How can personal, intimate stories of identity be translated to the public and political ground? Can public 'staging of fear' lead to establishing of democratic relations between creators and the audience instead of hierarchical ones? To what extent can the performance arts and reflections on them provoke a complex and critical statement about the pressing problems and serve for a real social change? etc. These questions will express the thematic context of the planned work sessions (*Mapy strachu*, 2016).

The project consisted of two five-day work sessions, featuring masterclasses led by professional artists, along with lectures and discussions. Each masterclass involved the formation of a group comprising a director, playwright, set designer, musician and four actors. Together with a Polish director and playwright, they collaborated on creating a performative piece. These sessions were held in Lviv and Kharkiv. The subsequent stage of the project entailed developing the performance, which would subsequently be showcased in various cities across Ukraine, including during theatre festivals. Two extra seven-day sessions in Kyiv and Lviv were allocated for these preparations.

The *Maps of Fear/Maps of Identity* (*Mapy strachu/mapy tożsamości*) project, in both its scope and the number of artists involved, significantly exceeded all previous laboratories organised in Ukraine by Wichowska. Each session attracted approximately 40 people. According to Apchel, almost all of the most active and engaged artists from across the country, deeply involved in the transformation processes of Ukrainian theatre, were in attendance.

> Most likely, in no other circumstances could such a meeting have been organised. Despite being geared towards a limited group of participants, it proved highly effective, surpassing the impact of performances by renowned creators with audiences of 1,500. During these gatherings, creators not only conducted workshops, but also engaged in discussions about their objectives and direction. This led to

the emergence of shared ideas, culminating in performances held in their own venues that attracted diverse crowds, including individuals from different artistic backgrounds. Furthermore, these leaders kept their team members informed about the project[33].

The initial two working sessions, conducted in Lviv and Kharkiv, primarily focused on the participants meeting one another, followed by an exploration of their individual identities. They endeavoured to contextualise their personal narratives within the political and social landscape, investigating how portraying fear theatrically aids in its confrontation. The objective was to establish a secure environment where creators could authentically pursue their aspirations without feeling constrained or compelled to compromise. Conversely, the gradual process of overcoming fear and establishing one's identity, coupled with independent thinking, aimed to foster acceptance of others who similarly possess the right to autonomy in their judgments. Jewgenija Nestorowich[34], one of the lecturers and workshop facilitators, highlighted that:

> This could perhaps be termed uncompromising theatre – in that the performers on stage didn't consider the director (there wasn't one), commercial success, or the audience's reactions in the hall. However, those who argued vehemently in the initial days, with no common ground within the project, eventually learned (and quite successfully!) how to chart paths to understanding – if not compromise, then at least an effort to comprehend the Other (Nestorowich, 2016).

One of the projects in the workshop segment was the performance titled *Maps of Identity: The Language of Hostility* (*Mapy tożsamości: język wrogości*). It was authored and primarily performed by Anton Romanov, an actor from the Kiev-based PostPlay theatre. The project, set in an abstract space and executed with minimal technical resources, centred on the theme of everyday life choices, which would allow one to be honest with themselves whilst granting others the right to do and be the same. According to Romanov, 'the expression of our freedom can sometimes infringe upon the freedom of others, so it's essential to avoid causing harm. This is particularly crucial during times of war when every individual's blood is equally red, underscoring the priceless value of human life' (Nestorowich, 2016). During the performance, there was no separation between the audience and the stage. Other participants

---

[33] Information obtained during an interview with Olena Apchel, conducted by the author of the text, on October 10th, 2023.

[34] Jewgenija Nestorowich is a Ukrainian cultural manager, editor, critic and writer. With extensive experience as an independent cultural manager, she has contributed to over 30 international projects and festivals. Additionally, Nestorowich has led numerous original courses and workshops focused on cultural criticism and creative entrepreneurship.

in the project surrounded Romanov and followed him during the action. At the start the performer announced his intention to undress completely, and anyone who disagreed could leave at any time. Those who remained were asked to write their names on Romanov's body. Then, he introduced himself using what he considered the most fundamental, yet often challenging to express publicly, identifying information: 'I am an artist, I am Ukrainian, I am Orthodox, I am gay...'. Following Romanov's example, all the other participants wrote similar statements to define themselves. As the performance unfolded and individuals became more open, they were able to include increasingly personal and challenging-to-publicly-articulate information. At some point, however, Romanov showed his passport to the Ukrainian artists in the room, revealing dual citizenship – Russian and Ukrainian[35]. He was therefore not only Ukrainian but also Russian, representing the aggressor nation, which unsettled some participants and led to Romanov facing their rejection. At this juncture, the actor handed out needles to everyone, requesting that they harm him by piercing his body. This marked the conclusion of the performative workshop. The performance, much like Milo Rau's plays such as *La Reprise*, was based on strong emotions, affect, and even risk, which compelled not only the audience but also the other participants in the project to engage with what was happening on stage. The goal was to break taboos and the audience, confronted with fear, aggression and disgust, simultaneously confronted themselves. Acting as passive observers in the play, who could only contribute to causing pain to the performer, they themselves became somewhat complicit. The powerful impact of this initiative was evident in the lively discussion that ensued, bravely tackling challenging and sensitive issues in both Poland and Ukraine. These included moral, social and national differences as well as the mutual distrust among residents of eastern and western Ukraine. Additionally, the conversation delved into complex individual circumstances where superficial judgments, rooted in incomplete information, hurt people.

As part of the project, artists also extended their performances beyond the traditional theatre spaces into urban areas. This component of the programme was titled *The Parade of the Brave*. Five performers walked the streets with their mouths taped shut and carried blank banners. At the peak moment, they inscribed on them slogans such as: 'I am Ukrainian. I hate Ukraine, I am an actor. I hate theatre, I am Russian. I hate Russia, I am gay. God loves me'. The central banner proclaimed 'We have left'.

---

[35] Romanov hails from Crimea, which explains his dual citizenship. During Euromaidan and the Russian occupation, he took a pro-Ukrainian stance, resulting in his forced departure from his hometown of Simferopol by the Russians. Following February 24th, 2022, he enlisted in the Ukrainian army to serve on the front line.

Like the previous laboratories, the *Maps of Fear/Maps of Identity* project also tackled topics aimed at acquainting participants with contemporary Polish theatre and performative arts. Once again, Marcin Kościelniak was among the lecturers, exploring the repercussions of artistic decisions made by creators during political tumult in Poland, including the triumphant protests and the birth of Solidarity in 1980, the imposition of martial law by the communists in 1981, and the period of systemic transformation after 1989.

However, the most significant social impact was generated by the performance prepared during the last two sessions of the project. It was a performative, post-dramatic spectacle, the script of which was created during rehearsals and improvisations. Although two playwrights – Joanna Wichowska from Poland and Dmytro Levytskyi[36] from Ukraine – were invited to prepare it, along with two directors, Agnieszka Błońska from Poland and Roza Sarkisian from Ukraine, they served only as curators, while the entire team was credited as the authors and creators of the performance. The performance bore a surprising and ambiguous title: *My Grandfather Dug, My Father Dug, and I Won't Dig* (*Mój dziad kopał. Mój ojciec kopał. A ja nie będę*). Described in the programme as a precursor to the genre of 'trash-punk-post-theatre', it involved navigating through a chaos of signs, eclectic styles and seemingly mismatched aesthetic concepts. Thematically, it engaged with the discourse on Polish-Ukrainian history, rife with dramatic and bloody conflicts. On stage, five actors from various regions of Ukraine and Poland delved into their countries' pasts through the prism of their individual experiences.

The performance mocked and exposed contemporary stereotypical judgments and prejudices related to Polish-Ukrainian relations, present both in Poland and Ukraine. It ridiculed official pseudo-patriotic political narratives, the erection of countless monuments to heroes and victims, and the competition over the number of victims and the extent of suffering endured. The deliberate disorder, cacophony of sounds, and frenetic movements depicted on stage were intended to mirror the nature of Polish-Ukrainian debates, marked by oversimplifications, baseless grievances, and political distortion of history. Moreover, fundamental inquiries were posed not only about national and individual identities, but also about the right to maintain personal interpretations of the past and present, which would not conform to officially imposed narratives.

In the *Ukrainian Theatre* magazine Iryna Chuzhynova published the following review of the performance:

> The stage action resembles a carnival-like anti-world, where everything, whether seen or unseen, sacred or sinful, undergoes mockery (read: questioning).

---

[36] More information about Dmytro Levytskyi in the appendix.

This includes everything upon which the 'temple' of traditional Ukrainian and foreign theatre relies: psychological depth, pretence, playacting, sanctified knowledge of humanity, tired metaphors and civic pathos. Even the untouchable symbols of national faith, now transformed into true fetishes by the efforts of fervent patriots, are subject to criticism here. In 'My Grandfather Dug...', however, everything is just what it is: a rug is a rug, the earth is the earth, a cliché is a cliché. All statements are in the first-person singular: performers share their personal phobias, criticise the theatrical system for its dead conservatism, and try to prove that the stereotypical nature of our thinking, or the fear of exceeding the boundaries of customary beliefs, is one of the fundamental and perilous fears. The actors dance on a stage filled with earth, shouting, quoting Adorno, mimicking sexual intercourse, and knocking over a plastic silhouette of Lenin. They discuss their love for gingerbread, the events of May 2nd in Odesa, tumours and bleeding, and the broken 'Ukraine' bicycle. In the 'de-' section, they reflect on democracy, decommunization, demobilisation, and other popular topics. At the start of the performance the words 'Have we started yet?' appear on the screen offstage. This questioning tone persists throughout the entire spectacle, as if the actors are still seeking answers to the project's questions and continuously doubt if there's indeed any underlying drama driving the action. While the scenes lack a clear narrative structure, each one somehow engages the audience in the themes of patriotism, ideology and stereotypes (Chuzhynova, 2016).

The play *My Grandfather Dug, My Father Dug, and I Won't Dig* quickly gained significant artistic success following its premiere. It was invited to the prestigious GogolFest[37] festival in Ukraine and later embarked on a tour to the country's most prominent theatre venues.

Performers from different Ukrainian theatres (Kharkiv, Lviv, Kyiv, Odesa) and Polish theatres (Warsaw) came together to form an ephemeral group called Did Company for these artistic endeavours. The performance garnered numerous reviews and was widely seen as a groundbreaking artistic event in Ukrainian independent theatre. According to a survey by the Ukrainian Artistic Council *Dialog*, the show was the primary cultural event of 2016 in Lviv.

The UA Landing Project

The initiatives led by Wichowska garnered considerable attention in Ukraine, particularly among independent artists and theatre critics. Yet, Wichowska's primary objective was to foster even greater collaboration between Polish and

---

[37] GogolFest is an annual multidisciplinary international festival of contemporary art and cinema held in Kyiv. Dedicated to the famous writer Mykola Gogol, it showcases theatre, music, film, literature as well as visual arts.

Ukrainian creators. While respected figures from the Polish theatre scene, like Agnieszka Błońska, Marcin Cecko, Jan Peszek and Cezary Tomaszewski took part in the workshops and labs, Wichowska aimed to facilitate the presentation of contemporary independent Ukrainian theatre in Poland as well. Once again, the collaboration with the Theatre Institute in Warsaw proved highly significant, as it spearheaded another major Polish-Ukrainian project, this time hosted in Poland. Curated by Joanna Wichowska and Roza Sarkisian, the project, titled *The UA Landing* (*Desant* in Polish) was undertaken in Warsaw between November 2nd and 5th, 2017. Its name carried ambiguity, drawing from military terminology that resonated with the context of Ukraine at the time. Despite ongoing conflict, the world, including Poland, had somewhat overlooked the situation. Thus, the project's title aimed to jolt society into remembrance and awareness. Furthermore, it aligned with the wartime themes explored in many of the projects featured. The title aptly captured the artistic aims of the project too: a Ukrainian artistic landing intended to catalyse change in Polish theatre, spark interest and foster its enduring collaboration with independent Ukrainian scenes. Moreover, it aimed to diversify the predominantly monolithic and monoethnic language landscape of Polish theatre. While the invited performances were delivered in Ukrainian with Polish subtitles, all supplementary activities, including workshops, embraced bilingualism. Given the linguistic affinity between Polish and Ukrainian, mutual understanding was quite easily achievable, especially that in challenging situations Ukrainian artists with some proficiency in Polish could offer support to their Polish counterparts.

For Wichowska, who held a rather critical view of Polish institutional theatres, content with their relatively stable financial and organisational condition, and at the same time uninterested in new artistic inspirations, *The UA Landing* was intended to provide a revitalising impulse. This is how she spoke about it: 'I also have the impression that in Poland we are so focused on ourselves and our own problems, which is evident in theatre as well, that we are missing out on what Ukraine has to offer us. There is a definite need for movement in the other direction' (Soszyński, 2017). She expressed even stronger sentiments regarding the colonial, culturally superior attitude of Polish creators towards Eastern culture:

> We harbour a deeply entrenched sense of superiority and exhibit a syndrome of colonising the East. Poles arrive, engage in activities – be it presenting, educating or offering some form of financial assistance – and then vanish. We've contributed funds to impoverished Ukrainians, allowing ourselves to feel virtuous, while the remaining issues fail to capture our attention. It's disheartening (Soszyński, 2017).

The UA Landing project was intended to drastically change such an attitude:

63

We're reversing this trend right from the title of the review: now it's Ukrainians who are landing on our shores. [...] This review goes beyond just checking off the 'collaboration with Ukraine' box. This time, it's not us once again going there to promote Polish culture, as has been happening for years, but rather it's a revisitation – and not by people playing the role of students, but by competent, fantastic creators who have something important to say. And from whom we can learn. That's how it should be. Additionally, during the review, two wonderful actress-performers from Kharkiv, Oksana Cherkashyna and Nina Khyzhna, will be leading workshops (Soszyński, 2017).

Artistically, the Ukrainian theatrical representation was very strong indeed. Several of the best, most well-known, and esteemed independent theatre companies from Ukraine came to Warsaw as part of *The UA Landing*. The project's programme included: documentary plays such as *Goods* realised by the Theatre of the Displaced and based on the frontline experience of the author, director, and actor Albert Sardarian; *Autumn on Pluto* (*Jesień na Plutonie*) by a Lviv playwright and director Sashko Brama[38], based on interviews with senior citizens and performed using realistic puppets; performances drawing upon texts created together with actors and utilising their own experiences, such as *Defense Adaptation* (*Adaptacja obronna*) performed by actors from the Kharkiv Beautiful Flowers Theatre and war veterans in Donbas, and *My Grandfather Dug, My Father Dug, and I Won't Dig* by the Did Company group (a play prepared as part of Wichowska's earlier project *Maps of Fear/Maps of Identity*); a performative lecture *I Screw Your Festival or the Peculiarities of National Gentrification* (*Pieprzę Wasz Festiwal, czyli osobliwości narodowej gentryfikacji*) by the PostPlay Theatre from Kyiv; and an audio performance *Maidan: A Walk* by the Pic Pic[39] group from Kyiv.

---

[38]   More information about Sashko Brama in the appendix.

[39]   The Kiev-based theatre group Pic Pic was founded in 2016 by Ukrainian playwrights Dmytro Levytskyi and Petro Artemovskyi. Operating at the intersection of art, technology, tourism and urbanism, the artists specialise in theatrical projects carried out in urban spaces, focusing on participatory art. The group's repertoire features theatrical walks like *The Mendel Beilis Case* (October 2016), *Maidan: A Walk* (January 2017) and *Over the Abyss in the Rye* (December 2017). The authors characterise the first two projects as instances of immersive theatre. These walks aim to stimulate imagination, prompt reflection and offer new experiences concerning the everyday locations encountered by Kiev residents on their way to university or work. Pic Pic's activities can be classified as site-specific projects, marking the first implementation of such initiatives in the Ukrainian theatrical scene. They align with the principles of postdramatic theatre, which often eschews traditional text-centric structures, permitting the evolution and coexistence of diverse art forms that surpass conventional theatrical genres while retaining a sense of theatricality. Theatrical walks are projects that, in essence, extend beyond the traditional confines of the theatre building and rely on active participation from the audience. The theatrical

The programme was complemented by paratheatrical activities: workshops for actors, performers and dancers, as well as discussions on the relationship between theatre and society, theatre and the state and theatre and the artist.

The play *Autumn on Pluto* marked the beginning of *The UA Landing*. Its creator, Sashko Brama, gathered materials for the project at a nursing home near Lviv, where he recorded conversations with residents. In the performance, authentic recordings were used, and instead of real characters, large puppets were employed to faithfully represent the speakers. The set design was minimalist, presenting an empty space where the audience observed lonely, lost and forgotten elderly individuals, abandoned by the outside world. The title of the play was metaphorical, with Pluto symbolising the farthest and coldest planet in the Solar System and 'autumn' alluding to the twilight of life. In Brama's portrayal, the elderly characters have no prospects ahead of them; they can only reminisce about the past, awaiting eternity. Despite poetically addressing the painful social issues of modern times, the play provided some solace. Anna Korzeniowska-Bihun, who included another of Brama's plays, *Pork Liver*, in her selection of contemporary Ukrainian dramas (Korzeniowska-Bihun, Moskwin, 2015), wrote about it as follows:

> In the play, a mysterious voice declares, 'For the soul, neither the fact of birth nor death exists. It has never been born, is not born, and will never be born. It is unborn, immutable, primal, and eternal'. However, this hopeful transcendental notion is disrupted by an unexpected question: 'What will you do with your eternity?'. If the same as with your present – a bitter reflection suggests – then it will be meaningless. For Brama, the escape from this seemingly hopeless situation lies in Hindu mysticism, subtly woven throughout the play, offering the characters not so much salvation as solace (Korzeniowska-Bihun, 2018).

---

walk begins with a group of people organising to meet at a specified location through a social network. Each participant is provided with headphones and radio equipment, enabling them to receive instructions. The creators of the walk assert that their project encompasses three aspects: narrative, interactive, and performative, where participants assume roles as both actors and spectators. Immersion in the realm of audio recordings fosters a dynamic scenario situated between memory and history, fact and myth, private and public life as well as individual and collective experiences. The narrative unfolds virtually, allowing participants to interpret emotions, thoughts, and feelings through the urban landscape. The physical cityscape transforms into a theatrical setting, with buildings, sidewalks, fences, trees, traffic lights, cars and even pedestrians serving as elements of the scenery. Participants and passersby observe each other, giving rise to a phenomenon known as heterotopia, described by Michel Foucault and representing an alternate space.

The second of the performances utilising the form of documentary theatre –
Goods by the Theatre of the Displaced – referred to the war taking place in
eastern Ukraine at that time. Prior to *Goods*, the Theatre of the Displaced had
undertaken numerous other verbatim projects dedicated to this theme. In
this play, the narrative was drawn from the personal memories of the director and lead performer, Alik Sardarian, who served as a soldier and military
medic in Donbas. Sardarian recounted his wartime experience in a concise,
detached manner, employing minimalist techniques. He described how,
at a rescue point near Donetsk airport, a young Ukrainian soldier died in his
arms. Similarly devoid of emotion, he narrated the subsequent events, where
a group of Ukrainian soldiers opted to aid and rescue a wounded Russian
separatist. Soon after, one of those soldiers fell victim to the Russians, while
the saved separatist returned home unharmed through a prisoner exchange
in the war. Sardarian's narration was consistently paired with video projections – striking, authentic images capturing the deaths of Ukrainian soldiers,
the efforts of medics to save the life of a separatist, the exchange of prisoners
and the subsequent loss of another Ukrainian fighter. The contrast between
these vastly different forms of communication, Sardarian's stoic composure
and the emotionally charged, divisive scenes from the footage heightened
the dramatic impact of the events portrayed. The format of the performance
prompted questions about how to discuss and represent war. As noted by
Korzeniowska-Bihun:

> Sardarian distances himself from the official and public discourse surrounding
> war, including television propaganda and patriotic rhetoric. His play serves as
> a portrayal of death that occupies a space between the clinical detachment of a medic
> and the fear experienced by wounded soldiers. The author highlights the extent to
> which the narrative surrounding events in the eastern regions remains unspoken,
> ambiguous, and distorted. This prompts the question: what constitutes truth, and
> how should reality be described in a country where euphemisms dominate; where
> the ongoing war of several years is referred to as an anti-terrorist operation, and
> the aggressor is labelled a separatist? (Korzeniowska-Bihun, 2018)

Another production addressing the theme of war in Ukraine was the *Civil
Defense Training* (*Trening Obrony Cywilnej*). The Beautiful Flowers Theatre
collaborated with war veterans to create this play, where the former combatants not only contributed based on their memories but also performed
on stage. Their involvement had specific therapeutic goals, which they strongly emphasised during the post-performance discussion. The performance
centres on a civil defence lesson, intended theoretically to equip participants
with the skills to respond to armed enemy attacks. However, the crux of
the matter lies in the fact that when faced with the reality of an actual war,

the lessons imparted by the stern instructor – repeating rehearsed formulas akin to military drills – are entirely ineffective.

> The questions the teacher asks students to write in their notebooks have no answers in school textbooks: 'Who is a real man?', 'When will the war end?'. These classes fail to prepare students for life, let alone death. The stylized simulation of death, excellently portrayed by actors in the performance, bears no resemblance to the ordinary, one might say, mundane death on the front, enacted by a real soldier participating in the play (Korzeniowska-Bihun, 2018).

The performative lecture *I Screw Your Festival or the Peculiarities of National Gentrification* was intentionally crafted to provoke and shock viewers. While nudity on stage may no longer faze most theatregoers, the sight of copious flowing blood from a self-mutilating man can certainly terrify many. Nevertheless, such actions are quite characteristic of the PostPlay Theatre. The founder of the group, Den Humennyi, even received threats in Ukraine from audience members opposed to the artistic methods used by his theatre. During performances, it was common for a portion of the outraged audience to leave the room. While such situations did not occur on the stage of the Theatre Institute in Warsaw, the audience was definitely not prepared for what they would see. Their reactions varied: some accepted and appreciated PostPlay's innovation, while others strongly criticised it. However, a significant portion of the audience remained indifferent, which, for the creators of the performance, only confirmed the validity of addressing the presented topics on stage.

The stage design of the play was minimalistic. At the entrance, there was a desk with a computer where an actress sat. On the wall, a large screen displayed a presentation about the history of the PostPlay theatre, the manifesto of underground theatre and comments on the challenges of conducting independent creative work in Ukraine. In front of the screen, four actors were seated. After the presentation of the slides, the actual performance began. One of the actors removed his shoes and socks, then started building a tower with Jenga blocks. Soon, the other performers joined in. Minutes later, one of them began unpacking his luggage on stage, discarding all his belongings and proceeding to undress. Meanwhile, another actress approached the audience and abruptly rushed towards them, pushing and jostling between the rows. Another actress, dressed as a customs officer, arranged packs of cigarettes on the platform, further unsettling the audience's sense of security by throwing those cigarettes in their direction. A fourth actress filmed these events, projecting them on a screen hung on the wall. The bewildered audience witnessed these disjointed, seemingly unrelated actions. Eventually, after the actor had stripped completely, he took needles from a cosmetic bag of disposable syringes and started to pierce his fingers with them. He proceeded to inscribe slogans on large boards using his own blood: 'There is no war, I didn't kill anyone, I'm not a victim' and more. Once the blood on his fingers had dried, he pierced his tongue and used the blood flowing from it to cross out all the denials in the previously written slogans. Now, the audience could read: 'There is war, I kill one, I'm a victim' etc. (Sosnowska, 2018, pp. 107–111). At the conclusion of the performance, the actors left the stage individually, without returning for applause. As the audience departed the theatre, they encountered the artists stationed in various places along the pathway to the exit doors. The naked actor remained seated on the floor in the middle of the pathway.

The performance incorporated seemingly unrelated scenes that contained references to the contemporary situation in Ukraine. Chief among these was the indifference of the West, which has overlooked the horrors of the war unfolding there since 2014. In contrast to the media's repeated assertions of 'there is no war, there are no victims' etc. those fighting with their own blood testified to the reality: there is indeed a war, there are victims and innocent people are being shot. Many people in Ukraine live in a constant state of escape, amidst panic and gunfire, repeatedly packing and unpacking, abandoning all they own and migrating internally from the east to the west of the country. Additionally, Ukraine's landscape is marred by corruption, smuggling and illicit trade conducted by those deprived of livelihoods due to the war. And though cameras capture what unfolds around, the world watches impassively, treating it as just another media spectacle, without any reaction. The tragic heroes remain in their own country, where the war rages on, akin to actors after the curtain falls, while the audience returns to their safe homes, passing them indifferently on their way out of the building. The title itself provocatively questioned the purpose of the festival and the relocation of the Ukrainian population. The play also challenged the meaning of the changes attempted by Ukrainian underground theatres. It suggested that what emerges from trauma, from the experience of war, cannot lead to any constructive outcome but rather to entities that, in their self-destruction, seek a form of escape from a seemingly hopeless situation (Sosnowska, 2018, pp. 107–111).

In terms of its artistic value, *The UA Landing* was truly successful. It marked the first instance in Poland where such a comprehensive showcase of Ukrainian independent theatre was presented. Curators Wichowska and Sarkisian offered insights into the selection criteria for performers and plays:

> The performances we'll present at *The UA Landing* make a clear statement: I won't hide behind the fourth wall of the stage, I won't play a character in a story. I'll speak for myself, about myself. [...] First, we invited projects created outside

institutions – we believe the most interesting things happen there. Second, all of them address the act of creation itself – they engage in some form of self-analysis, both critical and self-critical. We were interested in theatre that feels the need to foreground the personalities of the creators, which opposes the illusion prevailing on Ukrainian stages. This illusion is challenged by all the invited artists in various ways. In today's era, concealing oneself behind pre-written texts and expensive stage setups is no longer acceptable – all of these harbour a kind of insincerity that doesn't align with the circumstances. Naturally, we sought out artists, whom I refer to as citizens, who feel accountable for what unfolds around them – in their country, society, and environment – and are eager to address it through theatrical or performative means. These statements vary greatly in form. That was the premise: if we want to organise a Ukrainian theatre showcase in Poland, we must do it comprehensively, without the ambition to exhaust the subject, but with the ambition to acquaint people here with various phenomena (Soszyński, 2017).

The success was not complete, however. As recalled by Sarkisian, despite the presence of many audience members, what could be felt was a lack of representation of Polish artists. The audience included theatre critics, experts in Ukrainian studies, representatives of the Ukrainian community in Poland, and, most importantly, individuals within the Theatre Institute's network of acquaintances and colleagues. However, it was challenging to initiate dialogue or establish cooperation with specific creators, including those representing independent scenes in Poland similar to those in Ukraine[40]. However, implementing this required a change in the formula of the festival itself. As Sarkisian claims: 'Wichowska was well aware that after *The UA Landing*, another step was needed to elevate the presence of Ukrainian theatre in Poland to a new level'[41]. Unfortunately, the implementation of such a plan proved to be extremely difficult. At that time, it became evident that Polish theatre was closed off to new initiatives related to the eastern part of Europe. Wichowska tirelessly reached out to directors of Polish theatres, producers and directors, trying to spark interest in the topic of independent Ukrainian theatre. She explained the refreshing, innovative trends it embodied, but received no response. While her interlocutors promised to consider the idea and respond soon, they never followed up.

At last, in 2019 Joanna Wichowska was approached by Agata Siwiak[42]. Siwiak, an independent curator and producer, had a deep interest in critical,

---

[40] Comment obtained during an interview with Roza Sarkisian, conducted by the author of the text on October 18th, 2023.

[41] *Ibid.*

[42] Agata Siwiak is a curator and producer of theatrical and interdisciplinary projects. She serves as an adjunct at the Institute of Theatre and Media Arts at Adam Mickiewicz University

social theatre and performative arts. She was familiar with Wichowska's work in Ukraine, as they had collaborated on several projects before. One notable collaboration was at the Polish Theatre in Poznań, where they organised a large international festival called *Bliscy Nieznajomi* (*Close Strangers*). Siwiak suggested teaming up with Wichowska for the twelfth edition of this event[43].

The *Close Strangers* Festival

The *Close Strangers* Festival made its debut on the Polish theatre scene in 2007. Held annually at the Polish Theatre in Poznań, its thematic concept aimed to serve as a platform for discussing contemporary issues spanning history, culture and the relationships among European nations. Each edition centred around a distinct theme, often delving into significant, difficult, uncomfortable and socially or politically controversial topics. These encompassed the struggles of nations burdened by unjust histories, the portrayal of marginalised individuals and groups, the dynamics of modern family life, the overlooked lives of ordinary people and the notion of a collective European identity. In 2019 the *Close Strangers* Festival enjoyed a strong position on the theatrical landscape of Poland, drawing in sizable audiences annually. It showcased numerous compelling theatres from both Poland and abroad, with its reputation further solidified by its organiser, the Polish Theatre in

---

in Poznań. With her work as a curator, she navigates the intersection of various media, critical practices and socially engaged art. Since 2016 she has held the role of artistic director for the *Close Strangers* Festival at the Polish Theatre in Poznań. Between 2018 and 2019, she carried out her own project titled *RePresentations: New Education* (*RePrezentacje: Nowa edukacja*) as part of the Biennale Warsaw. For this initiative she received the first prize in the category of *Artistic Institutions and Museums* (*Instytucje artystyczne i muzea*) at the Warsaw Artistic Education Award presented by the City of Warsaw. Between 2012 and 2017 she led a theatre collective at the Children's Home in Szamocin. In 2015 she organised her own series titled *Interventions* at the Polish Theatre in Bydgoszcz. She authored and curated the social-artistic programme *Wielkopolska: Revolutions* (*Wielkopolska: Rewolucje*), organised by the Wielkopolska Regional Government (2012–2014). Additionally, she curated the *Trickster 2011* project, a performative programme of the European Culture Congress in Wrocław. Between 2008 and 2009, she was the artistic director of the interdisciplinary Festival of the Dialogue of Four Cultures in Łódź, dedicated to the idea of multiculturalism. From 2004 to 2007 she was associated with the National Old Theatre in Krakow, where she served as the director of the international Intermedia Theatre Forum *baz@rt*. From 2002 to 2004 she worked at the Polish Theatre in Wrocław as the programme coordinator for the Wrocław Forum of Contemporary Dramaturgy *EuroDrama*.

[43] Agata Siwiak shared this information on January 17th, 2024 during an interview with the author.

Poznań, renowned as one of the nation's premier venues. Siwiak offered her insights on the festival's pivot towards Ukraine:

> We will explore the diversity of theatrical forms of our neighbours, drawing inspiration from literature as well as historical archives, avant-garde traditions of the early 20th century, dark cabaret, choreography and modern music. We will encounter young, uncompromising creators whose voices are attentively listened to by audiences in Lviv, Kharkiv and Kyiv. We will also watch performances from Warsaw and Rzeszów, which address the presence of Ukrainians in Poland and our relationship with 'foreigners'. In guest performances, film screenings and audience discussions important social, political and cultural themes will resonate: the condition of society after the trauma of war, violence, nationalism, patriarchy, corruption as well as modern slavery. We will track possible versions of memory and contemporary relations between both nations and inquire about potential forms of emancipation in response to the burden of history and imposed norms. We will discuss the reality in Ukraine itself and the situation of the Ukrainian minority in Poland (Gabryel, 2019).

Thanks to Wichowska's contacts in Ukraine, the organisers gained significant financial and organisational support from the Ukrainian Institute, a state agency established in 2017 under the Ministry of Foreign Affairs of Ukraine. Its purpose is to represent and shape a positive image of Ukraine worldwide. In 2019, the Institute implemented as many as 85 cultural projects outside Ukraine, including the Ukrainian Festival of Contemporary Music in New York, the Year of Culture Austria-Ukraine 2019, presentations of Ukrainian-language audio guides in museums worldwide, concerts and networking events. It also played a very important role in popularising Ukrainian drama and theatre in Poland, being involved in numerous projects there, even after the full-scale Russian invasion in 2022. The festival's curators were Siwiak and Wichowska, jointly responsible for its programme. Their collaboration extended beyond one edition of the festival. *Close Strangers* expanded its scope to include Poland's eastern neighbours for the next two editions in 2020 and 2021. Since Wichowska took over the festival has undergone several changes, notably abandoning the principle of exclusively inviting repertory theatres. They expanded to include independent stages, performative actions and ephemeral projects created by artists from various backgrounds, including Polish-Ukrainian collaborations. Additionally, there was a much greater focus on non-theatrical projects like performative installations, film screenings and discussions.

In 2019 the festival invited four performances prepared by artists from Ukraine and two from Poland. It featured several individuals who had previously participated in Wichowska's workshops in Ukraine and *The UA*

Landing project. It was therefore another opportunity for them to strengthen their collaboration. It's difficult to find one common thread in the programme. The performances showcased various poetics, employing very different artistic means. Some referred to history, some to Western European literature, while some addressed the issues faced by contemporary Ukraine and Poland alongside the part of Europe that was condemned to the communist system and the colonial policies of Soviet Russia for years.

The Publicist Theatre[44] from Kharkiv was one of the most recognisable avant-garde groups among those invited, both within and outside Ukraine, commenting on social and political issues in their country. To the festival in Poznań the Publicist brought the performance *Red Wedding* (*Czerwone wesele*), based on the idea and dramaturgy of Victoria Myroniuk[45]. After the October Revolution, the term 'red wedding' referred to a secular ceremony celebrating the new, revolutionary order, inspired by avant-garde ideas of freedom, community, equality, liberated sexuality and emancipation. The performance was a whimsical reinterpretation of this secular, Soviet ritual. The artists employed diverse stage formats, including a talk show, re-enactment resembling a 'living newspaper' – an amateur revolutionary theatre display and a musical, showcasing various approaches to working with documentary and historical material. The ironic exploration of pre-revolutionary ritualism's ideas and aesthetics aimed to examine the relevance of historical concepts in present-day Ukrainian society as it continues to break free from the shadow of its Soviet past. Through this lens of history, the creators tackled a pivotal issue facing contemporary Ukraine: the role of the decommunisation process. An integral element of the performance was the music composed by Alexandra Malatskovska[46].

The second Ukrainian ensemble, the First Theatre[47], is based in Lviv. Established in 1920, it has undergone numerous organisational changes over

---

[44] The Publicist Theatre, also known as Театр 'Публіцист' or Theatre 'Publicist' Kharkiv, is an independent authors' theatre renowned for theatrical experiments in Kharkiv. It serves as a hub for alternative creative education and actively participates in urban cultural events. The theatre was founded in the mid-1980s as a student theatre, stemming from popular amateur theatre groups of the Soviet era that promoted the predominant ideology of the time. Today, in the modern environment of Kharkiv, Publicist is known as one of the most important alternative theatres. In its performances it tackles important social issues, engages in a critical revision of the past (including the Soviet past), seeks modern theatrical forms and explores new ways of communicating with the audience.

[45] More information about Victoria Myroniuk in the appendix.

[46] More information about Alexandra Malatskovska in the appendix.

[47] The First Theatre (Перший Театр) was founded in March 1920 in Kharkiv as the First Academic Ukrainian Theatre for Children and Youth under the name Theatre of Tales. It was

the years, transitioning from a theatre primarily for children and young audiences to its present-day identity and image of an experimental, avant-garde theatre that emphasises the contemporary fusion of diverse artistic practices, approaches and concepts. The First Theatre is highly receptive to collaboration with other independent theatres and directors. This led to them connecting with Roza Sarkisian and Joanna Wichowska, resulting in the production *Beautiful, Beautiful, Beautiful Times* (*Piękne, piękne, piękne czasy*), inspired by Elfriede Jelinek's novel *The Excluded*. Sarkisian directed the play, while Wichowska served as the dramaturge. *Beautiful, Beautiful, Beautiful Times* premiered in Lviv at the First Theatre and was enthusiastically received by both the audience and critics to the point that it has soon gained the status of a cult performance in Ukraine. The performance was subsequently invited to a number of theatre festivals in the country and abroad. In the performance the story described in Jelinek's book served as a starting point for reflection on post-war society infected with violence. The traumas of war breed widespread aggression, evident not only in the streets but also hidden behind the doors of proper, middle-class homes. Sarkisian and Wichowska tackled topics concerning the mechanisms of violence, highly relevant for contemporary Ukraine, and questioned the extent to which society can break free from the normalisation of wartime atrocities and aggression.

> Although the performance transports viewers to late 1950s Vienna, the story being told actually unfolds here and now: on a specific stage, in a specific city, today. The creators of the performance problematise theatre as a space where social processes, structures of violence and power relations are reflected on a micro-scale. They contemplate the future: after all, the post-war era is still ahead of us (First Theatre, 2018).

The play *Psychosis,* also directed by Roza Sarkisian, drew inspiration from the works of Sarah Kane's drama, along with the poetry of Ann Sexton and Sylvia Plath. Sarkisian invited actresses from different Ukrainian theatres in Kyiv, Kharkiv and Lviv to take part in the production. Among them were two exceptionally talented and esteemed artists in Ukraine, Oksana Cherkashyna[48]

---

staffed by a group of students and collaborators of the prominent Ukrainian stage reformer of the time, Les Kurbas. In 1944, the theatre was relocated to Lviv, to the premises of a former Jewish theatre, where it became a hub for renowned directors, both from Ukraine and abroad, such as Serhiy Danchenko, Volodymyr Opanasenko, Ada Kunytsia and Mark Nestantiner. During this period, it earned recognition as an independent and innovative theatre. The First Theatre regularly collaborates with acclaimed artists from Ukraine and other countries, including Andrii Prykhodko, Vadym Sikorskyi, Sashko Brama, Bohdan Polishchuk, Cosmin Matei, Natalia Vorozhbyt, Iryna Garets and others.

[48] More information about Oksana Cherkashyna in the appendix.

and Alexandra Malatskovska, who had previously participated in Wichowska's workshops and *The UA Landing* project. The performance was presented in Poland at a time when Sarah Kane's immense popularity in the country had slightly diminished. Earlier, her plays were sought after by prominent Polish directors such as Grzegorz Jarzyna, Krzysztof Warlikowski, Paweł Wodziński, Paweł Łysak and Maja Kleczewska. These artists focused mainly on interpreting the psychological aspect of suffering, seeing it as a key element of individual sensitivity and the state of an individual when confronted with society. Sarkisian aimed to offer a slightly different interpretation of the play. She wanted to steer clear of overly simplistic autobiographical elements, the portrayal of illness, or the play as a testament by the author. Above all, she was keen to avoid excessive poeticising of the text and instead emphasised the black humour present in Kane's works. As a result, the audience witnessed:

> 'A black cabaret about illicit love and death', 'a bipolar show', 'a psychedelic bachelorette party', 'a feminist revue', 'a manifesto of emancipated femininity'. The performance celebrates the strength of women: conscious and wild, rebellious and cheeky, suffering and laughing at their own suffering, reckless and unromantic. On the stage, there is a constant play with boundaries: pain, 'normalcy', theatrical form, societal taboos. All of this serves the deconstruction of the myth about the place of women in society (Psychosis, 2019).

Psychosis appealed even more to the pressing issues in Ukraine and Poland than the first two performances of the festival. In both countries, traditional, conservative norms operate in patriarchal societies, reserving limited freedom of choice of social roles for women. In this respect, the performance contributed to the discussion that progressive Polish theatres were having with the conservative government and church.

The next Ukrainian performance, *Restaurant Ukraine*[49], constituted another strong voice opposing patriarchal society. It was directed and performed by two outstanding Ukrainian actresses and performers, Oksana Cherkashyna

---

[49]   The Ukrainian performance resonated with one of the two Polish projects at the Festival *Modern Slavery*. It drew inspiration from the alarming findings of the Global Slavery Index report, which revealed that there were over 181,000 modern slaves living in Poland in 2016. They came from very diverse countries: Ukraine, Belarus, Korea, the Philippines, China, Vietnam, but also from Poland. In terms of the number of 'modern slaves', Poland ranked among the top countries in the European Union. The artistic team of Biennale Warszawa conducted an investigation to determine the origins of such statistics as well as the situations, places and stories associated with them. They also attempted to address why this phenomenon remains invisible and is rarely discussed in public debate. This initiative culminated in a performance-exhibition.

and Nina Khyzhna[50]. Dramaturgical development was handled by Dmytro Levytskyi[51]. *Restaurant Ukraine* was a play addressing real and psychological corruption, the enslavement of individuals and particularly the plight of women within patriarchal power structures. Set in the context of Ukrainian oligarchs' lives, it also delved into the world or theatre and the experiences of women, especially actresses, in Ukraine. The script evolved during rehearsals, with a significant portion relying on direct improvisations by the performers, drawing from personal memories of real events.

> The requirement to create a play about corruption triggers an actress' stream of consciousness and a series of performative hallucinations, during which childhood memories, personal traumas, idiosyncrasies, fears, anger, feelings of professional unfulfillment and helplessness are revealed (*Restaurant Ukraine*'s webpage, 2019).

The festival concluded with a performance by the Wanda Siemaszkowa Theater in Rzeszów titled *We Won't Give Lviv Back* (*Lwów nie oddamy*). Even the title itself could be seen as provocative, suggesting a call to revise history and reclaim the Ukrainian city of Lviv for Poland. This tactic was deliberate, devised by the play's director, Katarzyna Szyngiera, who humorously and

> somewhat cunningly portrayed the contemporary relations between Poles and Ukrainians. The entire performance was constructed from brief, dynamic scenes, presented concisely and precisely, addressing historical narratives (including sensitive 20th-century issues and prehistoric events from a millennium ago) as well as mentalities, satirising xenophobia, the fabrication of new histories by politicians and nationalists on both sides of the border (Stern, 2020).

The play was crafted from documentary material gathered along both sides of the Polish-Ukrainian border by the director and two journalists, Mirosław Wlekły and Marcin Napiórkowski. They conducted street surveys, questioning Poles about whether they should apologise to Ukrainians for the occupation of Lviv in 1918, their perspectives on Polish-Ukrainian relations and potential measures to enhance these relations. The responses varied; some reflected enduring grievances and perceived injustices from the other side, while others signalled evolving attitudes and an acceptance of the coexistence of Poles and Ukrainians. The audience was also shown the results of surveys conducted in high schools in Lviv and Rzeszów. Students answered questions about the meaning of patriotism, the current relationship between Poland and Ukraine and the future of these countries. In the production by the Rzeszów theatre, artists from the Polish repertory theatre collaborated with Ukrainian actors from independent scenes. Oksana Cherkashyna

---

[50] More information about Nina Khyzhna in the appendix.
[51] All of them had previously participated in projects realised by Joanna Wichowska as well.

portrayed one of the main roles, that of a True Ukrainian. The playwright Olha Matsiupa also helped prepare the play.

The inaugural Polish-Ukrainian edition of the Festival is yet to result in a significant breakthrough in the relations between Polish and Ukrainian theatres. Siwiak noted that garnering interest from institutional stage venues in independent projects, which venture beyond the boundaries of mainstream Western culture, continues to pose considerable challenges. The same difficulty is mirrored in engaging the audience. Although the audience turnout for specific events at the Festival was generally high, the organisers had to put in considerably more effort into promotion compared to previous editions of the Festival[52]. Despite challenges, Siwiak succeeded in gaining approval from Maciej Nowak, director of the Polish Theatre, to dedicate the upcoming edition of the Festival to Ukraine as well. This marks the first instance of repeating a theme in the Festival's history. The curatorial text stated:

> In contemporary Poland, including Poznań, we coexist with Ukrainian men and women in a single community. For the first time since the post-war era, we are evolving into a multicultural society. Nonetheless, the question persists: do we possess sufficient understanding of each other, or are we merely perpetuating stereotypes? For this reason the Theatrical Encounters *Close Strangers* – which previously focused solely on Polish theatre and art – have broadened their scope. Since last year, the festival's audiences have had the opportunity to experience performances and projects by Ukrainian artists as well. This year's edition of *Close Strangers* is shaped by questions. One of them resonated during the Maidan revolution: 'If not you, then who?'. The rest will be posed during the festival: Who should give hope? Who should build community? Who should speak about what's painful? Who should trust? Who should 'make love, not war'? Throughout presentations, meetings and debates, we will be asking both creators and the audience about who is speaking and on whose behalf. We will explore who various stories belong to – whether it's a singular narrative or multiple narratives – stories viewed from diverse perspectives and influenced by both individual and collective experiences. While we will address painful events from the past, it's equally crucial for us to delve into conversations about the potential for constructing a new, improved world that transcends national boundaries, social classes and divisions. The 13th Theatrical Encounters *Close Strangers* will once again spotlight Ukrainians, with organisers revealing secrets and confronting commonly held misconceptions about them. They will openly address typically taboo topics, including women's issues, war, rebellion and revolution (Curatorial text of the *Close Strangers* Festival, 2020).

---

[52] Information obtained from Agata Siwiak during the interview conducted by the author on January 17th, 2024.

With even greater determination than the previous year, the organisers aimed to kickstart long-term collaboration between Ukrainian and Polish artists during the Festival. During the grand opening, Siwiak highlighted that nurturing creative friendships and advancing further joint Polish-Ukrainian productions were one of the Festival's key objectives. The COVID pandemic imposed substantial limitations on their execution, however, leading to a majority of presentations being conducted online. Nevertheless, Siwiak made efforts to ensure that certain events could still take place in person, albeit in small groups. Once again, the programme featured a variety of artistic forms including performances, readings, performative lectures, audio walks, multimedia installations and documentary films, all accompanied by discussions.

One of the highlights of the Festival was the performance of the play *Więzi* (*Bonds*) by the Polish The Wybrzeże Theatre in Gdańsk, written and directed by Olena Apchel, a Ukrainian playwright, director and curator who was invited by the Gdańsk theatre to helm this production. *Więzi* was inspired by Apchel's *Journals*. She highlighted that the artistic form of the performance evolved significantly during the collaboration with Polish actors. Initially Apchel envisioned it as a documentary project. The end result, a tragic farce, is regarded by the director as the best possible choice, however. Conversations with the team made Apchel realise that the topic of the Russian war in Ukraine had completely disappeared from the Polish media in 2018. Many people, including those involved in preparing the performance, were surprised to learn that the war in Ukraine was still ongoing. Prior to rehearsals there were several days of extensive discussions led by Apchel about the events unfolding in Ukraine. These conversations encompassed dramatic and tragic moments alongside humorous and absurd occurrences.

> The team listened with great interest to my stories, my accounts from the war. Together we concluded that a straightforward, factual presentation wouldn't have the same impact on the audience as a vivid narrative encompassing both the horrors and the humour associated with war[53].

Apchel started writing her memoirs in mid-2013, amid escalating political tensions in Ukraine. She continued to chronicle subsequent events, trying to grasp the unfolding situation as more questions emerged with no easy answers. Even within Ukrainian families, there was disagreement. One faction supported the liberal-democratic side, while the other aligned with the Russian perspective. Jarosław Murawski relied on Apchel's *Journals* to develop the content of the play. However, the final script didn't solely focus on images of war. Even the title *Więzi* is ambiguous. In Polish, it can be

---

[53] Information from the interview with Olena Apchel conducted by the author on October 10th, 2023.

derived from words like 'to bind', 'bonds', or 'imprisonment', suggesting forms of enslavement of individuals or entire nations. Conversely, *więzi* can signify forms of interpersonal closeness or close relationships. Apchel expressed her thoughts on this matter as follows:

> In this manner the play aimed to depict something more nuanced, prompting us to consider what true understanding among people entails. The resulting text centres on what lies 'in between': between older and younger generations, between political perspectives, between western and eastern Ukraine. I believe we're living in a beautiful 'in-between' period. In this performance, we strive to come together at the table for a conversation. In situations where reaching an agreement seems impossible, we find a way, although it demands considerable effort. Often, it's the simplicity of human love that aids us in this (Umięcka, 2019).

The play was showcased at multiple theatre festivals and Apchel was honoured for her direction at the Prapremiere Festival in Bydgoszcz in 2019. It garnered equally high praise during its presentation in Poznań as part of the *Close Strangers* event.

The Civil Defense Training, another performance showcased at the Festival concerning the Russian-Ukrainian war, was already familiar to the Polish audience from *The UA Landing* Festival. This time, it was adapted by Polish artists from the Contemporary Theatre in Szczecin, building upon the staging by the Ukrainian group Beautiful Flowers. Ukrainian actress Vira Popova, who has lived in Poland for many years but hails from war-affected regions of Ukraine, also contributed to the production. She integrated her own independent narrative into the performance, distinct from the original presentation of the Beautiful Flowers Theatre. Essentially, it served as a protest against the tendency to cast Ukrainian artists solely as persecuted victims in productions abroad. From the stage, Popova directly asked: Why are they invited to participate in projects as 'Ukrainian artists' rather than just as artists? Drawing from this, she crafted a micro monodrama within the performance. Directed by Jakub Skrzywanek, the play was presented in the format of a performative reading.

The production *Deaf Republic* (*Republika głuchych*) took the form of an accessible online performative lecture. It drew inspiration from the poetic narrative of *Deaf Republic* by Ilya Kaminsky – a distinguished poet, recipient of the Anisfield-Wolf Book Award (2020), academic lecturer, critic and someone personally affected by hearing impairment. The lecture featured excerpts of poems performed by the deaf artist Daniel Kotowski, actress Martyna Zaremba-Maćkowiak, original recordings by the poet and commentary by Anna Łazar – a translator and critic, discussing various themes from contemporary Eastern European culture. The narrative of *Deaf Republic* takes place amidst a state of war in the small town of Vasenka. Its inhabitants devised a unique sign language, incorporating elements from diverse cultural backgrounds including Russian, Ukrainian, Belarusian, Yiddish and American Sign Language. Additionally, some signs were invented by the residents themselves, as they endeavoured to liberate themselves from the grip of the authoritarian regime by crafting a form of communication beyond its control.

Traditionally a significant part of the Festival's programme has been dedicated to social issues, including the situation of women in Poland and Ukraine. One of the events drawing attention to these topics was the performative walk *This Walk*, prepared once again in Poland by Piotr Armianovsky[54], Dmytro Levytskyi and the Kyiv-based theatrical collective Pic Pic. In contrast to the performance they showed during *The UA Landing* Festival in Warsaw, this time the urban space selected by the artists to critically engage with was Poznań, with women's experience of the city becoming the main theme. The project concluded with a debate on the situation, rights and violations of those rights of women in Poland and Ukraine, supplemented by screenings of the films *Citizens* and *Close Strangers*.

Among the non-theatrical projects, reviewers paid special attention to the multimedia installation *Coincidence* by the Ukrainian-Polish couple Yulia Andriichuk and Patryk Lichota. The multimedia world they created, composed of sounds, images and multimedia technologies, transported viewers to the crossroads of Polish and Ukrainian cultures. The focus was on what is culturally shared and distinct, close and distant. Throughout the duration of the festival the installation was scattered throughout the theatre, serving as a kind of set, through which viewers moved during various festival events.

The second edition of the Festival dedicated to Ukraine received considerable coverage in Polish and Ukrainian theatre and culture publications as well as in daily newspapers. By that time a larger group of Ukrainian and Polish artists and ensembles had converged around the Festival, either directly participating or observing presentations, although the participation of repertory theatres remained notably lower. An interesting trend indicating that joint Polish-Ukrainian festival presentations have a broader resonance was the emergence of projects that participants undertook in Poland beyond the framework of *Close Strangers*. However, it's challenging to provide further insights about the audience due to pandemic restrictions and the implementation of many events online where viewers were largely anonymous and their numbers limited.

---

[54] More information about Piotr Armianovsky in the appendix.

Agata Siwiak's selection of the theme for the upcoming Festival was notably shaped by the socio-political developments in Poland and its neighbouring regions throughout 2020 and 2021. During this period Belarus experienced a surge in protests against the authoritarian rule of Alexander Lukashenko, which were met with harsh repression, leading to numerous arrests. Consequently, a significant influx of Belarusian refugees, including theatre practitioners, sought sanctuary in Poland. Simultaneously, Ukraine witnessed heightened tensions with an escalation in armed conflicts and a rise in anti-Ukrainian rhetoric emanating from Vladimir Putin's regime. Simultaneously in Poland, the nationalist authorities escalated their anti-democratic policies, while the ruling party amplified its public condemnation of sexual minorities and non-heteronormative individuals. Women protested against the severe tightening of anti-abortion laws and demonstrations emerged against actions challenging Poland's democratic, rule-of-law principles. Consequently, it was decided that the *Close Strangers* Festival would expand its focus beyond Ukraine to encompass the broader Eastern region. In the Polish theatre magazine *Didaskalia*, the rationale for this decision was articulated as follows:

> Agata Siwiak shifted her attention to the East, where, much like in Poland, a policy of precarisation prevails and affects an increasing number of people through social exclusion. Recognising the shared sentiments of anger, dissent against systemic violence and hope for change between our country and Belarus and Ukraine, Siwiak invited individuals from both the East and local creators and activists to collaborate in the festival, granting them creative freedom. She encouraged them to express anger and envision dreams. Working collectively and inspired by the concept of sensitivity, akin to Siwiak's approach, these artistic individuals didn't just recount painful stories or expose oppressors; they primarily pondered what lies ahead: how to turn anger into affirmation? How to live more authentically? Consequently, the festival's primary act of agency was an interdisciplinary exploration of a more empathetic socio-political alternative and a communal endeavour to conceive new, improved worlds (Cudak, 2021, pp. 353–354).

In her curatorial text for the Festival, Siwiak wrote:

> Today our hearts are closest to the divided Ukraine and to Belarus, where anger has stirred. The common dissent against violence binds our countries together – allowing us to exchange strategies of resistance while embracing empathy and sensitivity towards one another. Being close to each other (also physically, as there is an increasing number of people in Poland who have emigrated from Ukraine and Belarus, both for economic and political reasons), we can collectively design a better world/worlds. Because who else is going to do it if not us? We want to voice our hopes (and sometimes shout them out), believing that speaking them

aloud will increase their chances of becoming reality. In all projects presented this year the theme of dreaming of a safe place – be it home, city, country or shelter – will be prevalent. We will engage in discussions and work in the spirit of activism, emphasising responsibility for the planet (with projects primarily using existing materials and objects) and maintaining faith in long-term processes. This year's edition of *Close Strangers* is largely based on several-week residencies and collaborations between artists from the East, including those already residing in Poland, and local creators. The resulting works will be showcased at multiple locations throughout the city (Curatorial text of the *Close Strangers* Festival, 2021).

Joanna Wichowska once again contributed artistically to the organisation of the Festival. Alongside Siwiak, they decided to alter the event's format, placing a greater emphasis on intercultural collaboration among artists and the development of projects during its duration, rather than solely showcasing completed works. The programme featured predominantly installations, performative walks and performances, with only one theatre production included. Interestingly, this production was also developed using a collective team approach to work. Artists were invited to Poznań not only for the festival itself but also for several-week, sometimes even month-long residencies. During these residencies, they would prepare projects to be showcased later during the festival. The emphasis was on fostering collaborative efforts between artists from Ukraine and Belarus and Polish creators.

The *Close Strangers – East* Festival, in a broader and more categorical approach compared to previous editions, tackled social issues, primarily manifestations of homophobia. These themes were prominently featured in the *Plac Wolności* project by Roza Sarkisian, Joanna Wichowska, Dominika Mądry[55] and Kiju Szałankiewicz[56]. Throughout the Festival, a project comprising various performative activities was conducted. The organisers described it as follows:

'Freedom Square' is a performative research project conducted collaboratively with queer individuals in urban settings. Can a safe space be established for Poznań's LGBTQ+ community in the city centre? What would this ideal 'queer

---

[55] Dominika Mądry graduated from Theatre Studies and Interactive Media and Spectacles at Adam Mickiewicz University in Poznań. Since June 2017 she has been a member of the theatre team at the Scena Robocza Association. She also organises and produces queer projects in Poznań, including the *Queer Open Showcase* event held in 2019.

[56] Kiju Szałankiewicz, who uses gender-neutral pronouns, works in the field of visual arts and is associated with the queer community in Poznań. They studied graphic design at the Faculty of Arts at Maria Curie-Skłodowska University in Lublin. Their interests include VR practices, analog animation, intermedia activities and experimental graphics. In recent years, they have also been exploring the theme of utopian safe and sensitive spaces.

home' look like when publicly visible? How might the city respond to it? How will the boundaries between societal norms and deliberate challenges to them be navigated? Can freedom only be expressed and embraced in secrecy or can it integrate into urban daily life? Must we choose between a sense of security and freedom? (*Bliscy Nieznajomi: Wschód*, 2021)

As part of the project, a safe space was established in the heart of Poznań for LGBT+ individuals. This space not only provided a place for peace and relaxation but also served as a platform where individuals could openly express their views and participate in various artistic activities. Artists from Poznań's queer community performed during the concerts. Additionally, there were performances and discussions centred around ballroom culture. Furthermore, a national reading of queer literature took place, with actors from the Polish Theatre in Poznań participating.

Another festival project *Schron* (*Shelter*) also aimed to create a safe space. It was carried out by two Ukrainian artists Victoria Myroniuk[57] and Olha Skliarska[58], alongside their Polish counterparts Kornelia Trawkowska[59] and Agata Kiedrowicz[60]. The project was inspired by ritual practices on the one hand, and the concept of home as a safe space. Individual viewers were invited to participate actively in the event by entering the shelter, a tent made of colourful blankets, inside which Kornelia Trawkowska conducted a 'secular

---

[57] Victoria Myroniuk is an interdisciplinary artist, performer and theatre activist. She obtained her bachelor's degree in cultural theory from the National University 'Kyiv-Mohyla Academy' in Kyiv, followed by a master's degree in contemporary stage practices and visual culture in Madrid. Additionally, she pursued doctoral studies in the field of performativity and scenography in Brussels. She mainly focuses on interdisciplinary projects that combine performative, participatory and visual practices, exploring themes related to rituals, their boundaries and potentialities. Her artworks have been showcased at various festivals such as Zürcher Theater Spektakel, Festival Belluard Bollwerk International, La Cosa en Casa, Festival Les Nuits Blanches, ParadeFest, Festival of Young Ukrainian Artists, among others.

[58] More information about Olha Skliarska in the appendix.

[59] Kornelia Trawkowska is a theatre actress who graduated from the Ludwik Solski State Drama School in Krakow (PWST) (now Krakow's AST National Academy of Theatre Arts, Akademia Sztuk Teatralnych). Since 2016, she has been a member of the Polish Theatre in Poznań. She is also one of the initiators of a project aimed at combating violence during the creation of performances. Additionally, she collaborates with the acting studio STA in Poznań.

[60] Agata Kiedrowicz is a designer, curator and educator. She teaches at the School of Form, Academy of Art in Szczecin and at Collegium da Vinci where she directs postgraduate studies in fashion and new media. Collaborating with designers, artists, cultural and artistic institutions, she has curated numerous exhibitions, including Polish Design Island, Vienna Design Week, Brussels Design September and Łódź Design Festival. Working interdisciplinary, at the intersection of humanities, art and design, she explores sensory practices of artists and designers.

ritual'. The actress shared memories she recalls in challenging situations. She also encouraged her guests to share their own stories by asking questions: How and where can we find peace in the face of a global catastrophe? What measures can prevent it and save the world? What is most essential for us, what do we want to take with us when the external world is on the brink of disaster? The goal was to craft a collective narrative. It was envisioned as a tale of a better world, a safe haven where one could escape the challenges of daily life. The ritual unfolded amidst the scent of incense and the soothing sounds of Tibetan singing bowls.

As per tradition, during the *Close Strangers* Festival, a lot of attention was devoted to feminism, the role of women in society, the violation of their fundamental rights, manifestations of chauvinism and discrimination. These topics were addressed in a performative walk, prepared, as in previous festivals, by Piotr Armianovskyi and Dmytro Levytskyi together with the Pic Pic group and Polish artist Patryk Lichota. Also now, the main theme of the interactive walk through Poznań was experiencing the city through the eyes of women. The project was co-created with Polish women and immigrants, activists and women who have experienced or are still experiencing difficult life situations, manifestations of homophobia, chauvinistic or indeed racist behaviours.

One of the two Belarusian programmes also centred on the perspective of women viewing the surrounding reality, which they perceive as hostile and dangerous. The project *Belarus Lives* (*Žyvie Biełaruś*) was rooted in the real stories of Belarusian women who actively engaged in social protests against the regime of Alexander Lukashenko, advocating for the restoration of freedom and democracy in Belarus. The narratives brought to mind the heroic resilience of women and the hardships they endured due to the oppressive tactics of the Belarusian police, which included arrests, beatings and torture. Utilising previously gathered materials, including video recordings, the Belarusian creators developed a multimedia installation in a public space. Another form of resistance against the Belarusian regime was proposed by the Belarusian artist and activist Jana Shostak in the project *State of Emergency*. It was a battle through laughter and ridiculing evil in a stand-up comedy format. At the beginning of her performance, Shostak emphasised that: 'without laughter, there is no revolution'[61].

The thematic reference to all the projects, illustrating the threats experienced daily by individuals inhabiting this very eastern part of the European continent, was a debate: *No one will invent the world for us if we don't do it ourselves*. It focused on extreme situations, such as systemic human rights

---

[61] The quote is from the play.

violations, dictatorship, authoritarianism as well as homophobia, racism, chauvinism, the threat to life during the pandemic and the perspective of an ecological catastrophe. The aim was not to sensationalise fear or create an atmosphere of helplessness, but to showcase ways of resistance and opposition.

The theme of Sashko Brama's project *Pandemia.ua* also revolved around human confrontation with mortal danger. The Ukrainian playwright and director, already familiar to the Polish audience through the *Autumn on Pluto* project at *The UA Landing* Festival, collaborated with Maria Jasinska[62], Witold Oleszak[63], Rafał Ziąbka[64], Ostap Manko[65] and Marek Straszak[66] in creating his documentary performance.

The project commenced in March 2020, which coincided with the onset of the initial lockdown when conventional methods of engaging with theatre audiences became impossible. Brama and Jasinska embarked on a quest to explore new forms of interaction with the world. They then created the *WE* project, in which they collected documentary testimonials from the time of the pandemic: quarantine and self-isolation journals, reports about COVID emergency teams, portraits of doctors, volunteers and leaders of anti-war movements. They endeavoured to engage with diverse communities, investigating the dynamics unfolding amidst the pandemic's changes. The culminating result, showcased at the *Close Strangers* Festival, was a unique concert incorporating documentary videos in collaboration with musicians from Poznań's free improvisation scene: Witold Oleszak (piano, objects) and Ostap Manko (violin, electronics). The dramaturgy of the project was handled

---

[62]   More information about Maria Jasinska in the appendix.

[63]   Witold Oleszak is a musician, a member of para-theatrical and avant-rock groups. He has created illustration-based compositions for alternative theatre and conceptual graphic scores. Over the past decade he has been fully devoted to free improvisation. In 2021 he returned to composing graphic music and performing written music.

[64]   Rafał Ziąbka is a producer and curator of performative arts. His main project is the Poznań Improvised Orchestra, developed since 2017, where he serves as a manager, conducts and plays on radio receivers. As a curator, he primarily operates in the field of improvised music, sound art and bio art, collaborating with Agata Siwiak among others. In his work, he focuses mainly on open initiatives that go beyond institutional frameworks and seek audiences in his everyday environment.

[65]   More information about Ostap Manko in the appendix.

[66]   Marek Straszak is a visual artist who graduated from the Wrocław Academy of Fine Arts (Multimedia) and the Berlin University of the Arts (Art and Media). He is the founder of the visual studio Animateria. Throughout his commercial endeavours, he has undertaken a variety of audiovisual projects, including collaborations with Alter Art, Nike and Pernod Ricard. Additionally, he crafts analog-digital artistic installations, with a keen interest in video projection techniques, motion design and film.

by Rafał Ziąbka. Collages of film fragments and improvised electro-acoustic music created an ephemeral, pulsating reality, questioning the reality of recent trauma. The creators posed the question: Is the pandemic a dream from which we will never awaken?

The only theatre performance showcased at the festival, *The H-Effect*, directed by Roza Sarkisian, drew from chosen passages from Shakespeare's *Hamlet* and Heiner Müller's *HamletMachine*, interwoven with the personal experiences of Ukrainian actors and actresses. These individuals, compelled to make extreme choices due to the war in Ukraine over the past few years, brought their own narratives to the stage. The performance was set in the Ukrainian reality of debris and ruins left behind by the Russian occupiers.

> The performance is structured like a mosaic, weaving together stories, events, quotes from reality, memories and imaginations. War serves as the backdrop to the entire narrative. While it's challenging to discuss, remaining silent about it is equally impossible. Just like trauma, there seems to be no suitable language for it. Talking about war is like navigating a minefield. Yet, the participants of the performance undertake this effort. In their testimonials, we see the projection of a new world where a wartime hero is allowed to show vulnerability and a woman is not a helpless victim (*Bliscy Nieznajomi: Wschód – H-effect*, 2021).

The H-Effect played a crucial role in the extensive discourse surrounding the war in Ukraine, especially concerning how, post-conflict, despite personal traumas, societal psychological devastation and a diminishing trust in the adherence to moral norms, there remains the potential to reimagine an ethical-political vision for a better reality. Bartosz Cudak highlighted in his review:

> *The H-Effect* can be primarily understood as a practical application of the concept of affirmative politics according to Rosi Braidotti, which encourages the transformation of negative affects into positive ones. And while it might seem nearly impossible, in the performance, traumatic experiences are not only vocalised but there's also an attempt to replace them with a different ethos than the culture of trauma. In one of the scenes actresses and actors take turns describing how they imagine a new, better world. And although each of them has their own vision of socio-political alternatives, the common denominator is the possibility of self-determination and rejection of the heroic and nationalist narrative about war. Designing a new reality in this case is based on deconstructing the existing, often oppressive dominance (Cudak, 2021, p. 355).

The director, Roza Sarkisian, embraced a collaborative approach to crafting the performance. The script evolved during rehearsals, with the actors' monologues about the war drawn from their personal experiences, as each of them had some direct involvement in it[67]. The stage was minimalist, with much of the action unfolding in an empty, dimly lit space. Actors donned contemporary attire, offering insight into their characters and roles as the performance unfolded. Scenes were characterised by brief, impactful cuts, set to powerful, discordant contemporary music. Developed in collaboration with the Internationale Heiner Müller Gesellschaft in Berlin, the play garnered acclaim at various theatre festivals across Ukraine.

The three subsequent editions of the *Close Strangers* Festival, in which Ukrainian creators were so well represented, undoubtedly constituted a significant stage in the process of getting to know one another and to collaborate between independent, progressive Polish and Ukrainian theatre. Collaborative projects and the chance to witness captivating theatres and performances have enabled artists from both countries to recognise their shared perspectives. These include a critical examination of various facets of their surrounding realities, particularly sensitive social issues often ignored or intentionally marginalised by conservative societies and authorities. They also involve contemplating the role of contemporary theatre and the artistic methods it should employ to fulfil its objectives, alongside a critical assessment of traditional, middle-class theatre. In Poznań, actors, playwrights, set designers, visual artists, musicians, cultural managers, critics and theatre theorists came together. This contributed to the development of a meaningful network of Polish-Ukrainian artistic connections, which, while still in its early stages, was steadily expanding. Both groups were also united by a generational community – they were representatives of the young or middle generation who entered the world of theatre with hopes and enthusiasm, refusing to accept the routine and self-satisfaction characteristic of many repertory theatres. Throughout the festival's successive editions, there was a noticeable shift towards anti-mainstream theatre, particularly since Wichowska's involvement. This trend created a growing divide between the festival participants and the conventional repertory theatre. A prime example of this was the main organiser, the Polish Theatre in Poznań. Despite the theatre's artistic director, Maciej Nowak, being a strong advocate for independent and Ukrainian

---

[67] In the performance the following actors perform: Oksana Cherkashyna – an outstanding theatre and film actress currently working at the Teatr Powszechny in Warsaw. Roman Kryvdyk – an actor at the Lesya Ukrainka Academic Theatre in Lviv who participated in the Anti-Terrorist Operation in eastern Ukraine (aimed against illegal military formations that occupied parts of the Donetsk and Luhansk regions in the spring of 2014). Oleh Rodion Shuryhin-Herkalov – a costume designer and stylist, an LGBT activist and a trained director. Kateryna Kotlyarova – a graduate in political science, a documentary filmmaker of war crimes and a former soldier in the volunteer battalion Aydar. Jaroslav Havianets – a trained lawyer, a participant in the defence of the Donetsk airport, who studied acting at the Kharkiv University of Arts before the war.

theatre, the festival, in its format over the last three years, posed a significant organisational and financial challenge for the traditional repertory scene, even with support from the Ukrainian Institute. One report from the festival included some telling remarks:

> The authorities in Poznań are liberal, and the director of the Polish Theatre in Poznań, Maciej Nowak, is progressive. However, it's known that institutions govern themselves by their own rules. Institutional theatre in Poland tends to be patriarchal and hierarchical, with its primary goal being artistic success and economic prosperity rather than creating a better reality (Cudak, 2021, p. 353).

Consequently, the fourteenth edition of the *Close Strangers* Festival turned out to be the last. This was certainly a very unfavourable situation for Polish-Ukrainian theatrical cooperation.

The most significant Ukrainian creators involved in Polish-Ukrainian theatrical collaboration

A much greater loss for the joint efforts of Polish and Ukrainian creators was the death of Joanna Wichowska in March 2022, thanks to whom contacts between Polish and Ukrainian creators essentially began and were subsequently continued. At that moment, there was a void left by an artist who intimately understood and resonated with contemporary, independent Ukrainian theatre, all while being deeply involved in Polish theatrical circles, particularly those exploring and critically examining social issues. One cannot forget about Wichowska's inexhaustible energy, activity and creativity, through which the vision of Polish-Ukrainian projects was consistently developed and enriched by her. There was also a belief in her that the presence of what is most interesting and inspiring in Ukrainian theatre could enter the bloodstream of Polish theatrical life and would not be merely a matter of passing fashion. During one of the meetings and discussions accompanying the *Close Strangers – East* Festival, Wichowska expressed hope that 'the longer stay of artists in Poznań would result in deeper professional and interpersonal relationships that would remain alive even after the project's conclusion' (Wichowska, 2021). Her instincts proved right as Ukrainian artists indeed began to come to Poland for longer or shorter residencies or exchanges much more frequently than before; there were also significantly more joint Polish-Ukrainian theatre projects. Among the individuals involved in these projects, regardless of Wichowska's initiatives, were, among others: Olha Skliarska, Ostap Manko, Piotr Armianovsky, Dmytro Levytskyi, Alexandra Malatskovska, Sashko Brama, Maria Jasinska, Svitlana Oleshko and Mychajlo Barbara. There were also cases of individuals choosing to stay in Poland permanently, such as the Ukrainian theatre and film actor Artem Manuilov[68]. He first arrived in 2010, performing at the Gardzienice Theatre. After 2015, he decided to extend his stay, eventually collaborating with the Powszechny Theatre in Warsaw starting in 2018. He secured a permanent acting position there in 2022. Among the participants of workshops, labs and festivals organised by Wichowska, the activities of three artists resonated most strongly in the Polish artistic community: Roza Sarkisian, Olena Apchel and Oksana Cherkashyna.

Sarkisian was one of the key figures in workshops, labs and festivals organised by Wichowska. In 2017 she received a six-month artistic scholarship as part of the *Gaude Polonia* programme, which gave her the opportunity to collaborate with Wichowska on several important Polish-Ukrainian projects and productions in Poland. The most prominent among these productions was *Radio Mariia*, directed by Sarkisian in January 2022 at the Powszechny Theatre in Warsaw. Wichowska contributed as one of the authors of the texts and served as the dramaturge for this performance. *Radio Mariia* presented a futuristic portrayal of Poland in the year 2037, depicting a scenario where Catholicism had essentially faded away in the country. The story unfolds at Radio Mariia station, portraying the most conservative and politically charged version of Polish Catholicism in the 2021 Polish reality. However, in 2037, it transforms into a secular radio station, boldly confronting Catholicism for all its misdeeds and mistakes. The premiere was announced by the Powszechny Theatre as follows:

> Let's envision the future. Let's consider that the most unlikely scenarios could unfold. Let's imagine the unimaginable. For instance: the Catholic Church in Poland has vanished. There are no longer religious classes in schools, nor statues of the Polish pope in public spaces. Parishes accommodate refugees, and churches have been repurposed into concert halls (or supermarkets?). Human rights supersede the interests of adherents to any one religion. Being Polish no longer necessitates being Catholic. The term 'concordat' fades from the Polish lexicon. And so forth, and so on. How did this happen and what are the consequences of this breakthrough? Has the Church also vanished from our minds? Let's imagine that we're already there. In the future. That we're shaping it right now, here. Together we're crafting alternative models of society, culture and politics. Where are the boundaries of

---

[68] More information about Artem Manuilov in the appendix.

our imagination? What limits it? What keeps it from being radical? What stands in the way of utopia becoming reality? (*Radio Mariia*, 2022)

The performance was in the style of a political stage poster. Provocation, irony, elements of buffoonery and grotesque dynamically intertwined with serious reflection. Sarkisian utilised techniques typical of avant-garde political theatre, including film projections. Actors, portraying radio presenters, performed on stage under their real names and, akin to a live radio broadcast, endeavoured to maintain direct contact with the audience in real time. The set design of the performance was simple and minimalist: a table with microphones, a pair of chairs, speakers, a camera and film screens. The themes of the play, which cast important figures of the Polish Catholic Church, with Pope John Paul II at the forefront, in a negative light, along with feminist and LGBT accents, corporeality and sometimes blunt language, caused a real storm and scandal, especially among radical right-wing Catholic circles. Protests would take place directly outside the theatre, with Catholic associations sending letters to the Minister of Culture and National Heritage urging an official ban on the performance. Reviewers assessed the play and Sarkisian's directorial work completely differently, however. It was one of the most extensively reviewed theatrical productions in Poland at that time. Critics highlighted Sarkisian's artistic maturity and nuanced approach to the subject matter. The play's goal was not to provoke scandal or mount a 'blasphemous' attack on the church, but rather to address a deeply significant and painful issue for many Poles: the state of the Catholic Church in their country.

In the performance the main role was played by Oksana Cherkashyna, one of the leading actresses in projects organised by Wichowska, appearing in productions such as *Psychosis, We Won't Surrender Lviv, Civil Defense Training, My Grandfather Dug, My Father Dug, and I Won't Dig, Restaurant Ukraine,* and *The H-Effect.* Cherkashyna, already a recognised actress in Ukraine, appeared in Poland in 2018 at the invitation of Katarzyna Szyngiera to perform in the play *We Won't Surrender Lviv* at the Wanda Siemaszkowa Theatre in Rzeszów. The play was subsequently featured in several Polish theatre festivals, including *Close Strangers*, and earned Cherkashyna some of Poland's most prestigious theatre awards in 2019. After successive performances at the *Close Strangers* Festival, towards the end of 2019, director Agnieszka Błońska offered her one of the main roles in the play *Devils (Diabły)*. Wichowska was responsible for the script and dramaturgy. The play was inspired by the true story of nuns allegedly possessed by the devil in a convent in the French town of Loudun during the 17th century. In Poland this theme was explored in the 20th-century novel *Mother Joanna of the Angels* (*Matka Joanna od Aniołów*) by Jarosław Iwaszkiewicz and in the acclaimed 1961 film by Jerzy Kawalerowicz, which received numerous awards at film festivals, including the Special Prize in Cannes. Błońska's performance, based on Wichowska's script, however, only loosely followed the thematic framework of the literary and film originals. Instead, it strongly engaged with contemporary Poland, depicted as a patriarchal country governed by right-wing conservatives, with the Catholic Church attempting to control the consciences and choices of society. The production was uncompromising, challenging taboos, deliberately straddling the line between provocation and the principles of good taste. It underscored the rights of women, portraying their pursuit of independence, self-determination and freedom as their greatest sin. In her review of *Devils*, Agnieszka Kobroń wrote:

> Finally, on the theatre stage, we will witness portrayals of women who exude confidence in themselves and their sexuality, certainty in their beliefs and worldview and assurance about their role in the world. The demonic aura attributed to them in Agnieszka Błońska's performance enables them to step out of the shadows and express themselves authentically. They speak truthfully, with strength and authenticity, transcending the boundaries of propriety and challenging every taboo. They take to the stage to talk about women directly, without pretence. Their mission, their manifesto [...], seeks to finally establish women on equal footing with everyone else, devoid of unnecessary divisions based on gender, orientation or any other factor. It's no longer a world of flawed women and strong men; the time has come for us all to unite as one cohesive group, working towards a shared goal (Kobroń, 2020).

Cherkashyna, in her portrayal of one of the nuns, received high praise from both audiences and critics.

> These moments seem like child's play compared to the scene featuring Oksana Cherkashyna, who caused quite a stir in the play *We Won't Surrender Lviv*. Charismatic Cherkashyna emerges somewhat as a person both 'from here' and 'from beyond', as a bold dismantler of national dogmas. One might get the impression that the creators of the performance strategically use the scene with the actress to provoke maximum controversy, perhaps positioning it as a milestone in 21st-century Polish theatre, akin to *The Curse* (*Klątwa*). The actress encourages the audience to envision her as Mary. She holds dildos in both hands, their buzzing amplified by microphones. In her monologue Cherkashyna talks about breaking the 'male anal inviolability', promising – to paraphrase words from *Pulp Fiction* – to 'get mediaeval on their ass'. In this context, it alludes to the Volhynian massacre, symbolising escalating aggression towards Ukrainian immigrants (Tomasiewicz, 2020).

In 2021 Cherkashyna became a permanent member of the acting ensemble at the Powszechny Theatre, where she played several significant and acclaimed roles, including in *The Heart of Darkness*, adapted from Joseph Conrad's novel. Her performance in the highly praised rendition of Anton Chekhov's *Three*

Sisters, a collaboration between the National Old Theatre in Krakow and TR Warszawa, directed by the renowned Belgian director Luk Perceval, also received wide social resonance. It premiered in May 2021. Perceval recognised that in today's world, Moscow no longer holds the status of a global centre or a 'promised land' that can inspire human dreams. In the production he aimed to highlight the theme of the 'decline of old Europe', embodied by the Prozorov sisters. However, the war in Ukraine questioned the relevance of staging a play in which the characters yearn for Moscow. A bold and controversial interpretive decision was therefore made to replace Moscow with Kyiv, and the titular three sisters dream not of going to Russia's but to Ukraine's capital city. Cherkashyna clarified:

> This approach was suggested by Luk Perceval and the dramaturge Roman Pawłowski. I won't attempt to explain their decision, but Luk constructed a setting from the start where the idea of a dream home in Moscow – especially in an era when you can buy a plane ticket for seventy euros and reach there in an hour and a half – seems somewhat absurd. Now, Moscow has shed all its positive connotations. Meanwhile, Kyiv has emerged as a symbol of the struggle for a new, independent Europe, free from regimes and political agreements (Kazimierczak, 2022).

The alterations from the original script of the play went even deeper. Cherkashyna portrayed Natasha in the performance, a character already somewhat estranged from the Prozorov family in Chekhov's text, not fully understood or accepted. Perceval aimed to enhance this sense of otherness, while also attributing Ukrainian nationality to the character. Here's Cherkashyna's view on this:

> During the rehearsals Luk told me that if my resistance is so strong, I should show it on the stage. That's why I wanted not only the Ukrainian nationality of Natasha to be visible, but also her humanity, her subjectivity. This is especially important now, when there are so many Ukrainian men and women in Poland (Kazimierczak, 2022).

For Cherkashyna, the language she used on stage held special significance, too. Recalling the performance, Svitlana Oleshko noted that at one point, the actress spontaneously transitioned from Polish to Ukrainian:

> During improvisation, Oksana began speaking Ukrainian, and it was her idea, not suggested by the director. She didn't conceal her Ukrainian identity in any way. She stood out with colours, styles of the constantly changing costumes, expressiveness, but also with language. As the atmosphere in the Prozorov household became more relaxed, she transitioned from carefully articulated Polish to her native language. It even reached a point where Natasha instructed her husband to translate what she had to say to the sisters. Natasha curses, mutters under her

breath, showing no interest in communication; she takes control of the situation. Cherkashyna's role relied heavily on improvisation. Her Natasha bursts onto the Old Continent with the force of the new Europeans, her Ukrainian speech overpowering the rehearsed foreign language conversations of the Prozorovs, drowning out their wilted monologues and dialogues[69].

The language not only identifies the character's nationality but also reflects the present circumstances. It embodies the convictions of Ukrainians regarding the position their homeland deserves within the family of European countries, which they perceive as somewhat indifferent to its fate. Cherkashyna speaks in Ukrainian also to 'shout out' from the stage that at a time when the enemy wants to take away Ukrainians' native language, throwing Ukrainian books out of libraries in the cities they occupy, preserving the language is part of the Ukrainian raison d'etre, a struggle to maintain national autonomy. It simultaneously shows that even far from their homeland, the goal of Ukrainian refugees – immigrants, including those who have had to perform abroad due to the war, is not to blend into a new culture, but to preserve their own. In 2021 Cherkashyna received additional prestigious acting awards, including recognition in the audience poll of the International Festival of Pleasant and Unpleasant Arts in Łódź. She was honoured there for her performances in *Three Sisters*, directed by Luk Perceval, and *The Heart of Darkness*, directed by Paweł Łysak. Becoming one of the leading artists at the Powszechny Theatre, she made a significant impact. However, in 2023, she opted to return to Ukraine following several interesting film offers in her home country.

Olena Apchel also decided to stay in Poland for an extended period. She first arrived in 2016 and had the opportunity to observe the work of many Polish theatres as part of a scholarship programme.

She was primarily interested in the youngest and middle generation of artists, creators of postdramatic, alternative, socially engaged theatres. Apchel considers her contacts with Krzysztof Garbaczewski and Ewelina Marciniak at that time to be the most fruitful and broadening her artistic horizons. After 7 months in Poland, she decided to return to Ukraine, however, where she actively joined the fight as a volunteer on the Ukrainian-Russian front, serving, among other things, as a paramedic. Apchel emphasises that her departure was also associated with a certain disappointment with Poland, but not with Polish theatre. The atmosphere in the country governed by radical right-wing ideology, marked by its anti-feminist, anti-refugee, anti-immigrant stance, homophobia and instances of racism, proved pivotal.

---

[69] Svitlana Oleshko during an interview conducted by the author on October 26th, 2023.

This sentiment was a mix of disappointment and sadness towards the Poles for electing such individuals to lead their country. I found it perplexing, particularly considering that in my everyday interactions, among my Polish friends and in theatres, I encountered a completely different attitude and mindset[70].

In 2018 Apchel was the artistic director of the Lviv Academic Drama Theatre. As she herself emphasises, her fondness for Polish theatre persisted, which is why, when she received an invitation from Poland's Wybrzeże Theatre in Gdańsk to direct the play *Więzi* (*Bonds*), she promptly accepted. The production was later showcased as part of the *Close Strangers* Festival. Yet, this was not the final project Apchel undertook in Poland. At the end of 2021, the Zagłębie Theatre in Sosnowiec featured the play *Kreszany* on its billboards, co-written by Apchel with Olha Matsiupa and Polish playwright Wojciech Zrałek-Kossakowski. Apchel also directed the play. The content of the play is quite provocative and may be controversial for some, especially considering the role of Christianity in Poland. This fairy tale-ritual creates a hypothetical reality, which could have emerged if in the 10th century, Grand Prince of Kiev Volodymyr and the historical first ruler of Poland, Mieszko I, had not decided to Christianise their countries.

> What if, the authors ask, the strongly patriarchal Greco-Roman mythology had not become our cultural model, at least in the part of Europe inhabited by Poles and Ukrainians, imposed in the educational system and cultural transmission? And what would our world, torn apart by war today, look like if we had a better understanding of Slavic mythology, in which, as suggested by Olena Apchel, women and their matrilineal cultural heritage played a more significant role based on caring for others and the land? (Bal, 2022, p. 35)

The play sheds light on the entirely forgotten Slavic mythology in both Poland and Ukraine. *Kreszany* therefore presents an alternative history of the Slavic world involving Poles, Ukrainians, Belarusians and Russians. It begins at the dawn of the world and spans to contemporary times, encompassing events like the Russian-Ukrainian war in Donbas in 2014. However, war is a side theme here. It is invoked in one of the scenes depicting a 'tryzna', which is a Slavic funeral rite. Olha Matsiupa was responsible for this part of the text. Specifically for this, she conducted interviews with Ukrainian women who have been fighting on the frontlines since 2014. Excerpts from these recordings were included in the performance. In Kievan Rus 'tryzna' had an exceptionally solemn character and was accompanied by various rituals and feasts. In *Kreszany* it was portrayed as a military ceremony

---

[70] Information obtained during an interview with Olena Apchel, conducted by the author of the text, on October 10th, 2023.

honouring a dead female soldier. On stage a circular structure was set up, leaning towards the audience, around which the actresses moved rhythmically, dressed in shorts and undershirts. Their movements, reminiscent of military drills, were interrupted by short messages from the musician on stage. His words echoed commands, prompting the actresses to don different pieces of modern military attire after each instruction. Subsequent scenes vividly evoked a military training ground.

> From stories about Slavic deities, we move with the heroines of the performance to the army, where orders are executed, grenades are thrown, shots are fired, tanks are repaired, land is de-mined, bulletproof vests are worn and aeroplanes are flown; to the army where fighters are haunted by dreams of people whose lives they took away. We arrive at the heart of the events with the heroines, events that leave scars on both the body and the psyche. One of the soldiers repeats the words like a mantra: 'The demarcation line is a scar that runs through me and bleeds'. The director incorporated another significant aspect into this scene: the general situation of women heading to the front. The clothing they received at the headquarters, designed for a male silhouette, was uncomfortable for the heroines. When someone finally considered their needs, they received numerous sanitary pads and tampons instead of appropriate attire (Tarasińska, 2023).

The production employed diverse artistic styles and aesthetics. The mythical realm, brimming with pathos and solemnity, was portrayed with a hint of irony and detachment. The distant, legendary past was interwoven with contemporary global and local concerns, juxtaposing Slavic mythology against the backdrop of the Greek and Christian worlds. The portrayal of the latter was critical, highlighting its role in stripping women of their rightful social standing and inflicting humiliation, suffering and pain.

The play premiered in December in Krakow during one of Poland's most significant theatre festivals, the Divine Comedy. Following this, *Kreszany* were staged not only in Sosnowiec but also in other theatres across Poland. The play reached its peak success at the Malta International Theatre Festival in Poznań. *Kreszany* became one of the most captivating and extensively discussed artistic highlights at this prestigious festival in Central and Eastern Europe, which hosts prominent and influential artistic figures from Europe and around the globe.

IV. POLISH THEATRE IN THE FACE OF THE FULL-SCALE RUSSIAN INVASION; HUMANITARIAN AND ARTISTIC SUPPORT – PHASE II

⌒

The full-scale Russian invasion immediately prompted symbolic gestures of support for Ukraine from Polish artists. This was accompanied by humanitarian aid actions, including offering theatre spaces to refugees. Quite quickly, theatres also began implementing projects, based mainly on contemporary Ukrainian literature as well as accounts illustrating the plight of the Ukrainian population amidst the ongoing war, through performative readings. At the same time, various institutions of Polish culture, primarily the Theatre Institute, initiated programmes intended to provide long-term material and artistic support to theatre professionals coming from Ukraine. The most significant in scale and importance were the residency programmes offered by the Theatre Institute in Warsaw.

The full-scale Russian invasion on February 24th, 2022 drastically altered the situation for Ukrainian artists, leading to a notable increase in their migration to Poland. These were no longer individuals seeking opportunities for artistic exchange, utilising projects offered by Polish theatre institutions to establish and expand Polish-Ukrainian theatrical connections. They were war refugees forced to flee their country, saving their own lives and the lives of their loved ones – children, parents... Very importantly, they did not see coming to Poland as emigrating to the promised land where they intended to stay permanently. The overwhelming majority of them repeated: 'we are only here for a moment, until we can safely return to our homeland', believing that ultimate victory will surely come, and fairly soon. In contrast to the standard actions of many immigrant theatres, which aimed to support refugees in the process of assimilation, the goals regarding refugees from Ukraine were diametrically different. Marco Martiniello highlights the issue of refugee integration, which usually unfolds through social, political, cultural and economic processes once they arrive in a new society. In this context, we're discussing a process deemed satisfactory when immigrants achieve a level of integration where their patterns of participation resemble those of non-immigrant citizens (Martiniello, 2006, pp. 4–6). Art, in this case theatre, is intended to support such integration processes. This was very evident, for example, in Germany and Belgium, where a policy of migrant participation in local culture was adopted, with theatres like the Maxim Gorki Theater and Theater der Migranten heavily involved (Totah, Khoury, 2019, pp. 3–4; Damery, Mescoli, 2019, pp. 59–60). The difference between the situation of migrants from the Far East or Africa in Western Europe and Ukrainian refugees in Poland is very well illustrated by a statement made by a Syrian refugee-artist, as cited by Cristina Cusenza:

> This feeling of living in exile will always stay with me. But you recreate your identity abroad, I feel more cosmopolitan. Of course everyone's attached to family and friends, but in terms of country, I've abandoned it to live in peace (Cusenza, 2019, p. 79).

It seems that none of the Ukrainian artists who arrived in Poland after February 24th would utter such unequivocal words, nor would they accept a programme of integration with the local Polish community or culture. For the vast majority of them emigration was a last resort, intensifying the wartime trauma due to doubts and feelings of guilt about whether they should have stayed in Ukraine. Is it ethical to perform on stage instead of fighting? Some, like Olena Apchel, even before 2022, and then in 2024, returned to Ukraine, directly supporting the fighters. For Ukrainian refugees who decided to leave Ukraine and perform on stage, performances, especially in the first months after the invasion, were meant to convey the truth about what was happening in their country, about the barbarism of the invaders, the tragedies of the people and the heroism of those fighting. They wanted to create a Ukrainian theatre of Ukrainian artists that spoke about Ukrainian issues in exile. The Polish theatre was fully aware of this and in no way attempted to implement an integration policy. It understood that its role was to support Ukrainian colleagues artistically and organisationally, but above all to provide them with platforms and give them a voice. This also had consequences in terms of the language that resonated from the stage at that time. Even if Ukrainian artists knew the Polish language, they wanted to speak Ukrainian in the theatre. It was a part of the fight for their national identity, culture, which the Russian occupier wanted to appropriate. Therefore, the vast majority of performances, in which Ukrainian actors appeared, were performed in Ukrainian, with Polish subtitles displayed on monitors. Besides its political connotations, the theatre also aimed to serve therapeutic functions. Ukrainian theatre scholar Maya Harbuziuk noted that both in contemporary Ukrainian drama and progressive theatre, the most characteristic element is the 'narrative of trauma', a trauma gradually intensifying since 2014, reaching its peak with the full-scale Russian invasion. This presented entirely new tasks for the theatre: the need to overcome and work through trauma:

> The sharp pain associated with the incurred losses triggered the need to create new methods of representing and processing the past. Today we can talk about two basic types of work with historical trauma. The first of these is called social theatre, which includes documentary theatre and witness theatre. Theatre of this type is focused on working with the newly acquired traumatic experiences of recent years. In such projects witnesses and participants of events themselves take part, telling the audience the stories of their lives, thus objectifying the traumatic experience (Harbuziuk, 2017, p. 121).

For performances created after February 2022, such tendencies will be very characteristic and also close to Polish stages, mainly independent ones, which have been using similar techniques since the 1990s up to the present day.

Symbolic gestures and performative readings

The Russian invasion resulted in a significant number of Ukrainian artists becoming refugees. Their decision to come to Poland was often not driven by artistic reasons, however. The intensified Russian attacks led women, often with children, to choose a place where they already had acquaintances and where they received information that there was somewhere to stay and settle. The Ukrainian artists who were already in Poland before the invasion very actively assisted their colleagues. In a way they provided a 'hotline', through which information on where to go and where to stay was shared. In this regard, Polish theatres also passed the solidarity test. Already on

February 25th, the vast majority of them issued appeals on their websites and social media, expressing solidarity with Ukraine and condemning Russian aggression. Efforts were also made to organise collections of goods and food to support Ukraine. Theatres began to serve not only as cultural institutions but also as centres for social assistance to the Ukrainian population. This included providing theatre spaces for temporary shelter for refugees, including those from the theatre community. For example, shortly after the invasion began, Andrzej Seweryn contacted Svitlana Oleshko, inviting her to Warsaw and offering not only accommodation in the theatre's guest rooms but also the opportunity to work. Initially, the director of the Arabesky Theatre refused, wanting to stay in Ukraine, but the dramatic situation in her home country prompted her to come to Warsaw with her sister and her children. Everyone found safe shelter at the Polish Theatre. Ukrainian actresses could also stay at the Nowy Theatre in Poznań, the Powszechny Theatre in Warsaw, the National Opera, also in Warsaw, the Polish Theatre in Bydgoszcz, the Puppet Theatre in Białystok, and numerous other venues.

On an even larger scale than in 2014, theatres across Poland provided support to Ukraine through symbolic gestures. Ukrainian flags were put atop of theatre buildings which were also lit up in yellow and blue colours at night. It became common for actors to hold Ukrainian flags in support of Ukraine and as a sign of condemnation of the Russian attack on it immediately after a performance, when taking a bow. There was not really a theatre in Poland which would not partake in such activities. What became particularly telling was the protest of a Russian playwright and theatre director – Ivan Vyrypaev – who had been living and working in Poland for several years. He would openly express his support for the Ukrainian nation in Polish theatres that were showing the pieces he had either written or directed. He also wrote a letter to Russia's President Putin, in which he renounced his Russian citizenship, having described Russia's invasion against Ukraine as a 'disgrace'.

Polish theatres swiftly initiated artistic endeavours to showcase Ukrainian cultural achievements to audiences. They selected existing Ukrainian dramas or stories for performative readings, aided significantly by an anthology of dramas authored by prominent contemporary Ukrainian writers, curated by Korzeniowska-Bihun. Despite prior efforts to promote Ukrainian theatre and drama by Wichowska or Siwiak, they remained relatively unknown in Poland. Works by Ukrainian authors were rarely staged, particularly by larger repertory theatres. The aforementioned anthology did not make much difference. Even the person who translated the plays acknowledged that very often when she would send the scripts to various theatre directors, many put them on a shelf without even reading them (Drozdowisko #59, 2022)[71]. Thanks to various performative readings, Polish audiences were now able to get to know the work of some of the most important, modern Ukrainian writers such as: Natalia Vorozhbyt, Pavlo Arie, Lena Liahushonkova, Natalia Blok, Olha Matsiupa, Neda Nezhdana[72], Serhiy Zhadan[73], Tamara Duda[74] or Oksana Zabuzhko[75]. The majority of those texts spoke of the war in Donbas, which had been attacked by the Russian troops in 2014. However, not all of them focused on tragic war experiences. For example, Liahushonkova's piece *A Kitten Peed on My Banner* (*Моё знамя обосцала кошечка*), whose first public reading took place at the Polish Theatre in Bydgoszcz in March 2022, tells a moving story about growing up in a post-Soviet, multinational Donbas.

An interesting form of performative reading was prepared at that time by the Kana Theatre Centre from Szczecin. They described it as a 'reading in transit'. The performance consisted of texts by contemporary Ukrainian writers: Serhiy Zhadan, Oksana Zabuzhko, Taras Prokhasko, Olena Astayeva, Oksana Grytsenko, Lena Liahusonkova and Olena Gapayeva. It was presented in various locations across Poland, with different artists from each city performing each time. The creators justified the choice of the 'transit' form of presentation in the following way:

> The temporariness, variability and constant movement have been accompanying us for several months in a particular form. Transit has become the daily bread of refugees, but also ours. In search of fixed reference points, despite newly charted maps, we hold our breath to read Ukrainian literature. We turn over in our minds, juxtapose and repeatedly recite aloud fragments of texts by selected authors, discovering their new or deeper hidden contexts, forgotten layers, current meanings and what they won't write about in newspapers. 'We should trust the word.

---

[71] Unfortunately, Ukrainian drama wasn't well-established in the world. It isn't really surprising, given that in Ukraine itself theatre directors focused on classics and world novelties, whilst completely ignoring the works of their own contemporary authors. Korzeniowska-Bihun also notes that Ukraine did not have to be ashamed of its achievements, because its contemporary drama offered a huge wealth of diverse texts by extremely talented authors who, based on their own national experiences, referred to universal themes that would be perfectly understood outside of Ukraine. It was only the activities of the Ukrainian Institute, founded in Ukraine in 2017, that caused some changes for the better, as evidenced by the presence of Natalia Vorozhbyt's work in the world of global culture. The film adaptation of her drama: *Bad Roads* (directed by the author herself) won numerous film awards in 2020, including the main prize for directing at the Venice Film Festival.

[72] More information about Neda Nezhdana in the appendix.

[73] More information about Serhiy Zhadan in the appendix.

[74] More information about Tamara Duda in the appendix.

[75] More information about Oksana Zabuzhko in the appendix.

Just realise that it is true, unique and means nothing superfluous' – we repeat after Taras Prokhasko. 'We can be deceived by people, and it has happened more than once, but texts never deceive us' – we reflect along with Oksana Zabuzko. We read in transit – between texts, languages, sounds – to better 'remind ourselves of certain simple things. To recall what truly deserves belief, and what can be doubted'. Reading while in transit, alongside a graduate of the Kharkiv University of Arts and two independent musicians from Szczecin, we form ever-changing arrangements and actions engaging new venues, institutions and fellow readers (Fibich, 2022).

The majority of the readings of the mentioned works were quite minimalist in terms of their performance aspect. A simple backdrop, often black curtains with dimmed lighting, focused on the actors seated on chairs or a stage platform, aiming to help the audience concentrate solely on the words. It was common for not all stage events to be shown: stage movements were often limited to simple gestures or the rotation of actors' positions on stage. Performative effects were primarily achieved through voice modulation while delivering the script – ranging from quiet whispers to loud shouting. Even in Matsiupa's play, where the main character engages in a lot of physical exercises, the actress portraying her remains stationary, running in place without moving around the stage. However, her emotions are conveyed through the intensity of her running, which reflects increasing anxiety and, at one point, horror.

According to Oksana Cherkashyna, performative readings were then a significant element of support for Ukraine by Polish theatres. She pointed out that Putin's and the Russian authorities' goal in this war is not only the physical destruction of the Ukrainian population along with the country's economic potential but also the obliteration of Ukrainian identity and national culture. Erasing them from the consciousness of societies worldwide. In this respect the presentation and promotion of Ukrainian culture, including its dramatic output, became a weapon in defence of this identity, showing the autonomy of Ukrainian culture, its distinctiveness from Russian culture and at the same time demonstrating that a country with such cultural potential as Ukraine aspires to join the European family not by chance (Majcherek, 2022).

Ukrainian artists swiftly engaged in artistic initiatives as a form of protest against the war. These decisions were challenging, given the shock and psychological trauma they experienced in response to the conflict and the need to leave their homeland, homes and often loved ones. Svitlana Oleshko's experience, settling in the guest rooms of the Polish Theatre, epitomises this struggle as she grappled with concerns for her loved ones back in Ukraine and the progression of the war. She was mentally exhausted, having endured ten continuous days of bombardment just before leaving Ukraine. The theatre director, Andrzej Seweryn, then planned to stage a performative reading of excerpts from the book *Wormwood Planet* (*Планета Полин*) by Ukrainian writer Oksana Zabuzhko. The author herself was also in Warsaw at the time. As Oleshko recalls, Seweryn enthusiastically encouraged her, almost compelling her to get involved in the performance preparations, persuading her that work would be the best way to overcome the trauma of war[76]. Oleshko eventually agreed and selected appropriate excerpts from Zabuzhko's book, adding authentic messages that appeared in Ukraine to protect the civilian population during bombardments, such as how to secure a residence or build a makeshift shelter. Seweryn's advice proved effective, and Oleshko regularly participated in artistic activities at the Polish Theatre, later preparing further presentations of Ukrainian literature, including Serhiy Zhadan's poems and an evening of contemporary Ukrainian poetry.

Kateryna Penkova[77], a Ukrainian playwright who has been in Poland since 2020 but has maintained collaboration with the Kiev Playwrights' Theatre, which she co-founded, also participated in preparing a performative reading dedicated to the Russian invasion. Additionally, Maria Kardash, a young Ukrainian actress who was in Katowice in February 2022 as part of a theatre project, and Olha Matsiupa were involved. Artur Pałyga, a playwright at the Silesian Theatre in Katowice, had a scheduled meeting with Kardash to discuss the possibility of collaboration between the Silesian Theatre and Ukrainian actors. They were thinking about long-term cooperation but the situation demanded quick decisions because both of them felt that support for Ukraine and joint actions were needed immediately. After consulting with the theatre director Robert Talarczyk, it was decided to organise performative readings as quickly as possible. Pałyga's idea was for them to consist of current notes, chat conversations, event journals from the war, written in Ukraine. Kardash posted an announcement requesting texts to be sent to Ukrainian websites. The response was almost immediate. Kateryna Penkova also offered assistance. Since the invasion began, she has been running a chat room with her colleagues from the Playwrights' Theatre[78] who were in Kyiv

---

[76] This description is based on information obtained from Svitlana Oleshko during an interview with the author.

[77] More information about Kateryna Penkova in the appendix.

[78] The Theatre of Playwrights is an independent authorial theatre in Kyiv, established by a group of Ukrainian playwrights in 2020. It constitutes a platform for presenting texts, training and exchanging experiences among playwrights as well as enhancing the role of the author in Ukrainian society. The artistic director of the theatre is Maxim Kurochkin. The Theatre of Playwrights emerged as a space for the dominance of lively and sincere dramatic texts, free from theatrical clichés. It was a response from a young generation of Ukrainian playwrights trying to reform the conservative Ukrainian theatre. The venue aimed to open its stage to progressive, socially engaged texts by contemporary playwrights that Ukrainian institutional repertory theatres were unwilling to perform. Among the founders of the Theatre of Playwrights

Shortly afterward, another co-founder of the Playwrights' Theatre, Olha Matsiupa, who was living in Lublin at the time, sent additional chat excerpts. It was a daily exchange of information, thoughts, expressions of concern, fear for loved ones and anger at the surrounding reality among several members of the Theatre of Playwrights, such as: Pavlo Arie, Olena Astasieva, Natalia Blok, Andrii Bondarenko, Vitalii Chenskii, Olena Gapayeva, Yuliia Honchar, Oksana Grytsenko, Iryna Harets, Maxim Kurochkin, Lena Liahushonkova, Olha Matsiupa, Yevhenii Markovskyi, Kateryna Penkova, Olena Shevchenko, Liudmyla Tymohienko and Natalia Vorozhbyt. Their chat, intertwined with reports, poems and journals from others who submitted their texts, formed the foundation of the performance, with Pałyga moulding its dramatic structure. Everything was swiftly translated into Polish. The reading, featuring actors from the Silesian Theatre, occurred on March 10th and its recording was posted online. It was subsequently repeated a few times.

The performance was called *Notes from the war* (*Notatki z wojny*) and took place in front of the Silesian Theatre's building, which had been lit up in blue and yellow – Ukraine's national colours. Actors dressed as civilians would go up onto a make-shift stage and read out the aforementioned reports, letters and messages from various internet fora against the simple yet symbolic backdrop. Usually one of the actors would speak at one time. At times, however, a few of them would join and read out comments, posts or other internet exchanges together. A choice was made not to use any other theatrical techniques, given how emotionally-charged the drama already was. The material used, which came from various parts of Ukraine and random Ukrainians, wasn't ordered thematically to constitute a logically coherent whole. Instead, images of bombardments and of loved ones dying would be interspersed with those representing everyday activities, which needed to be done, in spite of the raging war. Audiences were exposed to remarks that were philosophical in nature and aimed at finding any sense and rationale behind what was taking place. They could also hear about/witness the moving goodbyes with men who went to fight or the animals that had to stay behind. Last but not least, they were exposed to pieces of advice and warnings sent into the ether to keep people safe.

The characteristic techniques of documentary theatre were also applied in the performance *We Pray for Everything to Be Fine* (*Módlmy się, żeby wszystko było dobrze*) by Teatr Druga Strefa (The Second Sphere Theatre)[79]. In this case, however, the performative reading was preceded by a documentary

---

were: Pavlo Arie, Natalia Blok, Natalia Vorozhbyt, Maxim Kurochkin, Lena Liahushonkova, Kateryna Penkova and Olha Matsiupa.

[79] It premiered on March 17th, 2022.

film shot at one of the Warsaw train stations, where interviews were conducted with individuals from Ukraine residing in Poland who, after February 24th, decided to return to Ukraine to defend their homeland.

What was striking was the lack of pathos or heroism in those contributions. Most of the interviewees said that they were going home, because it was under attack. When asked, if they were afraid, they would usually say: 'what am I to fear, I'm going home'. The actual performance started with a Ukrainian song performed by Ukrainian artists. What followed was, once again, the reading of various messages from Ukraine, which were delivered by four performers, sat by lecters, in dimmed light. The messages originated from Chernihiv, a city which had already been occupied and completely demolished by the Russians by the time *We Pray for Everything to Be Fine* premiered. The choice of Chernihiv wasn't completely accidental. Ukrainian director Andriej Bahirov – an acquaintance of Sylwester Biraga who directed the Second Sphere (Druga Strefa) Theatre performance – came from and worked in that city. The script was based on authentic messages, including many from either Bahirov himself or the Ukrainian friends of the Warsaw-based theatre. Similar to those used by the Śląski (Silesian) Theatre, the theatrical techniques utilised when staging *We Pray for Everything to Be Fine* were very simple indeed. As the messages were being read out, the sound of a siren, accompanied by calls to hide in a nearby shelter, could sometimes be heard in the background. The performance finished with a symbolic scene of a woman saying goodbye to a man leaving for the front. The man's daughter, wife and mother were played by the same actress. Each of the three women was experiencing her own suffering and tragedy, highlighted by a very moving performance as well as small, symbolic props.

Russian drama and plays dedicated to Russia in Polish theatre after February 24th, 2022

Polish theatres often turned to dramas by Russian writers, especially classics. As a result of the Russian invasion, however, directors faced the problem of what to do when a play by a representative of the aggressor country is on the bill. Particularly for repertory theatres, making quick changes, such as removing a title from the repertoire, is not easy to implement. Polish theatres often turned to dramas by Russian writers, especially classics. As a result of the Russian invasion, however, directors faced the problem of what to do when a play by a representative of the aggressor country is on the bill. Particularly for repertory theatres, making quick changes, such as removing a title from the repertoire, is not easy to implement. Various strategies were employed in response, for example the actions concerning the previously mentioned production of *Three Sisters*, directed by Luk Perceval and staged at both the National Stary Theatre in Krakow and TR Warszawa. With the invasion, both theatres not only did not withdraw the production but quickly reinstated it into their current repertoire. They realised that in the new reality, the interpretation offered by Percival, especially the character played by Oksana Cherkashyna, gained even greater significance and relevance, serving as a bitter reckoning with the state of Russian culture. Cherkashyna, by introducing changes to her text, further ensured that the performance directly addressed the events after February 24th, 2022. In one of the scenes, her character Natasha cries out to the audience: 'Where is Europe? Where is Europe when they're bombing my country?'.

In the case of the performance of *Nastia*, staged at the Powszechny Theatre in Warsaw, the play itself constitutes a strong accusation against Russian culture and society. After February 24th, it gained even stronger resonance. In December 2021, Belarusian refugee Yura Dzivakou directed *Nastia*, based on a story by Russian dissident Vladimir Sorokin, opposing Putin's regime. The text itself is rather unique – brutal and cruel, and in which metaphors are taken literally, almost naturalistically.

Sorokin's story depicts a manor house in the Russian countryside, at the turn of the 19th and 20th centuries, where a family of intellectuals and landed gentry throws a party to celebrate the 16th birthday of their daughter – Nastya. What starts as a series of idyllic images, full of references to classic motifs from the Russian realistic prose, slowly turns into a nightmare. It turns out that a celebratory party attended by friends of the family is planned as a feast, during which the host's daughter, Nastya, is baked and eaten. She'll be consumed by her own family – members of the Russian intelligentsia. The world filled with norms and rules will ingest her during a polite, high society conversation. The dispute is of a philosophical nature about the value of human life and sense in nonsense, and its participants declare that they are always guided by reason, care and openness to other people. The overall message of the performance was universal. It showed what mutual hatred and stereotypes, as well as the cultivation of violence rituals, can lead to. The performance was about the dangerous instincts inherent in people, which are released in moments of crisis. Fundamental was the question about the limits of indifference to evil and the possibility of rebellion and escape in a situation of oppression.

From the very beginning, *Nastia* generated extreme emotions among those who watched it. However, the reception of its performance changed radically, without the need for any changes in staging, after February 24th, 2022. Here are some of *Nastia's* director's reflections on the topic: 'When we started working on Sorokin's story, none of us knew yet that there would be a war. And this text turned out to be prophetic. Sometimes I think that maybe I should stop doing theatre, since theatre has such power' (Dubrowska, 2022). A review like this followed:

> The first shows – just before the Russian aggression against Ukraine – had a completely different tone. A few months prior, they seemed like an exhausting nightmare, a delusion in the style of an author who has accustomed his readers to the depictions of Russia in the darkest of colours and to seasoning his plots with hatred for the post-imperial yearnings of the Russian elite. It did look like an artistic quirk, but not anymore. The image of a Russian manor, almost idyllic, where children learn French and manners, gives the impression of a prophecy. [...] It is a diagnosis of a violent system and the people infected with and by it; one that breathes real horror. [...] During rehearsals, between the first show in December 2021 and the final premiere in April 2022, a devastating war started to rage and it turned out that Sorokin's prose is not a sick, mad dream, but a precise record of being immersed in the depths of the so-called Russian soul. The result is a spectacle that is extremely topical and disturbing, with a dramatic question as to how long will this odium of violence and hatred follow Russia? Will it ever be thin enough for the world to breathe? Just six months ago, such a performance seemed to be some sort of bloody excess, a reverberation of the once fashionable brutalism. But not today, when, upon entering the theatre, you can glance at a screen and almost accidentally see the footage from Kramatorsk, where Russian troops dropped cluster bombs on a train platform full of people (Miłkowski, 2022).

The Warsaw Second Zone Theatre also leveraged the presence of a Russian actress, Valentina Sizonenko, in their ensemble. She had participated in Russian protests in Moscow's Pushkin Square against the country's invasion of Ukraine. She helped in the creation of the script for the performance, based on the chat of the people gathered there, a large number of whom, including Sizonenko, were arrested. The performance was titled *3 Pushkin Square* (*Plac Puszkina 3*). The audience[80] becomes part of the stage events. Upon entering the theatre, their clothes, bags and mobile phones are taken away. Then, they are led to a small, windowless room, and the doors are locked after the last person enters. Inside, there are no stage or seats for the audience, only a few wooden boxes. The room is dimly lit and unkempt. For the next few minutes,

---

[80] The audience comprises a maximum of a dozen or so people.

the audience waits expectantly for the actors to emerge, but they don't appear. Suddenly, a group of people starts conversing. One of them paces nervously from one end of the room to the other. It turns out that these individuals are the actors from the play, who were arrested during the demonstration. The rest of the audience, unaware, unwittingly assume the role of co-arrestees.

The dialogues authentically capture the mood of the Russian opposition: rebellion against Putin's regime and the invasion, along with the fear of beatings during interrogation and the potential for further repression. One of the prisoners, who was arrested by chance while going shopping without any intention of participating in an illegal demonstration, epitomises a common mindset prevailing in Russian society: unquestioning belief in state propaganda alongside deeply hypocritical views regarding Russia's supposed epochal mission in the modern world, which serves to justify all injustices and wrongdoings it commits. By showcasing extreme attitudes and perspectives, the performance offers a glimpse into the diverse spectrum of Russian society. Adding to its credibility is the fact that its script is drawn from authentic statements made by real individuals. Moreover, *3 Pushkin Square* amplifies the voices of Russians who lack a platform in the local media to express themselves. While they may represent a minority, they challenge the notion that all of Russian society is characterised by a lack of empathy, selfishness and indifference to the injustices perpetrated by their country.

The example of the Juliusz Słowacki Theatre in Krakow shows that Polish theatres also tried to use Polish classics addressing issues related to Russia to express protest against the invasion of Ukraine. Several months before the Russian attack, in November 2021, the Juliusz Słowacki Theatre premiered Adam Mickiewicz's *Dziady* (*The Forefathers' Eve*). A Polish national romantic drama and a cornerstone of Polish romantic mythology, Mickiewicz's *Dziady* is a very special play indeed. It was written during the time when Poland was absent from the map of the world for over 120 years. This was due to it having been partitioned between Russia, Austria and Prussia towards the end of the 18th century. It is indeed Russia that's criticised most severely in Mickiewicz's well-known piece. *The Forefathers' Eve* (*Dziady*) has stood the test of time and, in spite of being first published in 1822, remains relevant even today. Whenever *Dziady* was being performed in communist Poland, it was perceived as an opposition against Poland's oppressive government, which closely collaborated with the USSR, and which exercised total control over Poland's political and cultural life. The 1968 performance of *Dziady* directed by Kazimierz Dejmek in Poland's National Theatre in Warsaw led to huge student protests that quickly spread across the whole country.

In 2021 at the Słowacki Theatre, Maja Kleczewska, the play's director, levelled *Dziady*'s anti-establishment critique against Poland's post-2015 right-wing government as well as the catholic church, whom it accused of hypocrisy and of using its links to those in power to hide its own sins, such as cases of sexual abuse by the clergy. Kleczewska made references to Polish nationalist hooligans, anti-LGBT sentiments as well as the lack of respect for women's rights in a workplace demonstrated by the Polish government passing one of the harshest anti-abortion laws in Europe. In addition, she cast a female actress (Dominika Bednarczyk) in the main (and male) role of Gustaw-Konrad. Mickiewicz's famous prison scene paints a picture of young men – students of the Vilnius University – who are persecuted by the Tsarist power in the 19th century. In Kleczewska's version, it's young women, mothers and grandmothers who find themselves in that prison, immediately bringing to mind the scenes of beatings and arrests of women who took to the streets in 2020 to protest against the new anti-abortion bill. Once again *Dziady* – this time from Kraków – became a mirror to Polish reality.

When the Russian invasion began the creators of this important and widely discussed performance didn't want to cast a blind eye to what was happening in Ukraine. Not many changes were made to the actual performance. What was added, however, was a short, poetic piece of 36 verses, called by Mickiewicz himself *To my Russian friends* (*Do przyjaciół Moskali*), which is quite often not performed as part of *Dziady* as it doesn't really affect the rest of the play. The way Mickiewicz treats Russians in that passage is two fold. On the one hand, he speaks to those who opposed the cruel Tsarist regime, which usually meant them being horribly persecuted. On the other, he paints a picture of some Russians who are totally loyal to those in power, due to being driven by fame, career and/or money. In Kleczewska's version it was a Ukrainian actress that read out the aforementioned address. The Russian invasion against Ukraine gave it a number of new meanings. In part, it spoke to those parts of the Russian society that organised and took part in the anti-Putin and anti-war protests. Some of it, however, was to resonate with the majority of Russians, supporting their president and tuned in to the powerful Russian propaganda, which glorified the war, whilst casting Ukraine, its people and their culture in the worst light possible.

It's not to say that with the emergence of the new, post-February 24th, 2022 reality, Kleczewska's *Dziady* has lost its relevance to what had been happening in Poland. It didn't. If anything, the play gained yet another, international meaning, particularly with reference to Putin's Russia. Not only does one of its main characters, Tsarist senator Nowosilcov, embody the ruthless, unaccountable Polish government post-2015, but with his cynicism and cruelty he also resembles a new Russian emperor – Putin – who aspires to rule the world. The original main protagonist of *Dziady* – Gustaw-Konrad – is a poet and a rebel who incites the whole nation to fight for freedom.

Meanwhile, Kleczewska's Gustaw-Konrad comes across more as a tired observer, filled with pain at the sight of Poland of the 2010s, on top of witnessing an even greater and more harrowing tragedy – the devastating war in Ukraine.

Regardless of the strategies adopted by theatres, a few days after the invasion began, the question arose in the public forum about the justification of presenting Russian literature and music by Polish cultural institutions. This was in spite of the fact that rather than serving as part of the Russian propaganda, those displays were predominantly used to criticise the Russian invasion. On February 28th, 2022, the Polish Minister of Culture and National Heritage officially supported the appeal of the Minister of Culture and Information Policy of Ukraine to impose sanctions on Russia also in the area of culture. He stressed that in the face of an unprecedented military aggression by Russia against Ukraine, which is a close neighbour and ally of Poland, cultural cooperation with Russia was no longer possible in any way. On March 2nd, he further clarified his position, emphasising that there should be no room in Polish cultural institutions for any institutional cooperation with representatives of the Russian regime. Russian artists who have not clearly and unequivocally spoken out against the aggression of the Russian Federation against Ukraine, and have not condemned it, should not be guests of Polish stages, participants in artistic programmes or cultural projects. In light of the crimes of war in Ukraine, the Minister also strongly recommended refraining from showcasing works of Russian culture and Russian artists.

The response to this appeal was immediate, as none of the artists in Poland had any doubts that any cooperation with Russian cultural institutions would be highly immoral, given the situation. Polish thespians have terminated their contracts with Russia. Highly regarded directors Krystian Lupa and Krzysztof Warlikowski have cancelled their artistic trips to Moscow, including to the Golden Mask theatre festival with their latest performances: *Imagine* and *Odyssey: A Story for Hollywood*. Russian composers have almost completely disappeared from the repertoire of opera houses and philharmonics in Poland. The director of the Grand Theatre in Warsaw justified this decision in the following way:

> We are located in Warsaw, a city where the historical memory of the first bombs falling during World War II is still alive. We are feeling the pain of the war in Ukraine, as well as the suffering of the Ukrainian population. We express our admiration for the heroism of Ukrainians fighting to defend their homeland. War is nonsense, a simple return to barbaric rules. The difference, however, is that instead of stones, trained armies use the achievements of technology to kill people. Furthermore, they destroy cultural objects and the achievements of generations. We and our colleagues, friends, like all compatriots, are shocked by this catastrophe. People I know from both countries, with whom we have worked many times, creating opera

works together in an international group of artists, were suddenly placed on two sides of the barricade. Great-power mythomania and the arrogance of the rulers of Russia turned two close nations against each other. This is pure evil which will be judged by history as such. Together with the team, we have decided to cancel the upcoming premiere and all subsequent performances of *Boris Godunov*. Let this silence be a voice of solidarity with the people of Ukraine (Kruszyńska, 2022).

At the same time, the director of the Grand Theatre (Teatr Wielki) in Warsaw explained that the Russian literature and music, whose authors have nothing to do with Putin's regime, were not at fault here. He emphasised that it should be remembered, however, that on the international stage Russia very often harnessed its literature and art in the service of ideology. In order to create a cult of a strong, enlightened and proud state, the Russian propaganda often made references to the contribution of their well known writers and com-posers to the development of culture in Europe. It thus became obvious for Polish artists that in the face of another manifestation of Russian colonialism and aggression, such as the attack on independent Ukraine, for them to hurt the sanctions must touch many aspects of life, including culture.

Interestingly, drama theatres were treated much more liberally than music and opera in this regard. One of the appeals of the Polish creators of culture, published on March 16th, 2022, contains the following excerpt:

One can only question the logic of removing Russian performances prepared by Polish artists in Polish theatres. However, we have to respect the decisions of the directors of cultural institutions that cancel performances of and by Russian classics as a gesture of solidarity with Ukraine. Whilst they do not question the achievements of the Russian culture, they also do not want to propagate the culture of a country whose yet another leader lied and trampled on Russia's great cultural heritage, spreading the cult of his power, conquests and finally open war (Wyszomirska, 2022).

The Ministry of Culture and National Heritage itself, which earlier called for a boycott of the Russian literature and music, noted in March:

The situation is completely different with dramatic theatres, where the Russian repertoire is present in both classical and contemporary forms. As we know, Anton Czekhov is the second most popular playwright in the world (after Shakespeare) also in Poland. It is hard to imagine *The Cherry Orchard* disappear-ing from the Witkacy Theatre in Zakopane or the Polish Theatre in Warsaw. It is an existential art that has nothing to do with Russian imperialism. What is more, in *Three Sisters* – including on its National Theatre poster in Warsaw – we even have an image alluding to the march of an army to a garrison in one of the Polish cities. This can be downright alarming! At the same time, Opole's Kochanowski Theatre is showing the latest play by Ivan Vyrypaev, an outstanding Russian director and playwright. This author of *Top Secret Research* strongly condemned Russian aggression as early as its first day. He used the Polish daily *Rzeczpospolita* to do so (Cieślak, 2022).

Krystian Lupa was also against the categorical boycott of Russian literature in the theatre:

> We should definitely boycott artists who are currently working in Russia without any major problems: who write literary works, create plays, compose music under the regime. It doesn't matter if it's a kind of tacit tolerance on their part, even acceptance, or something else. However, I see no reason why we should remove the works of people like Fyodor Dostoyevsky, Leo Tolstoy and a whole range of artists of Russian culture, whose work, to a large extent, has shaped us. In this terrible situation, one must nevertheless maintain common sense in one's judgement (Cieślak, 2022).

Agnieszka Holland, a world-class film director, president of the European Film Academy, had a similar opinion:

> I support the boycott of Russian culture. Nevertheless, I also believe that the removal of great works of Russian culture from the world cultural heritage has no rational explanation and may lead to a spiral of blind nationalism (Karow, 2022).

There were many more voices of this type, although the artists' opinions were so divided that it would be difficult to say which side – supporters of an absolute boycott or its opponents – dominated.

The Poland-based Ukrainian artists were almost unanimous in their favour of the boycott. On March 1st, 2022, motivated primarily by the fact that Putin's regime abuses culture to carry out state propaganda, they issued an appeal addressed to artists across Europe, in which they called for the boycott as well as the imposition of cultural sanctions on Russia (Łozińska, 2022). Oksana Cherkashyna stressed that during the invasion all sources that help Russia to finance the war should be radically cut off, also through culture. At the same time, and referring to the opinions of some culture experts, she pointed out that the canon of Russian culture used to be and still is a carrier of a very aggressive narrative. She also unequivocally declared that she did not intend to attend Russian plays or perform in them (Kazimierczak, 2022). Svitlana Oleshko probably spoke the most on this subject:

> It is obvious to us that we have to separate ourselves from all Russian culture. A thick line. Entirely. Does art connect? No, it doesn't connect. Russian art is their weapon that always went before the tanks. This is a play about them, for them and created by them. I understand that in Polish theatres there are productions based on Russian literature. But I hope that soon, both in Poland and in the world, artists will understand it anew, read it as it is. Not great, not universal – as the world reads

it. Chauvinistic and imperialist. And I am honest in what I say. I graduated from Russian philology in Kharkov. I'm quite well versed in this. Powerful imperialist discourse. I know the propaganda of this literature and in this literature. It was never universal and added nothing to the world. However, I have the impression, and in fact I am sure, that very few people have actually read Russian literature with understanding. Dostoyevsky, Tolstoy – this propaganda is in them, only the world did not notice it. It didn't want to notice (Rigamonti, 2022b).

It is interesting that Andrzej Boreyko, the Russian artistic director of the National Philharmonic in Warsaw, was among the strong supporters of the boycott of the Russian culture:

I could never have imagined that there would be a war going on in the centre of Europe at the beginning of the third millennium. What I thought even less probable was that this war would be started by Russia, the country where I spent almost half of my life until 1989. And which I thought I knew and understood. But I don't understand today's Russia or those people who support genocide. And I will never change my mind. As soon as the war broke out, I decided to start the concert with the Ukrainian anthem. I also resigned from the planned performances of Russian music, although it is not easy for me. I believe that now it is necessary to play as many works and plays by Ukrainian artists as possible. Other artists and theatre directors are of a similar opinion. Russian culture is entering a time of a quarantine, at least. It is not known how long that isolation will last, but it is true that there should now be a boycott of artists from Putin's country (Moczulski, 2022).

Without a doubt the wide social resonance, instigated by the aforementioned discussion about the boycott of Russian culture, had an impact on the amount of plays by Russian authors that could be seen in theatres. For example, the National Stary Theatre in Kraków and the Stu Theatre in the same city gave up their respective plans to stage Russian plays. Furthermore, in the first of these theatres, Anton Chekhov's *Platonov*, which had previously been played with great success, was taken off the bill. In addition, during the Festival of Theatre Premieres in Bydgoszcz, all texts by Russian authors were also excluded, and plays by several Ukrainian authors were allowed in their place.

(Ukrainian) artists in residence

In the initial weeks following the invasion, it became apparent that the Polish theatre community lacked someone like Joanna Wichowska, who could co-ordinate assistance efforts for Ukrainian artists arriving in Poland. The need for organised support was first acknowledged by the Institute of Performing Arts. Almost immediately after the invasion began, on February 28th, they issued an appeal to the theatre community through the press:

> The artists from the Institute write that the Polish theatre can afford to welcome Ukrainian actors into its artistic ensemble, find resources for an additional performance that can be created by a Ukrainian director, provide housing for employed artists from Ukraine or a guest room during their work, and hire a person from Ukraine for a position in the technical or administrative team. The vast majority of public theatres are managed by local governments. In Poland there are 121 public theatres, according to the data from the Ministry's Raszewski Theatre Institute. If each of them took the initiative of the Institute of Performing Arts seriously, it would provide employment for at least over a hundred people. Or even several hundred. The effort required to do this is disproportionate to the benefits (Mrozek, 2022).

Support for this initiative was also expressed in the message presented annually on the International Theatre Day by the Polish Centre of the International Theatre Institute. The message was released on March 27th, 2022. It defined the goals and tasks facing Polish theatre, with the main emphasis placed on actions related to the situation in Ukraine (Adamiecka, Błasińska, Dutkiewicz, Dziekan, Kowalkowska, Strzępka, 2022)[81].

---

[81] Full text of the manifesto: 'This is a message for the time of war that is going on and for the time of peace that will come. A message for the theatre we know and for the one we will create. A message for the world we must change to save it. A message for life. When we think of 'theatre' today, the image of the Donetsk Regional Drama Theatre in Mariupol, smashed by missiles, comes first to mind, with a huge ДЕТИ sign on the square in front of the building. An image of a theatre-shelter that was not spared by the bestiality of the war caused by Putin. Immediately after we see images of the stage and the audience of the Dramatic Theatre named after Maria Zankovetska in Lviv, turned into a refugee house. And then images from Polish theatres, which became temporary homes for people fleeing violence and where intensive work is underway to help Ukraine. Collections, transports, activities for children, legal and psychological assistance, workplaces and artistic residencies are organised. When we think of theatre today, we also see actresses and actors who go out to the audience with Ukrainian flags, thus giving us the opportunity to jointly express our solidarity, our pain and anger. We see people gathered in the audience all over Poland, who join the fundraisers every evening, who respond

It differed significantly from earlier manifestos of this type, which tended to be quite general and very formal. This Manifesto addressed a specific

---

with ovations to the expressions of solidarity with men and women of Ukraine. We see seriousness, concentration, and emotion around us. We see how the meanings transmitted from the stage are intensively transformed, how the theatrical experience of community materialises in the real meeting of bodies – here and now. War tangibly allows us to feel that theatre is a gathering of fragile bodies that recognise their interdependence and the strength that comes from relationships. And fragility is what ignites revolution. Today, in the midst of the deepest crisis, an unbridled desire for change grows within us. War is a radical manifestation of patriarchy. So the patriarchy must end so that the wars against life will end. This will happen when we manage to transcend the logic of domination, power and subordination. When we break free from the vicious spiral of production-consumption-exploitation, we will move beyond the logic of efficiency and competition, beyond the capitalist-imperial fantasies of unlimited growth, conquest and violence. War will end when it becomes the rule of our societies to work together for life on Earth.It is in a theatre that we can imagine worlds that we cannot yet shape into social reality. It is here that we can design embodied utopias – provided, however, that we do it together. The principle of theatre is cooperation, and today it is clearly visible how important the quality of joint work is. The Polish theatre spontaneously became part of a new model of organisation – a bottom-up network of consciously practised interdependence. A new way of accepting refugees, a new guest-otherness. Part of the great workshops on the craft of co-living, which must include all refugees – those from the stations and those from the forests. Thus, the questions about the shape of theatre as an institution, its democratisation, empowerment and socialisation become all the more urgent. War does not cancel out old problems – rather it intensifies them and presents us with new ones. Theatre as an institution and as an imagined community must become fully open to the multiplicity of languages, needs, cultures, bodies, and desires. We must have the courage to think about it in new categories. The theatre of the times of the great movement of people and species is a post-national theatre, a living and direct laboratory of language for the society of the future, for the community to come. It is also a theatre of new rituals. Mourning and celebration, anger and joy. A celebration of life. We need theatre as a shelter, as a home for us and for those who will live with us. A shelter for the imagination that brings alternatives and creates new languages. A shelter for values. A shelter for human and non-human beings – when they want to be together, next to, close, body to body, breath to breath, close but strangers, everywhere, here and now – together. A shelter that is deep below the surface, underground, from which life beats and in which its pulse can be heard. A shelter, a place where people share resources and emotions. A shelter for humour that we cannot lose, because it would mean that we had believed in death. The theatre in Mariupol was demolished. It needs to be rebuilt. Before that happens, let's show Putin and those who follow his orders that the world sees their every crime and will judge each one. Let's send a message to the Russian society, which must recognise the truth and oppose the violence of its state. Let's put the inscription ДЕТИ in front of every theatre in Poland and in the world. Let this inscription-cry carry around the world: ДЕТИ ДЕТИ ДЕТИ... Let the criminal hear it and understand that it hits us all. Let Ukraine hear it and let it know that we are all with it. Let the world hear it and start working on a new future".

situation, expressing solidarity with Ukraine and condemning the Russian invasion, while focusing on what actions should be taken in the future. It strongly emphasised the need for sustained support for refugee artists – not just occasional efforts, but the creation of structural frameworks for long-term collaboration with Ukrainian artists in Poland.

Notably, the Manifesto redefined 'cooperation' as an opening to what is 'beyond' and 'between': post-national, multicultural and inclusive. This vision stood in stark contrast to the right-wing Polish government's emphasis on national, monocultural ideals and its resistance to 'outsiders'. In this government's view, an 'outsider' or a 'stranger' is often seen as an undesirable, threatening presence. In contrast, the Manifesto portrayed refugees as people who bring new perspectives, offering Polish theatre the chance to develop 'new rituals' and 'a new language of theatre' – not as threats, but as opportunities for growth.

For Ukrainian evacuees, Polish theatre was to become a 'shelter', providing not only material assistance and protection, but also a space to pursue artistic passions alongside Polish artists. This 'shelter' would be a place where people from different cultures could share their 'resources and emotions'. Additionally, it is worth noting that the Manifesto recognised refugees from Ukraine ('those from railway stations'[82]), but also from the Far East ('those from the forests'[83]).

The Manifesto did not go unnoticed. The direct reaction of Polish theatres was to place the inscription 'ДЕТИ'[84] in front of their buildings as a symbolic gesture of solidarity with the drama of people who died or were injured as a result of the barbaric bombing of the theatre in Mariupol by the Russian army. Almost all institutions in Poland joined this initiative. However, another project had much more profound consequences: the organisation of artistic residencies for refugees. Resulting indirectly from the postulates

---

[82]   The term came from the fact that trains constituted the most common means of transport used by the people escaping from Ukraine to Poland; furthermore, emergency support points were organised primarily at train stations.

[83]   The term referred to the hundreds of refugees from the Far East who had found themselves on the border between Poland and Belarus. Belarus, which, for reasons of a political game, controlled the entire action of transferring refugees to Poland, did not allow them to return after crossing the border illegally. The Polish authorities, in turn, decided to transfer such persons back to Belarus on the basis of the so-called 'push back', prohibited by international conventions. As a result, people camped in a small forest belt between the border, in the cold, without food, and Polish soldiers did not even allow for medical support or food to be supplied to them.

[84]   The inscription meant the Ukrainian word *children*. It was displayed on a theatre in Mariupol, bombed by the Russians, warning that the building had no strategic purpose, as civilians and children were sheltering there.

contained in the Manifesto, it has offered the Ukrainian people of culture a very real opportunity not only to find a safe haven in Poland, but also to continue their artistic activity.

The idea of artistic residencies for individuals from Ukraine has been undertaken, with financial support from the Ministry of Culture, by the Theatre Institute. The concept itself is not new; similar support was previously provided, for instance, to creators from Belarus who arrived in Poland due to the repression of Alexander Lukashenko's regime. In this case, however, the residencies were to be dedicated specifically to artists from Ukraine. It was emphasised that 'they will enable support for Ukrainian artists not only in terms of livelihood but also in the area of culture persecuted by the Russian regime, and will also contribute to strengthening Polish-Ukrainian relations in the field of theatre' (sk, 2022).

Each of the residencies was to last between one and six months. Its beneficiaries were offered substantive care by their host organisation/institution. Such care was heavily subsidised. In addition, the residents' costs of travel to the new place and living there were also covered. The goals of such residency were far-reaching. First of all, as early as at the application stage, efforts were made to match the artistic profile of the inviting institutions with the artistic profile of the residents. Additional funds were allocated for independent artistic projects carried out by Ukrainian artists, under the assumption that they would become part of the landscape of theatre life in Poland, attracting a wide audience in various cultural centres. Thanks to this, guests could establish further contacts, resulting in long-term cooperation. A whole network of artistic connections would be built, in which both Polish theatre and representatives of the Ukrainian theatre would look for what connects, what is new, creative and invigorating, and as a consequence, and as announced in the Manifesto, 'a theatre of new rituals' would be created. 'Mourning and celebration, anger and joy. A celebration of life'.

The Theatre Institute's residency project for artists from Ukraine continues uninterrupted as these words are being written, contributing significantly to the development of Polish-Ukrainian theatrical cooperation. In the inaugural edition alone, over 30 theatre institutions and several dozen Ukrainian artists participated, representing a diverse array of theatrical forms including drama, ballet, opera as well as playwrights, set designers and technicians. Over the first two years since the outbreak of the full-scale Russian invasion, the Theatre Institute has been the primary financial supporter of artistic projects involving Ukrainian artists through its residency programmes[85].

---

[85] It is also worth mentioning the financial and promotional support from the Ukrainian Institute operating in Ukraine.

Some theatre companies have additionally established their own, autonomous residency programmes, independent of that of the Theatre Institute. One of the most active and creative initiatives of this kind was the residency under the patronage of Theatre Directors of the Silesian Voivodeship, bringing together several theatres in one of the most industrialised and artistically developed regions in Poland. It is worth noting that, following theatre, residency programmes were also launched by the National Film Institute, including Ukrainian filmmakers and the National Institute of Music and Dance.

Among the Ukrainian artists who spoke up after arriving in Poland and commented on the residencies, not a single person questioned the purpose of their organisation. They primarily emphasised the stability provided by these residencies in a situation where their worlds were turned upside down upon finding themselves in a completely new environment, terrified by the events unfolding in their home country. Not only material stability (financial support, a place to live) was significant, but also a sense of relative psychological comfort, facilitating the recovery from the trauma that the vast majority of them had experienced. Olena Apchel emphasised the importance of not feeling pressured to engage in artistic activities within the residency. Some were not ready for it at that time. They had the option to immediately join the active work of the institution they found themselves in, opt for a small, one-time project, or choose to do nothing at all to cope with the stress caused by the outbreak of the invasion[86]. For Svitlana Oleshko, the opportunity to integrate with both the Polish and Ukrainian theatre communities was also extremely important. The Theatre Institute provided all residents with the chance, at the beginning of their residency, to spend three days together in Warsaw. They could meet acquaintances from Ukraine and get to know new people. It was during this time that ideas for joint artistic projects were born[87]. Olena Apchel mentioned a particular production where she invited two Ukrainian actresses, Nina Zakharova[88] and Kateryna Vasiukova[89], to the Zagłębie Theatre in Sosnowiec. They prepared a play there as part of the residency titled *Czuję do ciebie miętę* (*I Have a Crush on You*), which enjoyed success not only in Sosnowiec but also in other cities, including at theatre festivals both in Poland and abroad[90]. Natalia Blok strongly emphasised the significance

---

[86] Information gathered from Olena Apchel during an interview conducted by the author on October 10th, 2023.

[87] Information shared by Svitlana Oleshko during an interview conducted by the author on October 26th, 2023.

[88] More information about Nina Zakharova in the appendix.

[89] More information about Kateryna Vasiukova in the appendix.

[90] Information gathered from Olena Apchel during an interview conducted by the author on October 10th, 2023.

for those arriving from Ukraine of the mere opportunity to act, to perform on stage. During a time when the world collapsed for Ukrainian artists, they regained a sense of community and restored their creative dignity on stage. She also emphasised that the vast majority of them felt the need to speak out, to shout to the 'world' their disagreement with what was happening to their homeland. The residencies provided them with the chance for an immediate response, allowing for preparation, including performative readings or performances, almost immediately after the residency commenced. Blok also pointed out that theatres participating in the residency programme showed immense flexibility, making their stage available to Ukrainian artists despite their regular repertoire schedules[91]. When asked about the significance of residencies, Lena Liahushonkova replied, 'Now, it's our life. We plan it according to the residency schedule'[92]. Many artists were granted residencies on multiple occasions. For instance, Liahushonkova has established a lasting connection with the Polish Theatre in Bydgoszcz since her arrival in Poland, leading to numerous performances both domestically and internationally. For Roza Sarkisian Warsaw has become a friendly and much loved permanent base. Yet, despite this, she applies for additional residencies, through which she has already successfully completed numerous projects both nationally and across Europe. Having said that, for some artists Poland became just a stage in their artistic emigration. As Natalia Blok says, it was a fruitful, creative and fondly remembered time for her, but various circumstances led her to decide to move to Switzerland afterwards. The motivations behind Ukrainian artists leaving Poland varied greatly, and, as in Blok's case, it wasn't always due to Poland lacking favourable conditions for pursuing artistic aspirations. For some artists residencies served as a stepping stone to securing permanent positions in theatres across Poland. For example, Nina Zakharova and Kateryna Vasiukova, while staging performances during their residency at the Silesian Theatre in Katowice and the Zagłębie Theatre in Sosnowiec, earned recognition from the director of the former, who offered both of them permanent positions. In turn, Andrzej Seweryn appointed Svitlana Oleshko as a resident director at the Polish Theatre. Zhenia Doliak[93], after her residency at the Polish Theatre in Bydgoszcz, also secured a permanent position there and is currently performing in many productions in the theatre's repertoire.

---

[91] Information obtained from Natalia Blok during the conversation with the author on October 12th, 2023.

[92] Information from Lena Liahushonkova, shared with the author on September 10th, 2023.

[93] More information about Zhenia Doliak in the appendix.

Some characteristics of the Ukrainian artists in residence in Poland

The vast majority of Ukrainian artists who arrived in Poland were women, as men stayed in their homeland to fight for Ukraine. In the case of the residencies, they were entirely comprised of women, mostly young, some middle-aged. Their artistic backgrounds reveal that in numerous instances, even while in Ukraine, they were linked to smaller, privately funded institutions that operated independently from the constraints of the traditional, conservative Ukrainian theatre, which bore influences from Russian practices dating back to the Soviet era. In these smaller, self-financed institutions, they sought to explore a new theatrical language, aiming for a progressive theatre that embraced current and contemporary themes. These artists were accustomed to challenging working conditions, often dealing with poorly equipped theatres located in basements or clubs that they themselves had renovated. Additionally, they were constantly engaged in a struggle to secure funding for their artistic projects. Such individuals found it much easier to adapt in Poland, realising that demonstrating activity is necessary for the realisation of artistic projects. Roza Sarkisian believes that Ukrainian artists from institutionalised theatre settings in Ukraine, who have regular salaries and guaranteed pensions, lack such dynamism. They are accustomed to different work standards and, therefore, much less often decide to leave Ukraine. And even if they do, upon arriving in Poland, they do not necessarily seek artistic work there[94].

Among the Ukrainian artists who found themselves in Poland after February 24th, attention should be paid to the presence of emerging playwrights of the new socially engaged drama scene in Ukraine. One of them, Natalia Blok, arrived in Poland in March 2022, fleeing from the bombed city of Kyiv. Blok was a recognised playwright in Ukraine. Her texts had been previously nominated multiple times for prestigious international competitions. She collaborated with leading reformist Ukrainian theatres such as Dziki Teatr, Maj Busz Theatre and PostPlay. She was also a co-founder of the Playwrights' Theatre. The decision to stay temporarily in Warsaw was influenced by the presence of several acquaintances in the city, including Oksana Cherkashyna, who was performing at the Powszechny Theatre. As Blok recalls, she was keen on going to Poland precisely because the linguistic and cultural proximity of this country facilitated the continuation of her artistic activities. In Warsaw she was almost immediately offered collaboration with the Dramatic Theatre

---

[94] Information obtained from Roza Sarkisian, shared with the author on October 18th, 2023.

to prepare a performative reading of her play *Through the Skin* (*Przez skórę*). She also invited Oksana Cherkashyna to participate in the project. While in Poland Blok continued to collaborate with her colleagues from the Playwrights' Theatre who remained in Ukraine. According to her, leaving Poland and settling in Switzerland did not carry any artistic subtext. She fondly remembers the opportunity to work that opened up for her in Poland. In Switzerland, she continues to pursue various artistic projects, including international ones, while still collaborating with the Playwrights' Theatre[95].

Lena Liahushonkova is a representative of the youngest generation of Ukrainian playwrights. Although she doesn't have as many theatrical plays in her portfolio, she is considered one of the standout playwrights in Europe, as evidenced by the prestigious European New Talent Drama Award she received in 2022 from Schauspiel Stuttgart. At the onset of the invasion, she was in Kyiv, completing a play titled *A Kitten Peed on My Banner* (*Mój sztandar zasikał kotek*) in a shelter, during the bombing attacks on the city. Prior to departing Ukraine, she had three countries to consider: Germany, Lithuania or Poland. Opting for Poland, she already had some knowledge of Polish and had previously visited the country in 2021, where she participated and won the main prize at the Bydgoszcz Dramaturgy Festival *Aurora*. After arriving in Poland, she received a residency at the Polish Theatre in Warsaw, which organised a performative reading of her drama *A Kitten Peed on My Banner*. Subsequently, she obtained a residency at the Polish Theatre in Bydgoszcz, where she works at the time of writing this text. She also collaborates very actively with other Polish theatres. She is the most frequently staged Ukrainian playwright in Poland since February 2022. She debuted in 2018 with the play *Base* (*Baza*), which explores women and prostitution, presented at the Contemporary Art Festival. In Ukraine, she collaborated with two leading experimental theatres in the country: PostPlay Theatre and Young Theatre[96]. She is also one of the co-founders of the Playwrights' Theatre.

Oleksandra (Sasha) Denisova completed a course in documentary theatre at the Royal Court Theatre in London in 2010. She became a trailblazer in Ukrainian theatre for the verbatim play format, pioneering documentary theatre in Ukraine. She achieved her greatest successes working in theatres

---

[95] The information was gathered from Natalia Blok during an interview conducted by the author on October 12th, 2023.

[96] The Young Theatre (Młody Teatr) aims to capture the essence of the 1920s when the renowned Ukrainian theatre reformer Les Kurbas spearheaded the so-called Young Theatre movement. Today, it remains an experimental platform, delving into innovative modes of expression for contemporary and classic works alike. It frequently collaborates with international artists and engages in diverse international artistic endeavours. Notably, in 2014, the ensemble joined the European Theatre Convention.

in Moscow that opposed the Putin regime. From 2011 to 2014 she served as the deputy artistic director of the Moscow Academic Theatre named after Mayakovsky. In 2012 she won the Golden Mask Award in the experimental category for the production *Light My Fire* at the renowned and esteemed Moscow Teatr.doc[97]. She was the author of plays staged at the Meyerhold Centre in Moscow[98], the Moscow Art Theatre MCHAT, the Tver Drama Theatre and the Small Bronnaya Theatre. Shortly after the start of the Russian invasion, she arrived in Poland from Moscow, a city she had to escape in hiding due to the political repression she faced. In Poland she collaborated with various theatres, including Komuna Warszawa, where she staged the play *Six Ribs of Anger* (*Sześć żeber gniewu*) as well as the Polish Theatre in Poznań, where her play *The Hague* (*Haga*) was performed. Denisova was very actively involved in international projects and residencies. Her plays were showcased in various countries, including the United States, Australia, France, Germany and Bulgaria. The list of playwrights involved in various artistic projects in Poland after the invasion outbreak should also include Kateryna Penkova and Olha Matsiupa, who arrived earlier and also collaborated with the Playwrights' Theatre.

The Ukrainian female directors who arrived in Poland after February 24th, 2022, were primarily linked to experimental theatre scenes in Ukraine. Among them is Svitlana Oleshko, the founder and director of the Arabesky Theatre, who has been working at the Polish Theatre in Warsaw as both a playwright and director since relocating from Ukraine. Another director, Yulia Maslak[99], collaborated with Lena Liahushonkova at the Young Theatre in Kiev, directing productions and simultaneously serving as an assistant artistic director at the theatre. Upon arriving in Poland, she secured residencies at the Warsaw Studio Theatre and the Silesian Theatre in Katowice. Olena Apchel, mentioned earlier, was highly active in the Ukrainian performative scene. Her interest in Poland primarily arose from her participation in workshops organised by Joanna Wichowska in Ukraine. Since then, she has maintained fairly regular contacts with the country. At the time of the invasion outbreak, she was already in Poland participating in the Lane Kirkland

[97] Denisova (2022) herself described Teatr.doc as 'a cellar of freedom, an independent and boldly courageous theatre. It served as a home for all of us, where productions addressing topics such as the war in Chechnya, the LGBT situation in Russia, HIV carriers, Putin, Beslan and terrorist attacks were created. These productions featured uncompromising political texts that tackled the most painful issues, which conservative theatre didn't want to address' (Piotrowska, 2022).

[98] The director of this Centre, Elena Kovalskaya, a Russian, resigned from her position in protest against the Russian invasion of Ukraine, saying in a statement, 'One cannot work for a murderer and accept payment from them' (Piotrowska, 2022).

[99] More information about Yulia Maslak in the appendix.

Scholarship and collaborating with the Zagłębie Theatre in Sosnowiec. She subsequently undertook a series of theatre projects, serving as a resident at the Nowy Theatre in Warsaw. Apchel is part of the group of Ukrainian artists who decided to leave Poland. Her departure was due to a prestigious invitation in October 2022 from Berlin to serve as one of the directors and directors of Theatertreffen Berliner Festspiele. After completing her work in January 2024, Apchel returned to Ukraine.

Among the creators from Ukraine who actively engaged in theatrical activities in Poland, actors decidedly dominated. Despite the language barrier, they began to appear on stage relatively quickly[100]. They represented a wide range of theatres, from dramatic to revue and dance, even puppet theatres. Within this group, most individuals were associated not with powerful, state-funded institutional ensembles in Ukraine, but with smaller, offbeat experimental scenes. Valeria Kosmidis was involved with the PostPlay Theatre. Halyna Lozynska worked concurrently at the Les Kurbas Theatre in Lviv and the small experimental Lviv scene Teatr Wolny OKO (Free Theatre OKO; 'eye' in Polish). The former group, which consistently wins awards at international theatre festivals, utilises a range of theatrical techniques and psycho-physical actor training methods inspired by institutions like the Workcenter of Jerzy Grotowski, the Centre for Theatre Practices Gardzienice and the Saratoga International Theater Institute. For several years it has also collaborated with these institutions. In addition, Lozynska herself organised a series of lectures and performative workshops at Yale University, Columbia University in New York and the University of Pennsylvania.

Halyna Ryba also worked with the Teatr Wolny Oko, where she served as its artistic director. Kateryna Vasiukova was affiliated with two Kharkiv ensembles, Neft and Publicist[101]. Nina Zakharova, a theatre and film actress and choreographer, also worked at the Neft Theatre. Simultaneously,

---

[100] The similarities between Polish and Ukrainian languages make it relatively easy to overcome the language barrier. Moreover, theatres hosting Ukrainian artists made efforts to organise performances in a manner that would eliminate any language barriers when both Ukrainian and Polish performers were involved, such as providing subtitles for the audience.

[101] Neft was established in 2018 as an open, experimental artistic platform aiming to challenge traditional theatrical techniques through exercises, workshops and experiments. In their manifesto, young creators described Neft as a symbol of openness, experimentation, new forms and creative synergy. They set out to 'break standards, push boundaries and burn them to the core'. The Publicist Theatre is an independent authorial theatre renowned in Kharkiv for its theatrical experiments, serving as an alternative hub for creative education and actively engaging in urban cultural events. Through avant-garde expressions, it addresses social and political issues in Ukraine, experimenting with various forms such as documentary theatre, propaganda as well as musicals and talk shows.

she collaborated with Beautiful Flowers – an independent group formed in 2011 by graduates of the Kharkiv University of Arts. Maria Lozova[102] is primarily a dancer and choreographer who collaborated with Svitlana Oleshko at the Arabesky Theatre until Lozova's arrival in Poland in February 2022. She also prepared choreography for some performances at the Neft Theatre.

It's not feasible to showcase all the profiles of Ukrainian residents here. Despite the steady decrease in the wave of Ukrainian migration to Poland, their numbers continue to rise as new individuals opt to come for artistic residencies. Certainly, the scale of this process is currently much smaller. In total, today we can talk about a number of over 100 Ukrainian artists who have benefited from this form of support, with several dozen actively participating in the realisation of various theatre projects in Poland.

---

[102] More information about Maria Lozova in the appendix.

V. EFFORTS TO BUILD INTERCULTURAL RELATIONSHIPS – PHASE III

∽

Ukrainian artists who arrived in Poland as a result of the Russian invasion were relatively quick to resume their theatrical activities, staging performances. They were largely organised within the framework of artistic residencies. Initially, their primary objective was to stage dramas depicting events unfolding in Ukraine related to the war. While they often received support from Polish artists – directors, set designers, etc., the focus remained primarily on Ukrainian affairs. They considered speaking loudly on this topic their mission, a patriotic duty in a situation where they were forced to leave the country and couldn't actively support those fighting. Over time, with the dominance of performances focusing on documenting the war, Ukrainian creators began to ponder and discuss the future of Ukrainian theatre and drama in the face of the prolonged war. The purely documentary nature of the activities was deemed insufficient, further impoverishing the artistic aspect of the presentation. Without neglecting wartime issues, attention was drawn to a broader range of topics as well as a deeper social and existential reflection. This opened up opportunities for artistic relationships with Polish theatre creators, mainly from independent stages and smaller repertoire theatres outside the main cultural centres in Poland. The collaboration has revealed numerous common interests in both theatrical aesthetics and thematic artistic exploration between Polish and Ukrainian theatre. Consequently, phase III marks the inception of joint Polish-Ukrainian projects with an intercultural character, offering promising prospects for the future.

Performances involving female artists in residence – time to document

The first performances with the participation of Ukrainian female artists in (Polish) residence appeared on Polish stages a few months after the outbreak of the Russian invasion. The main problem that prevented the residents from joining the whirl of artistic work right away were not only social issues related to arranging a life in a new place, but also their mental state, resulting from leaving their home and loved ones in Ukraine, and the horrible uncertainty about their fate. Many of those artists suffered from the post traumatic stress disorder caused by the war.

The stories of the Ukrainian artists in residence are quite similar. For example, Tetiana Proskurina left her whole family in Ukraine: her husband and sons, who joined the frontline fight, as well as her elderly parents. Her inseparable prop after arriving in Poland was a mobile phone – listening to see if any information was coming from them and fear if everyone was alive. Julia Bukala, a student of the Kiev University of Arts, has been travelling from bombed Kiev to Poland for a week. She recalled:

> I was in Kiev when the first bombs fell on the city. Noise, clatter, loud explosions, shaking windows, sirens. From those days I will remember the sounds of suitcases on wheels that sounded the same as military planes dropping bombs. Those days were full of anxiety, fear, fatigue (moż, 2022).

When the war began, Kateryna Vasiukova was staying near Kharkiv. Her and her family had only fifteen minutes to grab the most necessary things and run. Her and her children spent 30 hours on the train before arriving in Lviv. The next stop after that was Poland. The management of the Zagłębie Theatre in Sosnowiec helped her find a flat. This is how she recalls the first days and months in Poland:

I didn't think I'd be here long. I didn't think anything, I was afraid of war. I spent two weeks like this. Doing nothing, feeling only fear. Now I feel helpless because I don't know how to work in the theatre. I don't know how to express the pain I feel. I don't know if my art will save the viewer or some other person. I don't know if I have the right to a safe space while my country is at war. I don't know when or if I'll see my husband or my children – their dad. I don't know why you should come to my show. I don't know if I should play for you either. My name and my age don't matter. There are thousands like me (Nowacka-Goik, 2022).

This is how Nina Zakharova described her condition in the first months after arriving in Poland: 'Sometimes I feel like I'm living in limbo. The emotions of fear are overwhelming. It's like I'm being wrapped in a heavy blanket, not allowed to breathe. Paralysed, you can't do anything but sit and be afraid' (Nowacka-Goik, 2022). Initially, Natalia Blok did not want to leave occupied Kherson. It was her fiancé, who stayed to fight, that convinced her. She came to Warsaw in shock, paralysed with fear and helplessness, especially when she found out about the Russian crime in Bucha. The fear was all the greater because her elder son was still in occupied Kherson. Sasha Denisova, who participated in the preparation of her play Six Ribs of Anger by the Second Strefa Theatre, recalled that during the rehearsals some Ukrainian actresses taking part in the performance were afraid of the drone flying over the stage (it was part of the dramatic action), because it made a sound similar to the bombing. This is how Oksana Cherkashyna described in an interview her condition after the outbreak of the invasion that found her in Poland:

Journalist: Are you asleep?

Cherkashyna: Since 5am on February 24th, I have a new sleeping pattern. I return home after the performance at approx. 22. I go to bed and set my alarm clock for two in the morning.

Journalist: Why?

Cherkashyna: To check what is going on in Ukraine, to check if everything is okay with my parents and sister in Kharkov, with my partner in Kiev. I check on them all the time. After two, I go back to bed and set my alarm for five in the morning. To check again. Then I sleep a little, but then I get up. It sometimes happens that I am on the phone all night, helping people who cross the border. Today I was waiting for a woman with her son. They came. They are with me.

Journalist: Do you feel no remorse that you are not there, at home, in Ukraine?

Cherkashyna: I do. [...] But if I am needed there in Kharkiv, I will go. I'm needed here right now. I talk to my friends about this strange feeling of guilt that hunts us for not preparing for war, that there was no tension in us. [...]

Journalist: What is the name of this state you are in?

125

Cherkashyna: In the past I didn't think I harboured any of the World War II traumas. But I have. Now I know that I have felt it since childhood. The Second World War, which also took place in Ukraine, was a trauma. This is the trauma of the entire Ukrainian nation. After all, in every family someone died then, every family had some losses. […] When Putin invaded Ukraine, I remembered that my greatest childhood fear was what would happen to me, what would happen to my family when the war broke out. I imagined that our apartment floats and flies like an aeroplane with us in it, safe. This vision saved me when I was six or seven years old. It calmed my fear. Now the war has broken out and our apartment in Kharkiv, where my parents live, has unfortunately not floated, my relatives do not fly it like a plane, they are not safe (Rigamonti, 2022a).

Almost all female artists experienced this type of thoughts and emotions, which prevented them from living a normal life, even though they had found a safe haven in Poland.

As a result, in many cases, the process of creating performances didn't start with artistic activities but with various forms of workshops, discussions and psychological laboratories. These activities allowed Ukrainian artists to gradually adjust to the new reality and begin their work. For example, Urszula Kijak, who directed the play *Life in Case of War* (*Życie na wypadek wojny*), had extensive experience conducting participatory workshops with individuals who had experienced various traumas. She worked with women, including victims of the civil war in Colombia, as part of the *Me Too* movement. In the first few weeks of the performance's production Ukrainian artists sat together with her at a large table and talked about topics completely unrelated to art[103]. They slowly reached a point where they decided they were ready to start working on the performance. As they later admitted[104], preparing the performance proved to be the best remedy for their traumas. Director Kamil Wawrzuta worked with the actresses of the play *Як Ви? Jak u Was?* (*How Are You?*) at the Second Sphere (Druga Strefa) Theatre in a similar way, gradually introducing them to the actual production. He approached the theme of the war in Ukraine, which was the content of the play, with great caution, delicacy, even tenderness. One of the reviews mentioned that, '[i]t was evident onstage that the director put a lot of empathy into ensuring the Ukrainian artists felt comfortable portraying the story of their homeland' (KMAG, 2022). In the case of the play *Six Ribs of Anger*, performed at

---

[103] Information obtained during a conversation with Urszula Kijak conducted by the author of the text on June 4th, 2022.

[104] Information obtained during an interview conducted by the author of the article with Olena Boryshpolets, Justyna Mohytych and Yevhenia Nepytaliuk on September 30th, 2022.

the Komuna Warszawa theatre, its author, Sasha Denisova, played a signifi-cant role in working on the emotions of the Ukrainian actresses. Due to her frequent work with documentary theatre forms, she also had extensive expe-rience working directly with people in difficult psychological situations, such as experiencing states of anxiety. Together with the director they began pre-paring the play with a several-day laboratory, during which she not only in-troduced the actresses to the aspects of documentary theatre but also worked on their emotions, preparing them to confront the reality of their war-torn homeland on stage.

Although numerous Ukrainian plays addressing the ongoing war have emerged since 2014, the scale of destruction and cruelty from the aggres-sor faced by Ukraine after February 24th, 2022, would be difficult to com-pare to previous years. For many reasons, works reflecting the most recent events couldn't be written immediately. Above all, society was preoccupied with ensuring its own security, both through internal and external migra-tion. Additionally, the trauma of war posed a significant obstacle to the cre-ative activities of playwrights. However, Ukrainian artists did not want to remain passive or refrain from addressing the events that had occurred. The texts were crafted directly on stage, drawing from firsthand accounts pro-vided by witnesses involved in the production, supplemented by testimonies from Ukraine. Forms of documentary theatre and verbatim techniques were utilised, drawing on authentic correspondences, interviews or social media posts. In this regard, the performances referenced both the working meth-ods that began to emerge after 2014 in progressive Ukrainian theatres and modern trends in European theatre, such as NTGent Theater by Milo Rau or the Maxim Gorki Theater. These were also techniques deeply rooted in con-temporary Polish theatre. All participants of the artistic project were involved in the realisation of various elements of the performance. The director was not solely responsible for the artistic shape of the production but rather played more advisory and coordinating roles. The dramaturg listened to the ac-tors' opinions, used their stories or improvisations and then edited the final script of the performance. The performances were based on a general vision, an idea that was then developed on stage during rehearsals. Projects often took the form of performance art, straddling the boundary between dramat-ic performance, dance theatre or visual arts. Most of them were hybrid in nature, combining personal statements from actors, film projections, audio-visual materials, lighting and laser effects and documentary photographs. This aimed to further enhance the realism of the depicted scenes and highlight the enormity of wartime cruelty. The residents also did not attempt to adapt existing dramas, including classics, to relate to the post-February 24th, 2022 reality. In their fairly common belief, traditional drama was not able to capture the horror and atrocity of what was happening in Ukraine, nor the emotions of the local population. None of the plays were able to express the anger or determination lurking within people whose homes were destroyed and loved ones killed for completely incomprehensible reasons. An important element of the performances was Ukrainian music, including folk music. In Ukraine folklore and folk singing have an identity-building, almost patriotic character, somewhat directed towards Russia, which has been trying for centuries to impose its own traditions and rituals on Ukraine. For Ukrainians, including Ukrainian youth, communal singing is a part of daily life. For example, after the premiere of *Life in Case of War*, the actresses spontaneously began singing together backstage to release the emotions associated with the performance and express joy at the successful conclusion of the show.

Initially the performances were characterised by a desire to directly address what happened in Ukraine after February 24th. Documenting the tragic events has therefore become the primary task. The resident artists themselves determined the content of the performances. In cases where Polish artists, like the director, set designer or dramaturge, contributed to the production, their role was primarily advisory and consultative. On stage the work mostly revolved around collective action. For Ukrainian artists the choice of theme was quite straightforward: their own experiences of war. At a meeting with the artists following the premiere of *Life in Case of War* a question was posed: Was it challenging for them to deliver a play revolving around war, war crimes and tragic events in their homeland? Instantly, a resolute response was given: 'Absolutely not. It would be difficult to play anything else. It's impossible to talk about anything else. We can't fight in Ukraine, but we can speak. We must tell the world what it's like there'[105]. The Ukrainian artists aimed to narrate the horrors of war, the brutality of the oppressor, but most importantly, they wanted to highlight the resilience and determination of Ukrainian defenders. It is very characteristic that none of the Ukrainian projects that emerged in the initial months after the outbreak of the full-scale invasion attempted to evoke pity from the audience or lament the fate of Ukraine in the fight. The central theme revolved around struggle, resistance and an unwavering determination to achieve victory. What surprised, and even shocked, Polish audiences was the prevalent use of grotesque humour, irony and mockery throughout the majority of the performances[106]. They

---

[105] Sentences uttered during a post-performance interview with performers of the play in May 25th, 2022 at the Horzycy Theatre in Torun.

[106] According to Yevhenia Nepytaliuk, Ukrainian humour and jokes became a problem for Russian soldiers, who couldn't understand how, right after city bombings and bloody battles, Ukrainians were joking about the situation on social media, making sarcastic remarks about

even appeared in the most tragic moments of the performances, reflecting a very characteristic trait of Ukrainian society: coping through humour with issues, tragedies and traumas. This was a form of self-defence, but also of building internal strength within society in the face of danger[107]. This helped with mobilisation, but also, as emphasised by Ukrainian artists, it is a national characteristic of society, which thus confronts the problems that affect it[108].

A very strong message in the performances was also directed towards Europe and the world, emphasising that the ongoing war is not solely Ukraine's concern.

> This concerns everyone, all of Europe; it's happening in Europe and can reach others at any moment. Therefore, our goal, our mission, is to speak out about it loudly. To speak out so that the world does not forget about Ukraine. So that the situation after 2014 does not repeat itself when the world grew accustomed to the war in Ukraine and left us to fend for ourselves[109].

The desire for a direct, personal engagement with the war, while also serving as a warning to the world, a shout that it must not be trivialised, was perhaps the most characteristic feature of these performances.

It's also worth noting that the vast majority of the performances were carried out by women, as Ukrainian artists remained in Ukraine, participating in military actions. Women play a specific role in Ukraine. On the one hand, many contemporary artists, mainly from Ukrainian independent theatre scenes, address feminist themes, criticising the patriarchal hierarchy of Ukrainian society. In turn, in everyday life, women often shoulder not only the responsibilities of caring for the home and family but also make key decisions crucial for their loved ones. In a situation where men went off to fight, the scope of women's duties and responsibilities, both for daily affairs and those with a broader civic dimension, became even greater. In the performances that emerged on Polish stages such a feminine perspective is palpable. Speaking of fundamental matters, the fight for the independence of the homeland, the authors of the texts do not forget that this struggle consists not only of battles fought, war strategies, international political relations,

---

the invaders. In one post, addressed to his family, a Russian soldier asked: 'Why do they, no matter what we do to them, mock us?'.

[107] Information obtained during interviews with Ukrainian artists: Olena Boryshpolets, Yevhenia Nepytaliuk, Justyna Mohytych, Olena Apchel and Olha Matsiupa.

[108] Information obtained during an interview conducted by the author with Olena Boryshpolets, Yevhenia Nepytaliuk and Justyna Mohytych.

[109] Information obtained during an interview conducted by the author with Yevhenia Nepytaliuk.

but also the daily routine, coping with all the inconveniences that war brings with it.

An example of a performance that implemented the aforementioned forms of work was the play *Life in Case of War*, prepared by Ukrainian residents of the Polish Theatre in Bydgoszcz and later presented at various theatres and theatre festivals in Poland. The premiere was held on May 25th, 2022. It starred Olena Boryshpolets, Zhenia Doliak, Alona Karpenko, Justyna Mohytych, Yevhenia Nepytaliuk and Yasia Saienko. They were a mix of professional actresses and individuals with backgrounds in music, visual arts and literature. The performance was directed by Polish artist Urszula Kijak, with Lena Liahushonkova overseeing the dramaturgical structure and Wojciech Faruga, the director of the Polish Theatre, handling the set design. The division of roles was not strictly defined since the production evolved on stage, allowing each participant to influence the script, final text and its staging. As mentioned, they were thus drawing on working methods used by various European theatres of migration. The adopted solutions were particularly akin to the work on the production *Munich-Damascus: Stories of One City* prepared in 2018 at the City Theatre of Munich. Similarly to the German production where Syrian performers began rehearsals shortly after arriving from Syria to Germany, Ukrainian artists have just arrived in Poland, fleeing from the war in Ukraine. The first weeks were spent in workshops with Kijak, aimed at processing the war trauma. The next stage was working on the script. It involved each of the performers sharing very personal memories related to the last few months of their lives in war-torn Ukraine and after arriving in Poland. These stories became the basis for the subsequent script. In addition to this, there were stories related to the invasion, memories, testimonies of individuals, documents and instructions found on social media and the internet. Liahushonkova, responsible for the dramatic structure, took part in rehearsals, collaborating with the performers to organise selected elements into a cohesive whole. The final form of the script was thus the result of the work of all participants in the project. *Life in Case of War* can be described as an interdisciplinary project, combining performative strategies, documentary theatre, verbatim with the form of public psychotherapy. The performance was presented in Ukrainian with Polish subtitles displayed on screens. Wojciech Faruga's scenography was minimalist and functional. It consisted of six black chairs, two round mirrors, a cartoonist's table and projections displayed on the wall, which became an important narrative reference in the performance. On the floor, an inscription in Ukrainian was pasted in capital letters made out of tape: 'children are here' – a clear reference to the bombed theatre in Mariupol.

The performance would begin in the theatre's foyer, where the spectators waiting to enter the theatre hall would be surprised by the wail of alarm sirens. The actresses, dressed in elegant office outfits, would then quickly and nervously direct the audience to their seats. The scenes that followed contained a mix of messages and posts taken from the Internet: at times extremely personal and dramatic, at other times funny, accounts of citizens of a country ravaged by war, would be contrasted with official, dispassionate instructions to protect people from its consequences. The latter, uttered with official seriousness by the actresses, were a form of a message/warning to those listening that this war could soon affect them; that it was real and close. The instructions corresponded with the clothes of the actresses who acted as experts: people conducting training, training in the event of war. The show was divided into parts whose titles were displayed on the screen, including: *How to Start a Tank, Toilet Princess, Chemical Hazard, Volunteer Collection Point, How to Make a Good Cocktail, No Home* and *How to behave during rape.*

The very titles suggest a mix of extremely dramatic and serious scenes with humorous ones. Using exaggerated gestures and movements, the actresses demonstrated how to operate a tank if it's abandoned by fleeing enemy soldiers. The video of their performance quickly became an internet sensation in both Poland and Ukraine, amassing tens of thousands of views. The instructions on how to behave during a nuclear bomb explosion sounded grotesque, as they indicated that in such a case, there isn't much left to do. However, in a situation where Putin kept escalating the threat of using such weapons, they sounded extremely serious, too.

The makers of the performance did not shy away from clashing the reality of war with luxury and splendour associated with the ruling class in Russia, but also the Western world, which, living affluently and peacefully in their homes, has no idea what the war in Ukraine entails. Images of this type were clearly visible in the episode *Toilet Princess*, in which one of the actresses, playing a person cleaning a public toilet at a metro station full of refugees in Kiev, uses a golden bottle and luxurious perfumes not to offend the sensibilities of the audience gathered in the room. The world of consumption, celebrities, lovers of exclusive brands from among the Russian dissidents or the local *nouveau riche* was parodied, but also the world of the West (hence the remarks addressed directly to the audience), whose *glamour* is mercilessly juxtaposed with the monstrous amount of excrement produced at the metro station acting as a shelter. There were more such deliberately used, grotesque-ironic episodes and references, showing that life during the invasion goes on with all its manifestations, tragedies, but also everyday life full of funny moments. It is interesting that, especially during the first performances, the Polish audience was not really ready for this type of images. Expecting

131

something filled with pathos and martyrdom, the first spectators were almost afraid to laugh, considering it inappropriate. Only subsequent presentations brought more spontaneous reactions from the audience, in which emotion and sadness were mixed with genuine laughter.

A few scenes from the play were particularly memorable. The first was striking in its brevity. One of the actresses announced that at this point in the performance, the artists planned to present the story of Bucha, a war crime committed in March 2022 by the Land Forces of the Russian Federation, where over 400 unarmed Ukrainian civilians were murdered in a real massacre. However, such a crime cannot be told, she commented, and after a long silence, the actresses moved on to the next parts of the performance. Equally emotional was the episode announced by the title appearing on the screen: *Volunteer Collection Point*. A young girl wearing a white dress with her hair down began to sing a Ukrainian song in a beautiful voice in the company of women dressing her. The song, sounding very nostalgic, was an authentic song that is sung in Ukraine during weddings, when the bride is dressed in her wedding attire just before the ceremony. Actresses with great solemnity recreated all the activities, except for one: instead of beautiful robes and ornaments, the bride was gradually dressed in the following attributes of a soldier going to war: a backpack, a helmet, a rifle… The wedding as a completely new stage in the life of a young girl was compared to going to war, referring to the multitude of Ukrainian women who joined the ranks of those fighting. The episode preceded by the title: *How to behave during rape* referred to one of the most brutal crimes committed in Ukraine by Russian soldiers. The text of the instructions was spoken by successive actresses extremely slowly, with great seriousness and calmness, as during a therapeutic session, with the message repeated many times: 'Keep calm, don't resist, because the enemy can kill you, remember, it's not your fault, your enemy is to blame'. The poignant scene ended with a punch line, which surprised the Polish audience: 'What to do when it turns out that you are pregnant as a result of rape and found yourself in Poland?'. There was a short, laconic and accurate answer: 'Fuck off from Poland'. The reaction of viewers was very different. Many nodded understandingly, remembering that a few months earlier the Polish parliament had introduced one of the most restrictive anti-abortion laws in the world, some were embarrassed, others were confused whether it was appropriate to laugh or rather cry at this moment.

The incorporation of visual elements into the performance proved an extremely interesting staging technique. Throughout the performance, one of the actresses sat at a huge table at the back of the stage, drawing pictures visible on the screen. They were drawings of various objects, including hospitals, schools, private houses destroyed by bombing, Russian ships destroyed by the Ukrainian army, pictures from the children's world – blocks, teddy bears, a train with a railway, etc. The camera positioned above the table allowed the audience to closely follow both the process of creation and the final effects on an ongoing basis. This act of drawing was accompanied by the painter's constant browsing of her mobile phone. The drawings were thus the images of the messages she'd found on the Internet. Such constant browsing of the mobile phone in search of any news about the war, the fate of loved ones, etc. has been a typical behaviour of the Ukrainians, especially women, after the invasion began. The drawings were also a kind of illustration for the course of events on stage, and in fact they entered into a dialogue with them, carrying new content and messages. And so, in the scene entitled *Dove of Peace*, a characteristic drawing of a white dove, symbolising peace, appeared on the screen. At the same time, one of the actresses uttered a dramatic monologue about being left alone with her five-year-old brother, because their mother died during the evacuation, and now they are sitting, hidden, hungry, and the only food they eat are killed street pigeons. Upon seeing the drawing of a beautiful white dove symbolising peace, the actress, full of frustration, would run up to the drawing artist and angrily take the sheet, then crumple, tear and throw it away. The cartoonist would not give up and draw another dove, which would be destroyed again and again. The sequence of such events was repeated several times, referring not only to the content of the monologue itself, but also to all the voices of world politicians and authorities who would often call for understanding and peace in the context of the ongoing Russian barbarism.

The gestures and stage movements of the actresses that accompanied the presentation of the instructions were meticulously refined, artificial, like the behaviour of training experts or stewardesses on planes, instructing passengers before take-off on how to behave in moments of danger. This type of game was contrasted with scenes in which the 'world of instructions' was switched to the real 'world of war', recorded in messages from the social media. The stage movement would then become disordered, chaotic at times. The actresses moved in different directions, there was no pre-planned order or purpose, which reflected the specificity and chaos of the war itself: constant escape, trying to save oneself, hiding from shelling and bombing, and finally everyday activities: cleaning, cooking, anxiously listening out to see if the air attack is coming back or not.

The director of the performance pointed out that in this feminist performance, created entirely by women, she wanted to convey a character trait that is very characteristic of Ukrainian women. She described them moving on stage as a 'bustle'[110]. Ukrainian women, even in such dramatic moments, tried to maintain control over everyday life, over the home. They were always busy, during the bombings, they protected the children, and in the short breaks between the air raids they ran to the kitchen, prepared something to eat, checked their savings, cleaned up. The acting means used during those episodes were frugal, maximally authentic, avoiding theatricalisation and pathos, also in the most dramatic scenes. The artificiality appeared only when the instructions were being read out. In the final scene, the artists remained silent, with silence punctuated by long, tiring sounds, including a monotonous, repetitive noise created by the rubbing of the microphone. This was accompanied by gestures, and the same gestures made by all the actresses at the same time summed up all those that had appeared earlier during the training throughout the performance. The sequences of movements and facial expressions would become more and more emotional, then they would lose their intensity and once again become even more intense. The repetitive sequences referred to the constant, heroic attempts to survive the war nightmare, internal mobilisation, determination and rage, and then falling into apathy and resignation, only to wake up again to fight. At that time, successive vertical lines, drawn slowly by the cartoonist, appeared on the screen, symbolising the passing days of the war. The scene lasted a long time, until the artist counted down the day of the war that fell on the day of the performance.

The theatrical performance *5:00 UA*, staged at the Silesian Theatre in Katowice, also took on an interdisciplinary form. It incorporated various performative strategies with elements of physical theatre, postmodern dance, singing, using verbatim technique. The title of the play referred to 5:00 in the morning, the time when the Russian invasion erupted in Ukraine and the first bombs fell on the country.

In the case of this performance, the script was developed during rehearsals. The premiere took place on June 23rd, 2022. Ukrainian residents led the preparations, including Tatiana Gerasymchuk, Maria Kardash, Halyna Lozynska, Anna Lysenko, Sofiia Mutylo, Dariia Novykova, Nataliia Pysarieva, Yerheniia Prysiazhna, Halyna Ryba, Kseniia Svistun, Kateryna Vasiukova and Nina Batovska. Here's what its director – Yulia Maslak – had to say about the performance:

> We decided that our personal experiences would be the basis of the performance. We want to share the story we experienced while escaping. It is common to all of us, and at the same time each of us has their own individual story. Most of

---

[110] Information obtained from Urszula Kijak during the interview conducted by the author on June 4th, 2022.

the monologues were written by the actresses involved in *5:00 UA*. They talk about escaping from Ukraine, about the war, about their stay in Poland. Working on the play was also a form of therapy for our whole group (Odziomek, 2022).

The plot centres around the artists' escape from Ukraine, their journey to Poland and the first moments of their stay in a new country. The main part of the performance, however, was filled with constant recurrences of the residents' memories of what they had experienced, what happened and is still happening in Ukraine, and the fate of their loved ones. Individual images were constantly changing, and the logic of their succession was solely determined by the emotions of the narrators themselves. The forms of artistic expression also changed. Performers continuously transformed from dramatic actresses into contemporary dance artists; having become the opera choir, they gave voice to a monologue by one of them, before reciting the text together or singing folk songs.

The journey in this performance was the dominant element that organised what happened and how it looked on stage. The scenography was extremely simple and minimalist: on an empty, dark stage, only a large screen was visible. In addition, suitcases of various sizes were placed in front of the stage, at the height of the first row of audience chairs. The scene resembled the huge hall of an old, dilapidated train station waiting room. At the beginning of the performance, the actresses took their suitcases, which from then on performed a variety of functions, not only those originally assigned to them. During the performance, those suitcases become barricades protecting the combatants, beds or a corner in the basement where you can fall asleep or hide from the bombing, and even a makeshift house when you have lost absolutely everything as a result of the bombing.

Even though *5:00 UA* was being prepared completely independently from *Life in Case of War*, many of the scenes dealt with the same themes. It was understandable, because, for example, the tragedy in Bucha, Mariupol, the criminal rapes of soldiers on civilians left an extraordinary mark on the entire Ukrainian community. Regarding the tragedy that unfolded in Bucha, the artists applied almost the same strategy as in the play *Life in Case of War*. Unable to find any words, they remained silent.

In the face of the tragedy of Mariupol – a bombed theatre in which hundreds of people, including children, were hiding – anger, frustration, but also helplessness were also felt in the actress' rendition of this subject. When telling the story, at one point she began to slap her face with all her strength, and then screamed in a terrifying way her protest and pain towards the children killed in Ukraine, as well as her own shame that she was safe in Poland at the same time. Equally uncompromising was the scene when one of the actresses drank water from the floor of the stage, which she had previously deliberately poured out, meticulously and greedily licking each drop. She explained that the starving in occupied Mariupol did not have such comfort, drinking dirty water from puddles after rain. Despite the image of death, destruction, human tragedies, powerlessness in the face of what is happening in Ukraine, what stood out in the performance was not so much despair and lack of hope as Ukraine's strength and determination in the fight for victory. A loud, shocking scream was strongly present in the performance, but more than pain and helplessness, it hid the warning towards the enemy: 'you are not unpunished'.

In the script, based on the experiences of the players themselves, there were also scenes related to the journey to Poland itself; apartments left in Ukraine, the fate of which is unknown; loved ones who stayed there. The stories were extremely personal. Some of the scenes took the form of monologues; in others all the actresses appeared, asking each other a lot of questions, bidding on whose story is more tragic, talking about what they have and haven't a right to as refugees in Poland, where is their place in the world of art, can they rebuild their lives in Poland, whether it will be a betrayal or not if they do not want to return to Ukraine after the war, whether they can start working on the play at all, when the war has just begun and the situation in Ukraine is constantly changing.

Also in this performance, some truly dramatic scenes were interspersed with those of a humorous nature, often taking the form of black comedy, revue or stand-up. The latter was used by one of the actresses explaining to the viewers what is the most effective weapon against attacking Russian drones. To the laughter from the audience, she advised preparing as many preserves as possible for the winter at home: jams, preserves, compotes, necessarily in large glass jars. When the drones were about to arrive, you had to gently, imperceptibly open the window, wait for the drone to approach the building and throw jars at it, thus destroying it. The humour of the situation was due to the fact that the story referred to an authentic story from the war with Russia, when an elderly Ukrainian woman destroyed a Russian drone with a jar of compote. In another episode, one of the actresses seriously advised the viewers to buy apartments only in the basement part of the buildings, or to adapt the basements for residential purposes, because during the bombing they would no longer be forced to flee to the shelter. An example of a revue/fashion show-like scene was one in which the actresses, dressed in very colourful, mismatched outfits, adorned with very visible labels of high end brands, paraded around the stage to the rhythm of loud music like models, loudly lamenting how they are supposed to live now, since all big fashion houses have withdrawn from Russia and they could no longer buy their beloved Chanel perfumes. It was an obvious irony in the face of all the voices of protest that were coming from Russia at the time in connection with the boycott of this country by most of the recognised brands. The scene was in stark contrast to the images of human misfortunes and dramas in Ukraine, showing the moral and intellectual emptiness of Russian society.

The stage movement in the performance was extremely dynamic, giving the performance a very coherent rhythm. Dramatic scenes flowed seamlessly into dance. Sometimes it was an illustration to the actresses' stories, sometimes a dance played a fully autonomous role in the performance. The individual scenes were as far removed from beauty and harmony as possible. Convulsive, ecstatic movements as well as acrobatically bent bodies of the performers reflected all the traumas hidden in the protagonists. In terms of inspiration, the artists referred to the Ukrainian dancer Larysa Venediktova, the creator of TanzLaboratorium, who implements critical and political dance practices following the example of the Ukrainian avant-garde and performance art. The dances, even more than the dramatic scenes, reflected the desire to show not only the tragedy of the Ukrainian nation, but also its strength and determination in resisting the occupier. This was particularly visible in the scenes of group and individual dance, which synthetically cast the viewer's imagination to the images of war. The theme of dying and falling was constantly recurring, but with a grimace of pain, the dancers stubbornly got up, reborn to fight. In some scenes the audience could watch the choreography from above, thanks to a screen and a camera placed above the stage. It gave the impression that the actresses lying on the stage were suspended in front of a huge, grey wall that prevented any escape. They were locked in the deadly trap of war, alone in their struggle and dying. Through dance, the nightmare of women raped during the war was also reflected. The convulsive movements of the actresses evoked a nightmarish practice. The scene returned several times during the performance, like the indelible trauma of people who experienced such crimes. The bluntness, brutality, pain and extremely emotional character emanated from all the dance routines present in the performance. The performative strategies used in them served to symbolically convey the nightmares associated with the war. The extremely dynamic, sometimes even ecstatic rhythm of the dance equipped such parts of the performance with an even stronger emotional message.

The final scenes of the performance referred to the end of the resident's journey, the arrival at one of the railway stations in Poland. This was accompanied by a silent, gesture-based scene where volunteers provided food and essential supplies to the visitors during their first days. In a scene that was very touching for the audience, one of the actresses spontaneously and very authentically thanked the Poles for their support, empathy and heart. The audience was moved by a fragment when the actress asked herself if she would be able to make such gestures as the Poles who were helping. After much thought, her answer was extremely honest: 'I don't know, but I would love to'.

Achieving the goal by the travellers was not, however, a 'happy end', a salvation for them, because the nightmares of war return, also in safe Poland. In the final scene of the play the motif of dance returns, this time evoking in a synthetic manner choreographic arrangements present throughout the performance: rapes, deaths, escapes... they return like war traumas, from which one cannot escape.

One of the earliest performances involving Ukrainian residents was the play *Як Ви? Jak u Was?* (*How Are You?*), presented at the small independent theatre Druga Strefa in Warsaw and debuted on April 28th, 2022. The title itself suggested the presence of both Ukrainian (*Як Ви?*) and Polish (*Jak u Was*) languages in the production. The phrase 'Як Ви?', typically used as a greeting, took on an entirely different meaning during the invasion.

> The Ukrainian 'How are you?' (*Як Ви?*) is no longer a polite greeting but a question filled with concern: 'Are you alive? Is it peaceful?'. This question, sent every morning, was directed to family members, friends, neighbours and colleagues who remained in Ukraine. It was the first task performed each day by those who fled to save their own lives and those of their children (Premiere of *ЯК ВИ? Jak u Was?*, 2022).

The director of the play and responsible for choreography, Kamil Wawrzuta, similarly to the performances described earlier, began preparing the show with meetings where Ukrainian participants shared their personal stories. These narratives ranged from the onset of the invasion, their decision to leave Ukraine and their initial months in Poland, to reflections on their childhood, adolescence and the beginnings of their careers. Personal threads intertwined with the fate of Ukraine, at times with joyful moments from the time when the country gained independence, moments of doubt stemming from the difficult process of political, economic and social transformation, to the days when war engulfed the country. The Ukrainian artists in *Як ви? Jak u Was?* want to share what they are going through, what they have experienced, about war, about what is simply important to them.

> The artists in *Як ви? Jak u Was?* aim to share their experiences, their journeys and reflections on war, focusing on what matters most to them. The play incorporates elements from their childhood and youth stories. The history of Ukrainian artists shows the uneven struggle against evil. The performance embodies everything that war takes away, namely love, joy, and above all, human life (Izdebska, 2022).

The script was directly inspired by these personal narratives. However, music, contemporary dance and singing took centre stage, evolving during rehearsals and improvisation. Monologues supplemented them, drawing from the artists' earlier stories. All of them: Maria Lozova, Daria Vadimovna Belikova[111], Alina Velcheva[112], Milaniya Medvedeva[113], Yelyzaveta Dzhuhostranska[114] were previously professionally involved in dance, with less dramatic experience. The reviewers highlighted their excellent skills while also noting the distinctions between the Polish and Ukrainian schools of contemporary dance. They suggested that collaboration between Poland and Ukraine could produce very interesting results for both sides (Izdebska, 2022). The musical aspect was handled by the immensely talented Alexandra Malatskovska, who had previously achieved great success in Ukraine. She is a composer, vocalist, pianist, actress and vocal coach. All the pieces were her original compositions, ranging from warm, melancholic and harmonious passages inspired by musical theatre to highly dynamic, atonal, densely layered sounds characteristic of contemporary classical music.

The performance *Every Minute Motherland* was entirely based on dance[115]. The director was Maciej Kuźmiński. The cast included dancers from both Ukraine and Poland. The premiere was held on August 25th, 2022. It was Kuźmiński's original project, subsequently showcased on numerous stages across Poland.

Kuźmiński develops his own method of movement called Dynamic Phrasing. This method is based on four pillars: two movement techniques – floor work, i.e. work with the floor, and work in standing, including the method of working with energy based on repetitive movements called the loop, drawing from the Chinese QiGong technique. The other two pillars are: the movement recomposition and reconstruction method called task basket, and the movement laboratory method based on improvisation. The main goal of Dynamic Phrasing is to connect with our own energy: both the one flowing through the body as a consequence of biomechanical conditions, and the one, which makes it possible for us to communicate in a non-verbal way and that we are part of a larger world. In stage practice, this meant that to a much lesser extent than in the previously described performances, *Every Minute Motherland* allows one to follow the plot of the action by giving the images precisely defined meanings. In this performance as well, Kuźmiński crafted a spectacle on stage utilising the dance improvisations of the participants. These improvisations were intended to convey the emotions linked to specific events of the war in Ukraine. Subsequent abstract

---

[111] More information about Daria Belikova in the appendix.

[112] More information about Alina Velcheva in the appendix.

[113] More information about Milaniya Medvedeva in the appendix.

[114] More information about Yelyzaveta Dzhuhostranska in the appendix.

[115] Cast: Daria Koval, Anna Myloslavska, Vitaliia Vaskiv, Anastasia Ivanova, Monika Witkowska, Szymon Tur, Maciej Kuźmiński, Judyta Pakulska.

choreographies communicated with the audience through emotions, above the verbal code of meaning. On a completely empty stage, devoid of any backdrop, we watched seven dancers. Dance sequences were separated by long pauses, after which the dancers slowly, with almost mathematical precision, took the right places on the stage. Whole group sets were interspersed with either solo or smaller group dances. Dynamic sequences, in which the harmony of the dance was disturbed by the rhythm of the changing music, forcing the search for new patterns or dance techniques, were intertwined with sets characterised by calmness, dignity, emanating a force that was able to order and override the previous chaos and confusion.

The performance allows for very different interpretations. However, some external centrifugal force seemed to be of key importance, the force of war, war fate, which again and again, in subsequent choreographic arrangements, tried to take control of the dancers, take over the physical and existential world, setting it in motion, chaos, questioning values, identity, sense of safety of the performing artists. What is most important, and what connects *Every Minute Motherland* with other performances described here, is the fact that the determining force, the ominous fate of war and aggression was not able to finally dominate the world of dancers, their artistic autonomy, freedom, it did not become the subject here, the main theme of the performance. That title/role went instead to determination, resistance, the power that lies dormant in people who can oppose war and evil.

Performances based on dramatic works created during the invasion – a time for deep reflection

As time went on, Ukrainian artists performing in Poland increasingly shifted away from creating scripts directly on stage during rehearsals, which relied on improvisations and stories from performers who were participants in dramatic events in Ukraine. Instead, they leaned towards producing dramatic plays that were written after February 24th, 2022. Many felt that the approach of promptly documenting wartime events, expressing emotional protest, and portraying war trauma on stage was becoming overused. However, they didn't have fully formed ideas about the direction Ukrainian drama should take next. The latter part of 2022 and throughout 2023 saw lively discussions within the Ukrainian creative community on this particular subject. These discussions unfolded in Ukraine, Poland and other countries where

Ukrainian artists were present. In September 2023 a special laboratory was organised with the participation of leading Ukrainian playwrights, including Lena Liahushonkova and Olha Matsiupa, to discuss how to write about war. The outcome was the creation of 7 different dramatic plays intended to meet new criteria. Interestingly, 4 of them did not focus on the time of the invasion at all; instead, some even reached back to World War II while still maintaining relevance. During the laboratory it was agreed that immediate documentation should be supplemented with a deeper reflection on the causes, consequences and social processes accompanying war. Armed conflict and traumatic experiences can provide a broader, more universal perspective, addressing political divisions that have become evident or even exacerbated, in Ukraine during wartime. This involves focusing on the psychological analysis of individuals caught in Ukraine's turbulent history, including recent dramas, and giving greater emphasis to the social issues of the contemporary world. Ukrainian theatre has inadequately represented these issues for years, including women's rights, LGBT rights and the individual's lack of agency in confronting the ongoing processes of globalisation, among others.

It is worth noting that these are topics that contemporary Polish theatre is also deeply interested in. In this way, there is an opportunity for intercultural understanding and joint projects addressing issues relevant to both nations. This lays the foundation for collaboration that extends beyond merely offering organisational support to Ukrainian refugee artists by Polish theatres, focusing instead on fostering substantive and creative cooperation. It should also be emphasised that the discussions held by Ukrainian creators about how to pursue their artistic ambitions in emigration during wartime, how to relate to the realities of war, corresponded with similar ones that occurred somewhat earlier in Western Europe in connection with the artistic activities of refugees from the Middle East. This was highlighted, among others, by Ruba Totah and Krystel Khoury whose focus was on the situation of Syrian refugees in Germany. Their initial artistic endeavours mainly focused on narratives directly related to the war, the experience of fleeing and forced displacement. However, over time those refugees began to feel that the local environment expected only such testimonies from them, which limited artistic creativity, freedom of expression and at the same time constituted an element of stigmatisation (Totah, Khoury, 2019, p. 5). Lena Liahushonkova recalled a similar experience in Poland when she was a resident playwright at the Polish Theatre in Bydgoszcz. She felt pressure, undefined by any official regulations or even suggestions from the theatre authorities, that as a Ukrainian playwright who directly experienced the horrors of war, she should write exclusively on such topics. Meanwhile, although she did not shy away from this most significant event in the lives of Ukrainians, she also had other ideas for her own plays in mind[116]. Roza Sarkisian highlighted that Ukrainian creators, at a certain point, started questioning whether presenting plays focused on wartime tragedies amounted to commercialising their own emotions on stage and engaging in self-promotion, catering to the expectations of Western societies. However, they were also conscious of the necessity of addressing the topic of war. When asked how one should approach writing about war, Sarkisian herself couldn't provide a clear answer[117]. At the same time Svitlana Oleshko emphasised that the way forward for new Ukrainian drama involves self-reflection, in-depth analysis and synthesis of the phenomena occurring in Ukraine, with the war at their centre. According to her, playwrights should prioritise the artistic value and a universal rather than opportunistic message in their works. Natalia Blok, who relocated to Switzerland after a temporary stay in Poland and collaborates with local theatres, cited her play *Das Leben ist unaufhaltsam* (*Life Cannot Be Stopped*), staged at the Theater Basel, as an example of such a non-opportunistic approach to the topic. It narrates the tale of two boys living amidst the invasion in the war-torn Ukrainian city of Kherson. While war plays an immensely influential role, shaping lives significantly, *Das Leben ist unaufhaltsam* primarily highlights young individuals aspiring to live, love and pursue their passions. Blok therefore advocates moving away from pure documentation of life towards universalizing events and seeking mystique in the surrounding everydayness[118]. Another acclaimed Ukrainian playwright, Olha Matsiupa, shares the opinion that drama and documentary theatre focusing solely on the theme of war have become anachronistic after more than 8 years of its duration. She considers the continuation of aesthetic changes in Ukrainian theatre, initiated after 2014 by young Ukrainian artists and writers, to be paramount. Therefore, the primary concern should be the artistic value of works, modern methods of work and staging. According to her, it's difficult to imagine nowadays that Ukrainian creators will forget about the war. While it will remain a prominent theme for a long time, they should also delve deeper into the traditions and roots of Ukrainian culture, making it simultaneously open and intriguing for contemporary audiences[119].

---

[116] Information obtained from Lena Liahushonkova during the interview conducted by the author on September 10th, 2023.

[117] Information obtained from Roza Sarkisian during an interview conducted by the author on October 18th, 2023.

[118] Information obtained from Natalia Blok during the interview conducted by the author on October 12th, 2023.

[119] Information obtained from Olha Matsiupa during the interview conducted by the author on September 10th, 2023.

The outcome of these discussions were additional plays written after February 2022, which started being performed in Polish theatres as well. One of them was Sasha Denisova's *Six Ribs of Anger*, produced at the Komuna Warszawa Theatre and premiered on June 26th, 2022. The performance directed by the young Polish artist Beniamin Koc featured Ukrainian actors such as: Maria Severilova, Justyna Wasik, Katerina Taran, Ania Lysenko, Tetiana Proskurina, Konstantyn Skiba and Aleksander Solovoniuk. The play was performed in Ukrainian with Polish subtitles displayed on screens.

Denisova, similar to many of her other texts, relied on the formula of documentary theatre. She utilised verbatim technique, interviews conducted by Ukrainian actresses performing in the show with refugees from Ukraine who found shelter in Poland, in the vast Ptak Warsaw Expo, a refugee centre. They lived in huge hangars, with approximately one and a half thousand women in each of them. Based on these interviews Denisova wrote the script for the play. However, she departed from the purely documentary formula of the art, introducing elements of fairy tales, legends, provoking reflection on both the contemporary condition of Ukraine and Ukrainian society as well as its past. In the play two narratives intersect: one portraying the trauma of the present and the other depicting a blissful Arcadia. The latter is temporarily lost, beyond reach, yet so deeply ingrained in Ukrainian tradition that, despite its utopian nature, it is anticipated as tangible and achievable.

The surprising title refers to the language of psychology, where specialists working with traumatised people believe that in reaction to trauma, especially war trauma, they go through six 'ribs' – six levels of anger: anger at the aggressor, anger at the war, anger at fate, themselves, and finally anger at those around them.

The protagonists of the play are five Ukrainian women living in a refugee camp. They come from places most affected by the war: Mariupol, Bucha, Chernihiv, Dnipro and the country's capital – Kiev. Each hides a tragic story: one is waiting for a call from her relatives fighting in the war, a signal that the child and husband who went missing while escaping from the bombing are still alive, etc. Denisova brilliantly portrayed the different characters and psychological profiles of these people: the apathetic mother of the missing child from Bucha; a dancing and energetic ballerina from Kiev, who with her activity tries to drown out the recurring image of her brother killed in front of her eyes by a Russian soldier; a kind elderly porter from Chernihiv, finally reached by her son from the front to communicate that it could be his last phone call, because he had found himself in Russian captivity; a philharmonic artist from Chernihiv filled with romantic optimism, and a blusterous mother of an unruly teenager (with whom she lives in the camp) – a woman who looks at everything extremely sceptically, and who doesn't shy away from offering blunt, even vulgar comments. It is she who carries the entire load of humour in the performance, commenting, for example, on almost every event with sharp, blunt profanity. And although she is the furthest away from any hope for a positive turn of events, the furthest away from empathy for her fellow residents, one person brings a dreamy smile to her face: the Ukrainian President Volodymyr Zelensky. She loves everything about him: beauty, courage, responsibility, although her infatuation is quite far from political issues and the role that the president plays in the war against the invader. Denisova allows herself quite a bit of self-irony, especially considering the tragic context of the play. In one of the scenes, President Zelensky appears to his admirer, hugs her, assuring her that he knows her very well, after all, he knows all his citizens perfectly. Saying goodbye, he does not hesitate to greet the Polish audience, shaking a dozen or so hands, while the whole scene parodies the former actor's and now president's passion for self-creation rather than referring to the martyrdom-like idealisation of him as a nation's hero.

Magical fairy-tale elements, referencing rituals and legends rooted in Ukrainian society, appear quite unexpectedly in the performance. When all the heroines have reached the last level of anger – the 'sixth rib' of anger at those who are around, i.e. at each other, one of them – an eternally optimistic, romantic girl from Kherson, who loves literature and music, tells the others the legend of the Cossacks[120], almost mythical heroes in Ukrainian culture, invincible soldiers. And the Cossacks return. Not in dreams, not in daydreams, but very real on stage, which in the performance is divided into three spaces. One is the large interior of the hangar where the heroines live. The second is marked by a huge screen, suspended in the side part of the stage, on which images corresponding to the content of the performance are displayed all the time. The third space, in the opposite part of the stage, is constituted by a white, slightly transparent curtain, behind which all the events outside the hangar take place: the psychotherapist's room, the prison from which the heroine's son calls, the space from which President Zelensky comes out. And it is precisely beyond this curtain, during the tales of brave Cossacks, that we see the outline of legendary heroes of Ukraine. Then we hear their voices and finally they emerge, finding themselves in the main space of the stage, reenacting scenes of the ultimate victory over Russia, now, in

---

[120] Cossacks (ukrainian козаки) – a name referring to a multi-ethnic group of people living in the steppes located south of the Ruthenian principalities, later also defining a type of military settlement in the borderlands of the Republic of Poland and Russia. Today's Ukraine considers the history of the Zaporozhian Cossacks to be an integral part of its own history and one of the most important sources of national identity. A direct reference to the Cossack tradition is found in the anthem of Ukraine. The origins of the Zaporozhian Cossacks date back to the 15th century.

contemporary times. The real and mythological realms intertwine at this juncture. While the latter appears to be merely a reflection of the thoughts and
hopes of the refugees themselves, the creators do not offer definitive answers in
this respect. Could it be that the Cossacks are indeed making a comeback?
The potency of this imagery, whether rooted in legend, myth, or perhaps even
real events, prevails over the 'sixth rib of anger'. At the end of the performance,
we see the heroines finally calm and happy, surrounded by their loved ones
who have found themselves and survived the chaos of war. However, the conclusion does not bring a simplistic happy ending; instead, it leaves a question
mark, whether we are truly witnessing a miraculous Ukrainian victory or
rather observing the effects of therapy that have transported the consciousness of the refugees into a world of dreams.

This is how Denisova herself justifies the weaving of mythical threads into
the realistic world of the play:

> And I thought to myself that refugee women cannot influence the situation,
> they can only help with their faith in victory, their magic spells – by imagin-
> ing witches, mythical Cossacks, they can somehow bring this victory closer.
> And I thought that I could turn these words into a theatrical play, and when I talked
> to my colleagues from theatres in France or Finland, they told me that this form
> would also be understood there. We Ukrainians are a European nation, but we
> tend to mythologise. This is our reality and it is historically determined. Just like
> in Latin American countries where the Catholic faith mixed with local beliefs.
> There were five churches in Ukraine, plus the Magdeburg Law and individual
> land ownership. Unlike in Russia. Old pagan beliefs have also been preserved.
> And all this wealth was hidden in a kind of casket. When I was studying in a Soviet
> school, we celebrated, for example, Kupala night, we looked for a fern flower, we
> threw wreaths, we jumped over a bonfire. These mythical Cossacks are also a real
> element for us. When the war started, a woman on a live TV program called on
> the Cossacks for help. Just like in my play (Biernat, 2022).

Denisova applied the verbatim technique in another of her plays, *The Hague*
(*Haga*), written after her escape to Poland, specifically commissioned by
the artistic director of the Polish Theatre in Poznań, Maciej Nowak, and
staged at that theatre. Denisova spent a lot of time talking to people staying
in refugee camps to gather information that she used in her drama, illustrating the process of Russian political elites after the war in Ukraine ended.
Going to the play, audiences could anticipate political theatre, presenting
a futuristic perspective on holding the primary perpetrators of the brutal
Russian assault on Ukraine accountable with factual precision. It's no coincidence that the Polish premiere announcements referenced the play *Responsibility* (*Odpowiedzialność*) by the Powszechny Theatre, which addresses

the accountability of those responsible for the inhumane treatment of refugees at the Polish-Belarusian border. The opening of the play at the Polish Theatre, introducing us to the lawyers who will participate in the trial – an experienced prosecutor in major international criminal cases and one of the best defence attorneys, known for representing mafia members in court, seemed to confirm these assumptions. However, the next scene quickly dispels the illusion of realism and straightforward documentation. It is then that the main defendants appear, representing the Russian elite: Sergey Shoigu (Minister of Defense of the Russian Federation), Ramzan Kadyrov (Chechen politician and commander), Yevgeny Prigozhin (founder of the Wagner Group), Valentina Matviyenko (Chairwoman of the Russian Federation Council), Margarita Simonyan (a star of the regime's media), Sergey Surovikin (general, military commander), Nikolai Patrushev (head of the Russian Federal Security Service), Vladislav Surkov (former advisor and propagandist of Putin), Yuri Kovalchuk (oligarch, owner of Bank Rossiya), and finally, Vladimir Putin himself. We observe exaggerated caricatures, with grotesque facial expressions and gestures that evoke pity rather than fear. The setting is also surprising, resembling an old classroom with traditional school benches, bearing no likeness to the International Criminal Court. The subsequent scenes increasingly veer towards grotesque, reminiscent of a fairground theatre or even a circus. We listen to the defendants' conversations with each other, their frenzied monologues, which expose the madness of the Russian elites. The scene where one of the defendants mentions the greatness of Russia and its culture using the example of the Bolshoi Ballet and the famous *Swan Lake* is characteristic. Suddenly, all the arrested dignitaries put on strange feathers and perform a caricatured, clumsily grandiose dance, mimicking a scene from Tchaikovsky's ballet. This fragment not only ridicules the Russian tyrants but above all shows how Russian culture, considered great, timeless, and admired by the world, becomes a tool of the aggressor's wartime propaganda. Denisova herself spoke about this:

> I've devised a separate bench for Russian culture. It's for the 'Mocking' theatres, for the influential figures of culture who either supported the war by concocting ludicrous justifications for genocide and shelling, or stayed silent, thereby multiplying the suffering and bloodshed of Ukrainians, my people (Piotrowska, 2022b).

The Hague is not just a performance that judges individual people, the political elite wielding power in Russia. It's an indictment against the entire nation. Already at the beginning of the play, the prosecutor declares this in her opening statement: 'Today we will judge not only individuals but the entire state, the social system that led to this dreadful war'. Denisova diverges from strict documentary accuracy here because the jurisdiction of the International Criminal Court in The Hague is limited to individual responsibility, not collective. However, in Denisova's play, realism, probability, adherence to regulations and procedures are not the focus. What holds more significance is the broader, universal perspective of the events portrayed. The key to understanding the deeper layer of the play is the absence of a judge in the ongoing trial. Meanwhile, for most of the performance, there is a little girl present on stage. She holds the characteristic judge's gavel in her hand, and it is she who will pronounce the final sentence for the war criminals. Similarly to *Six Ribs of Anger*, where the appearance of Cossacks transforms the realistic narrative into entirely new meanings, in this case as well, it is uncertain whether the unfolding events – the trial of the Russian elites – are happening in reality or perhaps in the mind of a child whose mother was killed earlier in a bombing when her apartment was being searched by Russian separatists. The trial would then be solely a projection of someone's thoughts, imagined, fabricated, which would justify the grotesqueness of subsequent scenes, an atmosphere completely inconsistent with the seriousness of a European Court. The girl serves as both a victim of the Russian invasion, narrating the ongoing trial and recalling her mother's tragic story, and as a figure suspended outside of time, crafting a fantastical vision of the desired and anticipated justice.

The Hague at the Polish Theatre garnered diverse reviews from Polish critics. Enthusiastic opinions predominated, praising the superb acting[121], remarkable and apt set design and makeup and the direction, helmed by the playwright herself who adeptly balanced between the grotesque, mocking, almost carnival-like comedy and the universal, solemn and tragic elements of the play. For some reviewers, these initial, mocking elements were deemed unnecessary and incomprehensible. In one such review, we read:

> Why such exaggerations, poses and facial expressions? Why the mocking performance of Swan Lake by the actresses and actors? Jokes about Pushkin and Doctor Zhivago? When the law proves ineffective and the prospect of justice rests solely on the remorseful consciences of criminals, the portrayal of their repentance and atonement seems like nothing more than a fantasy. So what does *The Hague* leave us with, then? With nothing more than empty laughter at the scorned might of Russia, but also at ourselves. With people still dying in Ukraine, and the likelihood of the aggressor's defeat or Putin's overthrow by Russians themselves still distant, mocking his empire appears premature. Depicting on stage the powerlessness of the law and the helplessness of the West, on the other hand, seems harmful (Dobrowolski, 2023).

---

[121] The performance featured Polish actors from the regular acting ensemble of the Polish Theatre in Poznań. The play was performed in Polish, without Ukrainian subtitles.

This perspective appears to arise from a deep-seated tendency in Poland, though it's becoming less common, to view art as having a didactic and martyr-like purpose. Any departures from politically, socially or culturally acceptable narratives spark controversy.

Following premieres in Poland, Denisova's play went on to achieve a series of remarkable international successes, being performed on various stages across Europe and in the USA. Peter Marks (2023), a reviewer from *The Washington Post*, described Denisova as 'the leading dramatic voice of the tragic war'. Those performances were put together by local theatre groups, featuring casts different from the Polish one.

The performance in Poznań, produced entirely by the artistic team of the Polish Theatre, marked the beginning of a new type of Polish-Ukrainian theatrical collaboration, which moved beyond solely staging performances with Ukrainian resident artists. Maciej Nowak's commissioning of a play from Denisova demonstrated an interest in Ukrainian drama from a significant and respected figure in the country's theatrical scene. Although larger-scale productions of Ukrainian plays by Polish theatres did not follow, a certain step was nevertheless taken. From time to time, Ukrainian dramas become part of the permanent repertoire of Polish ensembles and are presented independently of Ukrainian artistic residencies. One such performance took place on the stages of TR Warszawa, a significant repertory theatre in Poland. They staged the latest, at that time, drama by Lena Liahushonkova, titled *A Kitten Peed on My Banner*. Director Aleksandra Popławska incorporated two other plays by Liahushonkova, *Pipidówa* and *Gorky's Mother* (*Matka Gorkiego*), into her production. She titled the performance *A Kitten Peed on My Banner: Chronicles of Donbas*. The premiere, featuring actors from TR Warszawa, took place on April 28th, 2023[122].

Since making her debut as a playwright in 2018, Liahushonkova has steered clear of direct, documentary references to the ongoing war in Ukraine in her plays. Instead, she concentrates on depicting the broad societal and individual effects stemming from the Russian attack on the country. Feminist issues have been a significant theme in her plays, addressing the role of women in a conservative, patriarchal society amidst war. In adapting three of Liahushonkova's plays, Aleksandra Popławska specifically recognised these issues as crucial. The main character Lena, introduced to us as a teenager, hails from the small town of Stanica Luhanska in Donbas[123], situated right on the border with Russia. It's a place where everything is grey, backward and

---

[122] In the Polish-language performance, only Polish actors appeared: Jan Dravnel, Izabella Dudziak, Mateusz Górski, Magdalena Kuta, Lech Łotocki, Maria Maj, Sebastian Pawlak, Daria Polunina, Justyna Wasilewska, Julia Wyszyńska, Mirosław Zbrojewicz and Agnieszka Żulewska.

[123] Lena Liahushonkova was born in Stanica Luhanska.

steeped in stagnation and apathy. The landscape of Stanica Luhanska bears some resemblance to the Polish countryside, characterised by its ideological phobias, varying degrees of concealed antisemitism[124] and reluctance towards strangers, particularly 'gender deviants' (Miłkowski, 2023). The protagonist of the play is part of the LGBT community. Growing up in the Donbas province, she experiences her first romantic feelings and acknowledges her true sexual preferences, which are not accepted in her world. She dreams of breaking free, pursuing an acting career and winning awards at international festivals. Her journey was supposed to begin with studies in Moscow, but instead, she ended up attending university in Luhansk and then Kiev. There, she transformed from a provincial outsider into one of the leaders of the Orange Revolution. When she returns to her hometown as a mature individual, after the full-scale invasion, all she finds are ruins; people have either died or fled. Only her mother remains.

> The culmination of the performance is a staggering letter from the protagonist's mother, written in English with the aid of a dictionary. It serves as an address to the world, intended for delivery when Lena receives an award at Cannes. The letter holds the force of a silent scream, conveying the pain and suffering of a particular nation (Kulturalny Cham, 2023).

The director of the performance skillfully portrays the small-town atmosphere and its residents: the protagonist's Grandmother, grappling with advancing dementia and holding onto the traditions of a patriarchal society; the Grandfather, decorated with military honours and reminiscing about his youthful glory days, yet lacking faith in a brighter future; the Father, seeking refuge in a world of imagination; and the Mother, attempting to make ends meet by earning meagre wages in a mind-numbing job at the local factory, supplemented by small-scale trading of products acquired through connections at the stores. The roster of provincial 'personalities' is rounded out by the Teacher, driven by a sense of mission, 'a fervent patriot who educates generations of students and advocates for the legalisation of marijuana' (Kulturalny Cham, 2023). Additionally, there's a devoted admirer of the mother, with a rather dubious reputation, involved in various dealings with Russian intelligence. In her play Liahushonkova includes two of Lena's brothers positioned on opposite sides of the war barricade. One aligns with the separatist forces, firmly upholding what he perceives as the 'only correct Russian models and Soviet history' (Miłkowski, 2023), while the other fights for the freedom of his Ukrainian state. Before they perish, they will reunite at their mother's house, but even her pleas will fail to reach an agreement between them. Their

---

[124] The protagonist's family is of Jewish origin.

presence vividly underscores how the provincial setting of Stanica Luhanska reflects the wider challenges confronting modern Ukraine – the societal division into two conflicting groups, each deeply rooted in distinct cultural heritages and envisioning Ukraine's future in entirely divergent ways.

The TR Warszawa performance garnered overwhelmingly positive feedback from both viewers and critics alike. Subsequent shows were sold out, with both Polish and Ukrainian audiences in attendance. They had the chance to witness a broad spectrum of events in Donbas, spanning from the twilight of the Soviet Union, through the pivotal moments of the Kyiv Maidan, the 2014 war, to the full-scale Russian aggression in 2022. Embedded within these events was the internal turmoil of the main character, as she wrestled with her dreams, fears, rejection due to her sexual orientation and loneliness. The performance was also a portrayal of various human behaviours, meticulously depicted by Liahushonkova, particularly from a psychological standpoint, and brilliantly brought to life by the actors. We encounter individuals ensnared in the clutches of history, within the confines of a stagnant, provincial town, bound by traditions and stereotypes. Each of them seeks to break free in their own way, longing to escape and find happiness, yet it remains elusive to them. In this context, the greatest drama of Ukrainian society is unveiled – the division into two entirely contrasting, hostile worlds: one pro-Russian, earnestly believing in the happiness that an alliance with Russia could bestow upon Ukraine, and the other, which is already aware of the implications of Russian terror and colonialism. At first, it's a covert conflict, hidden in shame, but when war unleashes its relentless force, the presence of 'two worlds, two visions, two narratives of the same story on one land' (Kulturalny Cham, 2023) becomes unmistakably clear.

After *A Kitten Peed on My Banner* Liahushonkova collaborated with Kateryna Penkova to write another play, *Buka*, already in Poland. In it, the focus on war diminishes even more, which is why *Buka* constitutes the only piece performed in Poland where the Ukrainian writer dared to essentially overlook this fundamental issue for the entire nation. The authors believed that given the prolonged war in Ukraine, they had the right to address other highly significant societal issues as well[125]. In *Buka* we see the return of a patriarchal world, predominantly crafted for men, where it's incredibly challenging for women to defy the established societal norms. The titular character struggles unsuccessfully to mould her life according to her own principles. The press materials for the performance state:

---

[125] Information obtained from Lena Liahushonkova during an interview conducted by the author on September 10th, 2023.

Buka, written by Lena Liahushonkova and Kateryna Penkova, delves into the experience of womanhood in the 21st century. It challenges the idea that female characters should solely be depicted based on their external attributes or in traditional roles such as mothers, wives or lovers – always in relation to men. Buka rejects being defined through a masculine lens (Polish Theatre in Bydgoszcz, 2023).

The protagonist is 33 years old. Despite having finished her studies, she hasn't landed any lucrative or engaging job, resorting to childcare for income, even though she dislikes children. Despite her efforts, she faces financial struggles to make ends meet. Her personal life is equally unsuccessful, with her fiancé, heavily influenced by his mother who hates Buka, basically showing up only when he's in some emotional crisis and needs support. Buka is left with only casual, usually humiliating sexual encounters, and her lack of warmth and love is expressed through vulgar language and disdain for people. She shares an apartment with her roommate, Irka, who is her opposite. Unlike the rough and brusque Buka, Irka exudes warmth, trust, faith in people and hope for happiness in marriage, yet she also fears becoming an old maid. However, in the chauvinistic male world, her naive trust is brutally exploited, resulting in a double rape during a meeting that was supposed to mark the beginning of a wonderful romantic love affair with her beloved. *Buka* is a dark, joyless piece, illustrating the hostile world contemporary women must navigate daily, under the pressure of social expectations, prudish stereotypes and discriminatory regulations. The pessimistic tone of the play is not even softened by those fragments where the authors, through perfectly constructed dialogues, also introduce humorous elements. The overall atmosphere of the play is also imbued with the aura of post-Soviet Ukraine, which, although independent, still carries the burden of its not-so-distant past.

The performance by Liahushonkova and Penkova premiered on November 24th, 2023, at the Polish Theatre in Bydgoszcz. It marked another Ukrainian debut organised at this theatre as part of artistic residencies. In addition to Liahushonkova, the artist in residence of this theatre for the past few months has also been the director of the performance, Olga Turutia-Prasolova, a very young artist from Kharkiv who previously worked at the Kharkiv Academic Drama Theatre. The set design was prepared by Wojciech Faruga. Two actresses appeared on stage, portraying all the presented roles: Zhenia Doliak, previously a Ukrainian resident of the theatre in Bydgoszcz and at the time of the premiere, remaining permanently employed at this theatre, and Dagmara Mrowiec-Matuszak, a Polish actress of this theatre. The performance was delivered in Polish.

The premiere was a significant success, garnering an exceptionally high number of favourable reviews. Turutia-Prasolova's imaginative direction,

Faruga's set design, and the lighting were all commended. In one review, it was written:

> Director Olga Turutia-Prasolova brought a remarkable blend of drama, verbal and situational humour and dynamic stage movement to the entire production. All of this unfolds on a square platform surrounded by anthracite walls. The unified scenic design concept, along with Wojciech Faruga's costume designs, creates a black, metallic-silver space that reflects the emotions and experiences of Buka and Irka. It would seem that through the manipulation of light and shadow, Wojciech Faruga creates a semblance of a noir atmosphere, where words and mood become increasingly dense. This atmosphere is intensified by patterned, black-metallic, wide coats made of shiny jacquard fabric, which is a symbol of wealth and opulence. However, for Buka and Irka, their inner lives and the struggle for their own beliefs and views constitute their true wealth. This performance showcases how a unified and well-coordinated directorial vision, combined with acting, set design, costumes and lighting, triggers extensive associations in the audience, igniting their imagination and resonating with their personal experiences. The expert direction of Olga Turutia-Prasolova and the set design by Wojciech Faruga acquire deeper significance and layers through the evocative lighting direction by Katarzyna Borkowska. I haven't seen a performance in a long time where light itself could create such a poignant atmosphere, convey the moods and experiences of the stage characters and evoke a compelling atmosphere around them. The synchronisation of the lighting with the stage action is captivating. At times, it evokes the symbolism of sunbeams piercing through the clouds, as Buka and Irka question God… Then, it sharpens the edges of their spoken words… But there's also the red, sharp light surrounding the platform. Does it mirror the fire of Buka and Irka's suffering… (Słojewska, 2023)

The small square platform created by Faruga resembles a stage characteristic of stand-up performances. Doliak and Mrowiec-Matuszak, like stand-up comedians, present the lives of the main characters. The production is marked by tremendous dynamism, featuring swiftly changing scenes that evoke the pace of film editing, seamlessly integrated with the text. The actresses skillfully portray the intricate psyche of the characters, incorporating elements of physical theatre. Following rave reviews from both audiences and critics, the performance has become a staple in the theatre's repertoire.

The play *Czuję do ciebie miętę* (*I Have a Crush on You*) presented and acted by Nina Zakharova and Kateryna Vasiukova at the Zagłębie Theatre, was another instance where Ukrainian artists placed women's issues at the forefront. Zakharova and Vasiukova, together with the Polish writer Wojciech Zrałek-Kossakowski, wrote the text, and then, along with Jacek Jabrzyk, the resident director of the Zagłębie Theatre, developed it for the stage. The title of the performance (direct translation from Polish: 'I Feel Mint Towards You'), refers to a commonly used Polish phrase, which means: 'to feel sympathy, closeness, to be enchanted or in love with someone'. The play revolves around the relationship between two Ukrainian modernist writers and feminists, Lesya Ukrainka and Olha Kobylianska, a dynamic not fully elucidated by literary scholars. Vasiukova and Zakharova drew upon the mutual correspondence of these women. Throughout the performance, they embody these characters, reading the profoundly emotional, affectionate and captivating letters exchanged between Lesya Ukrainka and Kobylianska. However, this is only a small fragment of the performance. Zakharova and Vasiukova portray a variety of other, contemporary characters, woven into a narrative about Ukrainian women. These characters are depicted facing difficult life choices, having to cope with a hostile reality, including the realities of war.

The performance does not unfold in a linear, logically connected storyline. Thematic threads change and reappear, like in a kaleidoscope. Both actresses, portraying different female characters, also depict themselves on stage, narrating the story of Nina Zakharova and Kateryna Vasiukova's personal relationship, which is filled with emotional ups and downs. It begins with a distant, almost hesitant encounter during their first meeting at the theatre, then progresses into a formal correctness necessitated by their shared stage performances, and ultimately transforms into an exceptional emotional bond, female solidarity, and shared empathy towards the dramatic fate of their homeland. Their narrative parallels the relationship between Lesya Ukrainka and Kobylianska. The actresses employ a wide range of acting techniques and theatrical conventions. Scenes typical of physical theatre and performance are interspersed with excerpts from the correspondence between Lesya Ukrainka and Olga Kobylianska presented in a classical theatre convention. The performative actions transition into improvisations, allowing the actresses to have direct contact and dialogue with the audience, while symbolic elements of dance or mime resurface. In the minimalist set design, a large screen takes centre stage, displaying a photomontage of bombed Ukrainian towns throughout the performance. This screen almost assertively imposes itself on the observing audience, lending an interpretive dimension to all the events on stage. It helps viewers understand why, amidst moments of unexpected joy and happiness in the actresses' performance, there are lingering shadows of fears, traumas, pain and despair. Their climax comes at the end of the performance, which was previously staged in Ukrainian and Polish with scenes of verbal interaction with the audience. The final words are shouted by the actresses in English, marking the show's universal, timeless message. Thrown out to the world, fate, God: 'Why do people die?! Why should we die?! Why do I have to die?! Why should anyone die?!'. In *Czuję do ciebie miętę*, war remains in the background, subdued, mostly confined to cinematic presentations. Yet, its presence is felt, its destructive force influencing the actresses' performances and scenes of romantic fervour, fascination and happiness. Confronted with this force, the characters become utterly defenceless. All they can do in their helplessness is shout out the eternal, fundamental and unanswered question: Why?

The remarkable and deeply moving performance, staged in a theatre that may not be among Poland's largest or most prestigious venues, enjoyed significant success both domestically and internationally. It became one of the most talked-about Ukrainian productions in Poland following February 24th, 2022. After premiering in Sosnowiec, the production was invited to several national festivals, including the *Szczeliny: Women in Performing Arts Festival* in Wrocław and the International *Divine Comedy* Festival in Krakow. At the latter, it caught the attention of Peter Marks, the leading theatre critic at *The Washington Post* since 2002, who had previously covered off-Broadway theatres for *The New York Times*. Impressed by the performance, he wrote about it in *The Washington Post*, stating, among other things: 'The work is raw, elusive, gripping, a deeply moving brush with what I'd been seeking: art created viscerally, out of what was occurring across the border' (Marks, 2023). An important international success for the performance was also its invitation to Berlin in May 2023 for the city's International *Theatertreffen* Festival. The play became a permanent fixture in the repertoire of the Zagłębie Theatre, enjoying great popularity.

We are witnessing a new form of Polish-Ukrainian theatrical collaboration with the production of the monodrama *She Is War* (*Ona wojna*) at the Zagłębie Theatre in Sosnowiec. The performance was created in Lviv through the joint efforts of the Varta Theatre and the Publicist Theatre from Kharkiv. Both of these teams later reached an agreement with the Polish theatre in Sosnowiec to showcase the performance on its stage, thereby opening the door to further collaboration. The Polish premiere occurred precisely on the anniversary of the Russian invasion of Ukraine, on February 24th, 2023. Once again, Ukrainian theatre addressed women's issues, with the creators employing the verbatim method in the performance. The director, Konstiantyn Vasiukov (who is privately married to Kateryna Vasiukova, a resident artist at the Zagłębie Theatre, and later a permanent actress at the Silesian Theatre in Katowice), along with the actress in the monodrama, Svitlana Melnyk, began the production process by gathering documentary materials. They comprised interviews conducted in Ukraine with women of various social roles and statuses. Oleh Myhajlov then used this material to craft the dramatic text. In the performance, Melnyk took on multiple roles and characters, portraying the stories of 30 women in total. These include a volunteer supporting refugees, a physiotherapist rescuing abandoned animals in Ukraine, a volunteer who rescued a marine infantry soldier that defended Mariupol from Russian captivity, a woman living in Poland with three children who feels guilty for fleeing the country while others perish, and an LGBT activist sharing dramatic experiences with Ukrainian right-wing radicals, whom she fights alongside for the freedom of their homeland after the invasion erupted. Also featured in the play are less politically engaged characters, such as an actress and a celebrity who cannot comprehend what happened in Ukraine on February 24th and is determined to preserve her existing comfort, luxury and splendour at all costs. An important element of the performance is its visual presentation. It serves not only as an illustration of the events depicted but, above all, influences their interpretation. On large screens placed above the stage, films and photographs are presented, depicting Ukrainian women, wartime actions and destroyed Ukrainian cities.

Despite the creators of the monodrama employing techniques typical of documentary theatre, *She Is War* does not become solely a presentation documenting the Ukrainian reality after the Russian invasion. Above all, it's a poignant, at times tragic, at times incredibly humorous portrayal of Ukrainian society, composed of Ukrainian women and young girls. It's also a story of emigration, inequality, challenges, ways of overcoming psychological crises and restoring stability. It raises both contemporary and timeless questions, some of which are taboo in Ukrainian society, concerning gender equality, gender roles and the status of women. Amidst the backdrop of war, these inquiries acquire fresh significance: should women truly be stereotypically viewed as the 'weaker sex'? Do fear, pain, hatred and courage have any gender attribute at all? How does war affect gender biases, learned and perpetuated through generations? Will they disappear in the future due to the experiences brought by war or will they be further entrenched?

Melnyk played all of the roles in Ukrainian. Only in those moments of direct interaction with the audience did she also address them in Polish. The method of engaging the audience in the unfolding action made them integral to the society depicted in the performance. Consequently, Ukrainian reality transitioned into Polish contexts, highlighting contemporary issues such as respecting women's rights, ensuring equal treatment and addressing manifestations of chauvinism, which remain just as pertinent in Poland as they are in Ukraine.

The ongoing collaboration between the Zagłębie Theatre and Ukrainian teams led to the next production, *The Sea Will Stay* (*Morze zostanie*). This time, only the Publicist Theatre from Ukraine was involved in the preparations. The production was staged at the Zagłębie Theatre, with the premiere on November 4th, 2023. Directed by Kostiantyn Vasiukov from the Publicist Theatre, and written by Oleh Myhajlov, both of whom were also involved in *She Is War*. In the performance, Polish actors from the Zagłębie Theatre and two former Ukrainian residents of the Sosnowiec theatre, who later became permanent actresses at the Silesian Theatre in Katowice, Kateryna Vasiukova and Nina Zakharova, participated. Other individuals from the Publicist Theatre also assisted in the technical preparations. The director expressed the following in a press interview regarding the Polish-Ukrainian co-production:

> **Vasiukov:** When we decided to incorporate poetry into the work, I immediately thought of Kateryna and Nina. The idea for the performance was born back in Ukraine. I received funds from the German organisation Gesellschaft zur Verwertung von Leistungsschutzrechten to assist the artists and technical team of my theatre. We decided to allocate part of those funds for another project, originally planned for Ukraine. However, circumstances led me to Poland. On the anniversary of the Russian invasion, I presented *She Is War* in Sosnowiec – a collaboration between the Publicist Theatre from Kharkiv and the Varta Theatre from Lviv. Later, in collaboration with the management of the Zagłębie Theatre, we also staged *The Sea Will Stay* in Sosnowiec. We received four scholarships from the Theatre Institute in Warsaw as part of their artistic residency programme for creators from Ukraine and Belarus, covering the director, set designer, choreographer and composer.

> **Aneta Głowacka:** What are the scenographer Polina Kuznetsova, choreographer Inna Falkova and composer Volodymyr Ponikarovskyi doing now?

> **Vasiukov:** Except for Volodymyr, who came to Wrocław even before the war, everyone else has returned to Ukraine, to Kharkiv and Kyiv, where Denys Beliaiev, a visual artist who prepared the video for our performance, is also staying. Ivanna Skyba-Yakubova – whose poems we used in the performance – although she is constantly participating in various international events in Poland, Serbia, the Czech Republic and Germany, lives in Kharkiv, where she works as a cultural animator, curator and arts manager. Inna Falkova, who is not only a choreographer but also a performer and personal trainer, has transitioned into the field of psychology and psychotherapy. As a volunteer, she assists residents from frontline areas and towns liberated from Russian occupation. On these missions she is accompanied by her husband, a photographer documenting her work. We showcased his photos in the theatre foyer on the premiere day.

> **Aneta Głowacka:** Did you draw upon Inna Falkova's therapeutic experiences while working on the performance?

> **Vasiukov:** Yes. Inna's narratives were very important for our work. They influenced the atmosphere of particular scenes and the development of characters. Through her stories, Inna illuminated the internal struggles of individuals

enduring trauma. For instance, she highlighted how those with post-traumatic stress disorder often narrate their experiences with detachment yet tend to offer intricate details (Głowacka, 2023).

The Sea Will Stay is a play set in the vicinity of Mariupol. Oleh Myhajlov has woven a poetic narrative about two individuals living in the picturesque areas along the Sea of Azov. The city of Mariupol, named after Maria, the wife of Russian Tsar Paul I, practically ceased to exist due to the Russian invasion. The character at the centre of the performance is also named Maria. Her narrative mirrors a biblical parable in some instances, a grim fairy tale in others, and at times, a post-apocalyptic tableau. The coastal sand is a constant presence on the stage, while the arranged crosses represent the graves of those who fell victim to Russian soldiers. Living in poverty on the outskirts of the cemetery, the main couple's sole objective is to endure yet another day. The familiar world they knew ceased to exist: people either fled or were killed, birds perished, leaving only emptiness. Food is also scarce and the challenge lies in finding fuel. As a solution they resort to burning books, but only those of Russian literature. Images of the residents' daily life are interspersed with sudden appearances of patrols of aggressor soldiers with distinctive 'Z' signs on their uniforms as well as the sounds and flashes of air raids and bombings, heightening the atmosphere of horror and danger. The routine of their days is interrupted by the unexpected arrival of a lost goose, portrayed by one of the actresses without any bird-like costume. The couple takes it in and cares for it, deciding against using it as food. Instead, they choose to let it live. The presence of the goose triggers memories of a lost child for the woman, stirring up her longing for the daughter who left home long ago. It serves as a poignant reminder of a happier past that was shattered by the onset of war. In the play, the goose symbolises a profound attachment of the Ukrainian people to their homeland, even when it lies in ruins, much like Mariupol. Like geese, which mate for life and remain faithful until death, the characters refuse to abandon their homeland or leave the devastated Mariupol, seeing death as the only alternative.

In the performance the central role is played by the titular sea. It stays present throughout the entire play, thanks to highly realistic visualisations of the authentic shores of Mariupol. These are displayed on large screens suspended above and on either side of the stage. The sea provides a visual contrast to the devastated city, yet it also offers a poetic reflection, implying its enduring presence to safeguard the memory of the fallen, the ruins, the traditions, and culture. These elements, preserved within the sea's memory, will rejuvenate in the future. The poetic and metaphorical essence of the performance is underscored by the inclusion of poems by Ukrainian poet Ivanna Skyba-Yakubova, which are recited in their original Ukrainian by

Kateryna Vasiukova and Nina Zakharova. The actresses do not appear on-stage, however, but are instead integrated into the visual film projections. One of them is dressed in a white dress, the other in a black one, they are on a beach surrounded by dunes, symbolising the struggle between life and death that unfolds in Ukraine every day. *The Sea Will Stay* is yet another Ukrainian drama that steers away from the immediate documentation of war. It incorporates poetic metaphors and universal themes, depicting the bond between people and their homeland, the resilience of love, the enduring power of tradition and the importance of values that even the forces of evil, armed with planes, bombs and rifles, cannot conquer. Like the sea, which remains steadfast, so do the main characters persist until the end, bearing hope for future generations in this dark, post-apocalyptic world.

The year 2023 ended with a significant premiere for Ukrainian theatre in Poland: the remarkable performance of *Fucking Truffaut*, created by the newly formed close-knit ensemble of Ukrainian and Polish artists, Bliadski Circus Queelektyw. The Polish Reszka Foundation[126] produced the show, with co-production from two renowned theatres: the Polish Dramatic Theatre in Warsaw and the German Maxim Gorki Theatre in Berlin. The premiere took place in Berlin in November and in Warsaw in December 2023. The formation of Bliadski Circus Queelektyw was facilitated by pre-existing connections and collaboration among Ukrainian artists Roza Sarkisian, Alexandra Malatskovska, Olga Cherkashyna and Polish theatre curators Agata Siwiak and Dominika Mądry. The first three had previously met during their involvement in Joanna Wichowska's joint laboratories and projects in 2022. They had the chance to collaborate with Siwiak and Mądry through the *Bliscy Nieznajomi* (*Close Strangers*) festivals, which the two Poles curated.

Polish and Ukrainian members of the Queer community also joined the team, with two of them, Babcia and Vrona (Arek Koźmiński), performing alongside Alexandra Malatskovska and Roza Sarkisian in the play. Roza Sarkisian directed the production whilst the dramatic text was developed

---

[126] At the forefront of the Foundation are Agata Siwiak and Dominika Mądry, both former organisers of the *Bliscy Nieznajomi* (*Close Strangers*) Festival. The foundation's goals encompass several key aspects: embracing interdisciplinary artistic and research practices that unite diverse media, genres, and cultural perspectives; fostering collaboration with artists across different domains, representing various generations of creators, and amplifying their work; encouraging critical reflection on art from historical, social, cultural, and institutional standpoints; striving to cultivate a civil society and fortify local communities through cultural endeavours; ensuring the inclusion of marginalised groups through artistic, educational, research, and cultural initiatives; promoting intercultural cooperation, mutual respect, and the co-creation of content; and advancing audience democratisation by consciously integrating socially excluded groups into the artistic sphere.

by Krystyna Bednarek[127], a Polish playwright, theatre scholar and writer. The show was performed in Polish and Ukrainian, with Alexandra Malatskovska delivering certain lines and songs in English.

The bold title of the performance, inspired by the name of director François Truffaut, a trailblazer of the French New Wave, primarily highlighted his belief that any discourse about war ultimately glorifies it. In this regard, the performance served as a significant contribution to the ongoing conversation among Ukrainian creators about whether and how theatre can engage with the ongoing war in their homeland. Presented in the format of a cabaret, the show refrains from offering definitive answers. Instead, it raises important questions, shedding light on the propaganda surrounding the war in Ukraine, the hypocrisy of global elites who claim solidarity and support for Ukrainians, and the predicament of artists whose independence and creative expression are influenced by the audience's propaganda-driven expectations. In the review that appeared after the Berlin premiere of the performance, particular attention was paid exactly to this aspect of the show:

> A musical grotesque about the war in Ukraine consciously breaking away from previous presentations of this topic. While the issue of representing this war in theatre – previously depicted with varying degrees of patriotic pathos – is difficult and troublesome, Ukrainian director Roza Sarkisian and her Queelektyw (queer collective) present the war in the form of a campy revue, in which Alexandra Malatskovska, with a powerful voice and a face flirting with the audience, performs musical hits in English. Their recurring message can be encapsulated in the phrase 'Our war is your entertainment' [...]. The mood is deceptively provocative, the performance almost breaches taboos, but after a year and a half of war and the evident adherence to previous depictions of Ukraine in theatre, the small-scale production showcased at MGT [Maxim Gorki Theater – P.H.] signifies a turning point towards fresh engagements with this subject (Irmer, 2023).

In contrast to earlier Ukrainian productions, which claimed the right to unrestrained, even iconoclastic independence, on stage we witness mockery, irony and ridicule of wartime narratives, saturated with empty pathos and

---

[127] Krystyna Bednarek is a young Polish artist who has already made significant contributions to theatre projects, both in Poland and abroad. She participated as a resident in the inaugural edition of the Ephraim dramaturgical project at the Lausitz Festival 2021, where she co-created and staged the play *My Guardian Angel Doesn't Look at Me Anymore* (*Mój Anioł Stróż już na mnie nie patrzy*) for the residents of the Polish-German city Gubin collaborating with Maximilian Pellert. Additionally, she has worked with the Powszechny Theatre in Warsaw on productions like *Devils* and *Orlando: Biographies* (*Orlando. Biografie*) (directed by Agnieszka Błońska), as well as *Radio Mariia* (directed by Roza Sarkisian), where she contributed, alongside Joanna Wichowska, to the dramaturgical development of the play.

propagandistic falsehood. The Bliadski Circus Queelektyw's Cabaret accomplishes the deheroisation of war and false acts of patriotism, instead mocking the purported solidarity and support of Western societies for Ukraine during the invasion. The performance's social context is prominently displayed, with two of its performers, Babcia and Vrona, representing the queer community. Announcements for the show, featured on the Warsaw Dramatic Theatre's website, highlighted that

> the collective's primary artistic expressions include cabaret, serving as a response to turbulent times amidst the war in Ukraine, and queer, functioning as a space for love, resistance and subversion, enabling a radical departure from bourgeois taste and patriarchal norms. When the world is crumbling, we aim to gather with the audience to explore alternatives together. Bliadski Circus tunes into the pulse of Warsaw's streets and the tales and echoes from the besieged cities of Ukraine. On the stage of the Dramatic Theatre, it will engage with current events, serving as a platform for expressing complex and sometimes contradictory emotions, infusing the space with feminist narratives, drag humour, herstory, queer perspectives and self-irony. Bliadski Circus will resonate with freedom, manifesting diversity (*Fucking Truffaut*, 2023).

Also in this second aspect, the presence of non-heteronormative individuals in society, the performance uncompromisingly deals with widespread hypocrisy and prudery. In the Polish context, with deeply rooted phobias and lack of tolerance towards 'others', shockingly for the audience, a song played on the piano, sung, or even shouted by the artists, whose main theme is the vagina, resounds. The audience hears it just after entering the intimate theatre hall, while taking their seats. Throughout the entire performance, Babcia and Vrona appear in queer attire that starkly contrasts with the war theme. Amidst the madness depicted in successive episodes of the show, through various cabaret sketches and songs, they expose the limitations of commanders repeating clichéd military formulas that fail to address the tragic experiences of those in combat. While others indulge in the splendour of gifts from the West meant for defending the homeland, such as flashy, used clothes, and sing ironic war songs, brilliantly composed and performed by Alexandra Malatskovska, only Babcia and Vrona seem rational. They logically observe the 'falling world' and seek alternative ways to cope with its hypocrisy-filled madness. The media also constitutes the subject of ridicule and mockery. Roza Sarkisian, as a war correspondent, is present on stage throughout the performance, filming the most 'spectacular' as well as intimate moments of the war, recorded not to show the truth about it, but with the aim of monetising the prepared material through evoking emotions and squeezing out tears.

One of the performance's crucial elements is the visualisations displayed on a large screen suspended at the back of the stage. These visuals facilitate the integration of the actors with the transgender soldier, Antonina Romanova, stationed on the front line. There is no theatrical fiction involved. Romanova is a theatre artist and performer who has appeared, among other performances, in one of Joanna Wichowska's projects, *Maps of Fear/Maps of Identity*. However, she decided to leave the stage and join the defence of the country. In contrast to the common visualisations in Ukrainian productions about war, which primarily served to intensify emotions, create an atmosphere of horror, depict the cruelty of the aggressor and heroism of the fighters, Romanova's accounts are characterised by calmness, a desire to narrate about the everyday life of a soldier. Dramatic events intertwine with ordinary daily rituals as well as sometimes even comic situations brought about by war. The honesty of this message is striking; there is no pretence or falsehood, nothing that could be seen as an attempt to commercialise personal feelings or manipulate emotions. This is especially clear in the part where Romanova struggles to answer why she went to war. It's a challenge for her. She attempts multiple times to articulate her thoughts into coherent sentences. Yet, the question persists. She begins anew, only to eventually, feeling powerless, ask everyone on the other side of the screen: 'So, why didn't you go to war, actually?'.

Among the Ukrainian productions brought to life in Poland, *Fucking Truffaut* is extraordinary – celebrated for its originality and unyielding exploration of the ongoing realities of war. Its social relevance deeply resonates with the Polish context, where intolerance towards the non-heteronormative community, expressions of hate and acts of aggression, though not pervasive, remain palpable. This directly impacted the creators of the performance, who faced homophobic comments on online forums after the premieres. However, the show received a largely positive reception from both audiences and critics alike. Every performance was sold out. The Dramatic Theatre has decided to stage it again in February 2024, and there is a strong likelihood that it will become a permanent fixture in its repertoire. Discussions are also underway to extend its run at the Maxim Gorki Theater.

PROSPECTS AND SUMMARIES

The conclusion of the year 2023 marks the end of the period covered by this monograph. However, it certainly does not signal the end of Polish-Ukrainian theatrical collaborations, nor does it preclude further Ukrainian residencies in Polish theatres and the productions staged as part of them. Although it's been over 2 years since the full-scale Russian invasion began, Polish society seems to have adapted somewhat to the ongoing war on the eastern border, with other topics now making headlines in the media. However, since Joanna Wichowska initiated Polish-Ukrainian theatrical activities in 2014, they have continued in various forms, ensuring that Ukrainian theatre and drama remain part of Polish theatrical life. While they may not hold a dominant position, their presence is significant. Since 2014 in Poland it has been possible to see close to 70 performances or performative readings involving Ukrainian artists or created by them as well as a difficult-to-count number of joint Polish-Ukrainian projects, workshops and laboratories. Certainly, especially compared to previous years, this represents a significant change and a new trend. It no longer solely stems from the Polish side's desire to support Ukrainian artists due to the situation they found themselves in as a result of the war but increasingly is related to plans for joint artistic endeavours. Ukrainian and Polish creators, particularly those from independent scenes, have discovered shared interests in various areas. They delve into themes such as individual freedom in the modern world and efforts to restrict it, feminism, minority rights and human reactions to globalisation. They also share similar theatrical aesthetics, including the utilisation of verbatim techniques, theatre of testimony and visualisations. Increasingly, intercultural artistic projects are being realised, a good example of that being *Fucking Truffaut*, described earlier. The current intercultural dialogue between Polish and Ukrainian theatre would not be possible without the relationships established earlier during joint projects such as *The UA Landing*, *Maps of Fear/Maps of Identity* or *Close Strangers*. Previously, Agata Siwiak, Dominika Mądry and Roza Sarkisian collaborated, as did Piotr Armianovskyi, Dmytro Levytskyi and Patryk Lichota, along with Victoria Myroniuk and Olha Skliarska. In 2024, they intend to initiate new artistic ventures in Poland. Siwiak and Sarkisian will continue their artistic endeavours with the Bliadski Circus Queelektyw ensemble, showcasing *Fucking Truffaut* domestically and internationally. Siwiak and Mądry have taken on the role of curators for the prestigious international Festival of Many Cultures in Łódź (formerly the Festival of Four Cultures), where they plan to annually feature performances by Ukrainian artists. Importantly, these won't be mere guest appearances but festival productions, created in Poland by Ukrainian and Polish artists through several-month residencies.

In 2024, Myroniuk and Sklarska will present a collaborative project titled *The Clinic of a Broken Heart* (*Klinika ocalenia złamanego serca*), exploring a medical syndrome where symptoms resembling a heart attack manifest in individuals following the loss of something or someone. The script was penned by Myroniuk, and individuals from the local Łódź community, previously unaffiliated with theatre, will be invited to participate in the performance. Armianovsky, Dmytro Levytskyi and Lichota are also contemplating a collaborative project, though it's currently in the planning phase. Importantly, the artistic residency programme at the Theatre Institute in Warsaw for Ukrainian creators will persist in 2024, indicating the likelihood of more Polish-Ukrainian artistic endeavours. Polish repertory theatres are gradually embracing Ukrainian drama. In Warsaw's Polish Theatre, three notable premieres based on works by acclaimed Ukrainian writers were slated for 2024. In March *Kharkiv, Kharkiv* by Serhiy Zhadan, directed by Svitlana Oleshko, will debut, followed by *Maklena Grasa* by Mykola Kulish and *Planet Lem* by Oksana Zabuzhko. Svitlana Oleshko, serving as both playwright and director at the theatre, deserves much credit for this development. The Polish Theatre in Bydgoszcz is also gearing up to stage the newest play by Lena Liahushonkova, titled *The Order of Made Beds* (*Zakon pościelonych łóżek*). Fragments of this play were showcased through performative readings during the Theatre's Festival of Premieres in 2023. The drama has sparked significant interest and controversy already. This is because Liahushonkova, as one of the first Ukrainian playwrights, delves into the Russian aggression on Ukraine from the viewpoint of Russian women, particularly mothers of soldiers engaged in the frontline battles.

When discussing the shifts in how Ukrainian theatre is perceived in Poland, it's probably best exemplified through contemporary Ukrainian drama. Before 2014, it was largely obscure. Although Anna Korzeniowska-Bihun's collection of translated texts improved this situation, it didn't increase the presence of Ukrainian plays in Polish theatres. Having said that, contemporary Ukrainian drama is presently gaining more recognition through productions on Polish stages. The works of writers such as Liahushonkova, Denisov, Apchel, Matsiupa, and Zhadan are increasingly finding their way into the repertoire of Polish theatres, becoming regular features on their schedules. While it's challenging to equate this with the popularity of Western drama, Svitlana Oleshko highlights that more Ukrainian plays are being translated into Polish for future staging. Oleshko goes as far as to suggest that translators of Ukrainian dramas in Poland can expect job security for the foreseeable future[128].

The future of Ukrainian and Ukrainian-Polish projects should primarily be linked with institutions that have demonstrated the most commitment to this endeavour thus far. We're not referring to widespread representation, but rather isolated pockets on Poland's theatrical landscape. Smaller theatres and socially engaged stages are predominant, emphasising the importance of the mission behind public theatre activities. Two repertory theatres, while not considered among the nation's foremost stages, play a leading role by executing numerous social projects and extra theatrical programmes: The Zagłębie Theatre in Sosnowiec and the Polish Theatre in Bydgoszcz. Located at opposite ends of Poland, the Zagłębie Theatre in the southwest and the Polish Theatre in the northwest have hosted the largest number of premieres of Ukrainian plays featuring Ukrainian and Polish artists. The theatre in Bydgoszcz also ensures the representation of Ukrainian drama through its annual Festival of Premieres. Additionally, due to the presence of Ukrainian artists in their permanent ensembles, Ukrainian plays are also showcased at the Silesian Theatre in Katowice as well as at the Powszechny and Polish theatres in Warsaw. Following TR Warszawa's collaboration with Lena Liahushonkova for the premiere of *A Kitten Peed on My Banner: Chronicles of Donbas*, the Dramatic Theatre in Warsaw, which hosted the creators of the cabaret *Fucking Truffaut*, has recently emerged as a significant venue on the 'Ukrainian theatrical map' of Poland. The Polish Theatre in Poznań, showcasing *The Hague* and previously serving as a home to the *Close Strangers* Festival, can be added to this list, too. Groups like Komuna Warszawa, Teatr Druga Strefa in Warsaw and the Polish Theatre in Wałbrzych also express their willingness to collaborate with Ukrainian creators. However, these are primarily individual initiatives and the productions they've done have had relatively brief runs on theatre billboards. It's puzzling that theatres located in the eastern part of the country, closest to the border with Ukraine, show very little activity towards the Ukrainian community, despite the significant number of refugees residing there who could potentially constitute a substantial audience for performances. Apart from a few projects carried out by small private theatres, there is also a lack of interest in collaborating with Ukrainian creators shown by the theatre scene in Krakow, aspiring to be the cultural

---

[128] Information shared by Svitlana Oleshko during an interview conducted by the author on October 26th, 2023.

capital of Poland, with its two leading stages: the National Old Theatre and the Juliusz Słowacki Theatre. However, it's important to note that Krakow hosts the East-West Festival, featuring invited Ukrainian theatres. Additionally, there's the International Divine Comedy Festival, which has showcased performances by Ukrainian creators or based on Ukrainian plays for several years now.

Despite the fact that in 2023 we no longer see as many Ukrainian refugees coming to Poland, including representatives of the artistic world, and some of them have returned to Ukraine or left for other countries, there is still a fairly large group of theatre creators from Ukraine residing in Poland. These artists, when discussing their time in Poland, highlight the welcoming social atmosphere, particularly within the artistic community, and notably, a better appreciation of Ukraine's national and cultural distinctiveness from Russia compared to the West. Even individuals who have chosen to depart Poland, such as Natalia Blok, Olena Apchel and Oksana Cherkashyna, express their willingness to pursue artistic endeavours here in the future.

The outlook is promising, although there are certainly areas where more could be done. For instance, the Polish side has yet to effectively organise working conditions for Ukrainian creators to ensure greater stability in Poland. Residencies, in this context, only offer temporary solutions. The crucial factor would be providing the opportunity for a permanent position within theatre institutions, a proposal advocated by the Polish Institute of Performing Arts at the outset of the full-scale invasion. Agata Siwiak echoes this sentiment, stressing that despite any economic constraints, involving additional workers from Ukraine wouldn't pose a significant problem for Polish theatres, especially those with ample budgets and sizable teams. Siwiak adds that while collaborating with many Ukrainian actors, she has observed their excellent acting skills, often surpassing those of Polish actors in their ability to work with their bodies and music, which are crucial in contemporary Ukrainian theatre. Technical staff also demonstrate a high level of work ethic and professionalism. Therefore, the advantages of employing Ukrainian creators and theatre workers would be mutual[129]. Meanwhile, the presence of full-time employees from Ukraine in Polish theatres remains minimal. There are some notable exceptions, such as the Silesian Theatre in Katowice, which appointed two actresses almost at the beginning of the full-scale invasion: Nina Zakharova and Kateryna Vasiukova. Additionally, the Polish Theatre in Bydgoszcz employs Zhenia Doliak, while Svitlana Oleshko works full-time at the Polish Theatre in Warsaw. Moreover, Artem Manuilov has been

---

[129] Information obtained from Agata Siwiak during the interview conducted by the author on January 17th, 2024.

working for years at the Powszechny Theatre in Warsaw, alongside Oksana Cherkashyna, although she recently returned to Ukraine. Some observers of the Polish theatrical scene see the lack of greater openness of theatres to hiring refugees as a consequence of the pandemic and the financial crisis it caused. As a result, theatres have become less open to international cooperation, especially forms that could lead to breaking the monoethnic character of Polish stages. This also stems from concerns about competition from newly hired foreigners.

There is also a lack of an institution that could coordinate and support the organisation of Polish-Ukrainian theatrical activities. So far, the initiative has always been in the hands of individual entities, such as Joanna Wichowska, Agata Siwiak and Dominika Mądry, who have been attracting more enthusiasts and gaining varying degrees of support, whether short-term or long-term, from various cultural institutions. However, as Siwiak points out[130], such work absolutely exceeds the capabilities of individual persons in the long run. The organisational and financial support provided by institutions such as the Theatre Institute in Warsaw or the Ukrainian Institute in Ukraine is indeed crucial. However, it falls short when one takes into account the extensive administrative, promotional and substantive efforts required to foster a greater number of new and compelling projects as well as to ensure the comfort of artistic work for creators. Olena Apchel believes there's a need to establish an institution or society in Poland solely dedicated to Ukrainian theatre and artists in the country. This entity should oversee legal regulations, including safeguarding the copyright of playwrights and ensuring the legal status of Ukrainian artists in Poland. Additionally, it should organise theatrical projects that foster ongoing collaboration between creators from Ukraine and Poland, such as workshops and laboratories. Apchel highlights the significance of the economic dimension, which would fall under the purview of this new institution, ensuring funding while granting creators complete autonomy. In the discussion, she underscored: 'For contemporary art, you need to provide people with space, food and lodging, and then let them work without interruption'. Apchel highlights that obstacles to establishing such an institution may arise not only from challenges on the Polish side but also from internal conditions within Ukraine:

> While collaboration among Ukrainian artists at the institutional level is feasible, the challenge lies in cooperating in the realm of shared identity and national values.

---

[130] Information obtained from Agata Siwiak, *ibid.*

In Ukraine itself, significant divisions exist, particularly between the East and West of the country, characterised by differing attitudes towards language and history[131].

Lena Liahushonkova also addresses the divisions that impede collective action, succinctly stating that 'where there are two Ukrainians, there are three hetmans'[132], indicating the difficulty for her fellow countrymen to reach compromises. Consequently, Liahushonkova doubts the possibility of consolidating the Ukrainian artistic community in Poland. She anticipates that future projects will rely solely on individual connections between creators or individuals who are acquainted with each other. Most likely, such controversies could have influenced Sasha Denisova's decision to abandon a very interesting plan to establish the Reduta 22 theatre institution in Poland. It was intended to be a theatre of 'intercultural encounter', where Ukrainian, Belarusian and Polish directors, playwrights and actors would collaborate. Denisova announced this project:

> We are inaugurating the Reduta 22 Theatre (because 'reduta' refers to both a military fortification and to an incredibly important theatre that once existed) – for collaborative projects involving Ukrainians, Belarusians and Poles, here in Warsaw, a theatre representing diverse languages and cultures. The aim is for Ukrainian artists, playwrights and actors to integrate into the Polish cultural community, not merely as participants in residencies during times of conflict. This is a contemporary, socio-political theatre, infused with a new Eastern European energy. Our objective is not to isolate Ukrainians or exploit their wartime experiences for sympathy, but to fully engage them as participants in theatre. Ukrainian audiences will suffice here. Hopefully, we will also attract Polish audiences (Biernat, 2022).

It should be explained that the Reduta Theatre was one of the most important experimental groups in Poland, laying the foundations for modern theatre. It was founded by Juliusz Osterwa and Mieczysław Limanowski and existed from 1919 to 1939. It was the first theatre-laboratory in Poland, pioneering the search for new methods of acting, revolutionising the principles of preparing performances, including actor ethics. It is interesting that the idea of Reduta emerged during Osterwa's several-year stay in Ukraine, in Kyiv. There, he supposedly met with the leading figure of Ukrainian experimental theatre, Les Kurbas, and made plans for a joint artistic project. Denisova's initiative would thus be somewhat a realisation of those intentions for Ukrainian--Polish theatrical collaboration. It's important to highlight that the initiator

---

[131] Information obtained during the interview with Olena Apchel, conducted by the author of the text, on October 10th, 2023.

[132] Information obtained from Lena Liahushonkova during an interview conducted by the author on September 10th, 2023.

envisioned cooperation not merely as a response to the war and the inability of Ukrainian creators to return home but as a forward-looking, intercultural project. It aimed to address new challenges beyond the conflict's end. It's possible that Denisova's busy schedule, with successive premieres of her plays in theatres worldwide, hindered the realisation of the plan. What also needs to be acknowledged here, however, is that her extensive work history in Russia and her delayed departure from the country after the onset of the Russian-Ukrainian conflict have stirred controversy within the Ukrainian creative community. Consequently, it's rather challenging to envision Reduta 22 truly becoming a hub for joint projects involving Ukrainian creators. Denisova's idea is indeed worthy of consideration and execution. Agata Siwiak shares a similar sentiment. While collaborating on *Fucking Truffaut* with Roza Sarkisian, they envisioned an independent Ukrainian stage in Warsaw, equipped with its own theatre hall and excellent technical facilities, welcoming both Ukrainian and Polish creators. They believe this could significantly transform the situation for Ukrainian artists, providing them with a stable hub of artistic support and a dedicated workspace, eliminating the need to search for institutions willing or unwilling to realise their ideas. Siwiak reflects: 'We even fantasised with Roza that if the city gave us even a small stage, it would already be something. But for independent project realisation, to take the next step – a place must exist'[133].

2024 marks a decade since Polish and Ukrainian theatres have started showing significantly greater interest in each other and engaging in joint artistic endeavours. This paper delineates three primary stages of this collaboration. The initial phase comprised mutual acquaintanceship through workshops and laboratories organised by Joanna Wichowska, followed by the first major theatre festivals, initially hosted in Ukraine and subsequently in Poland. Even during these early stages, collaborative projects involving Ukrainian and Polish theatre creators, predominantly from independent scenes, highlighted shared artistic interests and pursuits for both parties. The second phase, triggered by the full-scale Russian invasion in February 2022, focused mainly on providing humanitarian and artistic aid to Ukrainian artists by the Polish theatre community. The goal was to offer immediate assistance to those fleeing the war and to establish organisational and artistic frameworks for future support. Over time (the third stage), projects arising from a shared creative community, convergent goals and forms of artistic expression of Polish and Ukrainian creators began to emerge more frequently. In this case, we can speak of the first intercultural projects addressing significant

---

[133] Information obtained from Agata Siwiak during the interview conducted by the author on January 17th, 2024.

contemporary issues. The collaboration mainly involved independent stages and repertoire groups focused on the social mission of theatre. The presence of leading Ukrainian playwrights in Poland and the emergence of new Ukrainian drama in recent years played an important role in subsequent stage productions. The year 2023 and the outlook for 2024 also suggest a gradually increasing interest in Ukrainian drama among significant repertoire groups in Poland. However, it's crucial to emphasise that the main objective of Ukrainian theatre in this country isn't integration. It doesn't aim to become a typical migratory theatre seeking long-term or permanent residence in a new state. The majority of Ukrainian artists in Poland strive to preserve their cultural and national identity, their language of creation, and after Russia's defeat, intend to return to their homeland. The connections they forged in Poland and their desire to sustain collaborative projects with Polish creators offer promising prospects for the future. Even two years after the onset of the full-scale Russian invasion, we can identify this as the third stage of Polish--Ukrainian artistic endeavours. Moving beyond performances solely documenting the ravages of war, Ukrainian creators, frequently aided by Polish artists, are now delving into depicting the wartime reality within a broader social, political and existential context. It is within these realms that the shared interests of contemporary Ukrainian and Polish theatre are notably pronounced.

The year 2024 holds promise, as mentioned, for a series of new initiatives, albeit accompanied by numerous challenges. However, hopes and expectations are primarily focused on the prospect of the next stage, where Ukraine would emerge victorious from the war. Ukrainian theatre groups would then be able to operate at full capacity, with actors currently engaged in military activities joining their ranks. This transition would also free artists from the traumas and constraints associated with the war.

It's possible that the efforts of numerous Polish and Ukrainian creators since 2014 will yield intriguing, surprising, and revitalising artistic projects, affirming that Polish and Ukrainian theatre share far more than mere collaboration prompted by wartime circumstances.

BIBLIOGRAPHY

Adamiecka A., Błasińska M., Dutkiewicz J., Dziekan M., Kowalkowska D., Strzępka M. (2022), *Orędzie Polskiego Ośrodka Międzynarodowego Instytutu Teatralnego ITI na Międzynarodowy Dzień Teatru* [*The World Theatre Day Manifesto of the Polish Centre of the International Theatre Institute* – J.L.], posted: 25/03/2022, https://www.instytut-teatralny.pl/2022/03/25/oredzie-polskiego-osrodka-miedzynarodowego-instytutu-teatralnego-iti-na-miedzynarodowy-dzien-teatru/, last accessed: 25/11/2022.

Bal E. (2022), '"Kreszany", czyli o testowaniu starych/nowych epistemologii napływających ze Wschodu' ['"Kreszany" or on testing old/new epistemologies coming from the East' – J.L.], *Didaskalia*, no. 168.

Barnard E. (2019), '"Cultural resistance": Can such practices ever have a meaningful political impact?', *Critical Social Thinking: Policy and Practice*, no. 11.

Basakin A. (2021), 'Teatr "Neft"', *Newsroom*, posted: 28/06/2021, https://www.newsroom.kh.ua/place/teatr-neft, last accessed: 15/04/2023.

Biernat J. (2022), '"Polska zmieniła się w rodzaj arki dla Ukraińców". Rozmowa z Saszą Denysową, scenarzystką przedstawienia *Sześć żeber gniewu*' ['"Poland has turned into a kind of ark for Ukrainians": A conversation with Sasha Denisova, author of "Six Ribs of Anger"' – J.L.], posted: 18/07/2022, https://e-teatr.pl/polska-zmienila-sie-w-rodzaj-arki-dla-ukraincow-27796, last accessed: 18/12/2022.

Bleiker R. (2000), *Popular Dissent, Human Agency and Global Politics*, Cambridge University Press, Cambridge.

Bliscy Nieznajomi: Wschód (2021), festival program [*Close Strangers: East* – J.L.], posted: 6/09/2021, https://teatr-polski.pl/bliscy-nieznajomi-wschod/, last accessed: 11/11/2023.

Bliscy Nieznajomi: Wschód – H-effect (2021), information about the play [*Close Strangers: East – H-effect* – J.L.], posted: 9/09/2021, https://teatr-polski.pl/bliscy-nieznajomi-wschod-h-effect/, last accessed: 5/09/2023.

Borkowska A. (2020), 'Chcę słuchać historii i opowiadać je dalej' ['I want to listen to stories and pass them on' – J.L.], ngo.pl, posted: 24/07/2020, https://publicystyka.ngo.pl/alicja-borkowska-chce-sluchac-historii-opowiadac-je-dalej, last accessed: 25/06/2023.

CBOS (2014), *Foreigners in Poland*, Research Report, August 2014, Warsaw.

'Charków-Warszawa – wspólna teatralna sprawa' (2015), ['Kharkiv-Warsaw – a mutual theatrical interest' – J.L.], Nasz wybir – portal dla Ukraińców w Polsce [Our choice – a website for Ukrainians in Poland – J.L.], posted: 7/07/2015, https://pl.naszwybir.pl/charkow-warszawa-wspolna-teatralna-sprawa/, last accessed: 26/11/2023.

Chuzhynova I. (2016), 'Mój dziad kopał, mój ojciec kopał, a ja nie będę' ['My grand-father dug, my father dug, and I won't dig' – J.L.], *Ukraińskij Teatr* [*Ukrainian Theatre* – J.L.], 25/09/2016.

Cieślak J. (2022), 'Polscy artyści solidaryzują się z Ukrainą' ['Polish artists show solidarity with Ukraine' – J.L.], The *Rzeczpospolita* Daily, no. 54, posted: 7/03/2022.

Cox E. (2014), *Theatre and Migration*, Palgrave Macmillan, London.

Cudak B. (2021), 'Czuła kuratorka, czułe osoby tworzące' ['Sensitive curator, sensitive curators' – J.L.], *Didaskalia*, no. 166.

Curatorial text of the *Close Strangers* Festival (2020), https://www.poznan.pl/mim/sport/events/wydarzenia-online-zdalne,c,117022/xiii-spotkania-teatralne-bliscy-nieznajomi-ukraina-online,120820.html, last accessed: 23/10/2023.

Curatorial text of the *Close Strangers* Festival (2021), https://teatr-polski.pl/bliscy-nieznajomi-wschod/, last accessed: 23/10/2023.

Cusenza C. (2019), 'Artists from Syria in the International Artworld: Mediators of a Universal Humanism', [in:] *Arts and Refugees: Multidisciplinary Perspectives*, ed. by M. Martiniello, Multidisciplinary Digital Publishing Institute, Basel.

Damery S., Mescoli E. (2019), 'Harnessing visibility and invisibility through arts practices: Ethnographic case studies with migrant performers in Belgium', [in:] *Arts and Refugees: Multidisciplinary Perspectives*, ed. by M. Martiniello, Multidisciplinary Digital Publishing Institute, Basel.

Dobrowolski P. (2023), 'Jeszcze nie czas' ['It's not the time' – J.L.], teatralny.pl, posted: 5/04/2023, https://teatralny.pl/recenzje/jeszcze-nie-czas,3728.html, last accessed: 10/09/2023.

Drozda J. (2015), *Opór kulturowy. Między teorią a praktykami społecznymi* (*Cultural Resistance: Between Theory and Social Practices* – J.L.), Wydawnictwo Naukowe Katedra, Gdańsk.

Drozdowisko #59 (2022), *ABC kultury ukraińskiej w Polsce – ukraiński teatr i jego siła oddziaływania na społeczeństwo* [*The ABC of Ukrainian culture in Poland – Ukrainian theatre and its impact on society* – J.L.], Teresa Drozda's podcast and conversation with Anna Korzeniowska-Bihun, https://www.podkasty.info/katalog/podkast/7697--Drozdowisko_Teresa_Drozda/_59_Anna_Korzeniowska_Bihun_ABC_kultury_ukrai%C5%84skiej_, last accessed: 5/01/2023.

DS (2023), *PiS straszy w referendum nielegalnymi imigrantami, a tak wyglądają dane od 2015 r.* [*Law and Justice threatens illegal immigrants in referendum, and this is the data from 2015* – J.L.], The *Business Insider*, posted 13/08/2023.

Dubrowska M. (2022), 'Przed wejściem na scenę dowiedział się, że w Ukrainie zginął jego przyjaciel. "To proroczy tekst"' ['Before coming on stage, he learned that his friend had died in Ukraine: "It's a prophetic text"' – J.L.], The *Gazeta Wyborcza* Daily, no. 61, posted: 15/03/2022.

Fibich W. (2022), 'W gazetach tego nie napiszą. Czytanie tranzytowe ukraińskiej literatury' ['They won't write about it in the newspapers. Transit reading of Ukrainian literature' – J.L.], posted: 18–19/10/2022, https://weronikafibich.pl/aktualnosci/wpis/1819-x-w-gazetach-tego-nie-napisza-czytanie-tranzytowe-ukrainskiej-literatury-rez-w-fibich,994, last accessed: 12/12/2023.

First Theatre (2018), The theatre's website: https://pershyi.com/uk/about/history, accessed: 10/12/2023.

Fucking Truffaut (2023), information about the play, https://teatrdramatyczny.pl/bliadski-circus-queelektyw, last accessed: 12/12/2023.

Gabryel S. (2019), 'Poznań: Spotkanie z Ukrainą, czyli Bliscy Nieznajomi w Teatrze Polskim po raz dwunasty' ['Poznań: Meeting with Ukraine, or Close Strangers at the Polish Theatre for the Twelfth Time' – J.L.], *Głos Wielkopolski* [*Voice of Wielkopolska*], posted: 9/09/2019, https://gloswielkopolski.pl/poznan-spotkanie-z-ukraina-czyli-bliscy-nieznajomi-w-teatrze-polskim-po-raz-dwunasty/ar/c13-14402821, last accessed: 7/12/2023.

Głowacka A. (2023), 'Teatr, który ocala' ['A theatre that saves' – J.L.], *Czas Kultury* [*Time of Culture* quarterly – J.L.], no. 5, https://czaskultury.pl/artykul/teatr-ktory-ocala/, last accessed: 12/01/2024.

GUS (2011), *Small Statistical Yearbook of Poland*, Central Statistical Office, Warsaw.

Harbuziuk M. (2017), 'Scena a przedstawienie traumy historycznej: dramaty/spektakle, twórcy/odbiorcy' ['The stage and representation of historical trauma: Dramas/performances, creators/audience' – J.L.], *Miscellanea Posttotalitariana Wratislaviensia*, no. 6.

Hołowninenko A. (2017), 'Кінець удавання: мапи ідентичності українського (a) театру' 'End of Pretence: Maps of Identity in Ukrainian Theatre' – J.L.], Театральний Портал (Portal Teatralny; Theatre Portal), posted: 4/03/2017, https://teatre.com.ua/modern/inets-udavannja-mapy-identychnosti-ukrajnskogo-a-teatru/, last accessed: 30/08/2023.

Irmer T. (2023), 'Leichensäcke mit Leichtigkeit', Theater der Zeit, https://tdz.de/artikel/f9bcedfb-ab10-4c5d-ada5-151a8ff8f455, last accessed: 3/01/2024.

Izdebska N. (2022), 'Як ви? *Jak u Was?* Najnowszy spektakl Kamila Wawrzuty /recenzja/' [review of Kamil Wawrzuta's latest performance Як ви? *Jak u Was?* – J.L.], https://kmag.pl/article/jak-u-was-najnowszy-spektakl-kamila-wawrzuty-recenzja, last accessed: 15/07/2023.

Karow J. (2022), 'Sztuka i lęk' ['Art and fear' – J.L.], e-teatr.pl, posted: 1/07/2022, https://e-teatr.pl/sztuka-i-lek-27327, last accessed: 12/12/2022.

Kazimierczak S. (2022), 'Zamknąć niebo' ['To close the sky' J.L.], *Teatr* [*Theatre* – J.L.], no. 4.

Kaźmierska M. (2016), 'Andrzej Pakuła, reżyser spektaklu o uchodźcach: Na "obcego" można zwalić wszystko' ('Andrzej Pakuła, director of the play about refugees: You can blame everything on the "other"'), *Gazeta Wyborcza. Magazyn Poznański* (The Poznań supplement of the *Gazeta Wyborcza* Daily), posted: 25/11/2016, http://poznan.wyborcza.pl/poznan/1,105531,21027040,andrzej-pakula-rezyser-spektaklu-o-uchodzcach-na-obcego.html, last accessed: 25/08/2023.

KMAG (2022), '*Jak u Was?* Najnowszy spektakl Kamila Wawrzuty' ['*How are you?* The latest performance by Kamil Wawrzuta' – J.L.], https://kmag.pl/article/jak-u-was-najnowszy-spektakl-kamila-wawrzuty-recenzja, last accessed: 16/12/2022.

Kobroń A. (2020), 'Diabły, reż. Agnieszka Błońska' ['*Devils*, directed by Agnieszka Błońska' – J.L.], Afisz Teatralny [Theatrical Poster – J.L.], http://www.afiszteatralny.pl/2020/02/diaby-rez-agnieszka-bonska.html, last accessed: 18/09/2023.

Korzeniowska-Bihun A. (2018), 'Krajobraz po bitwie' ['Landscape after the battle' – J.L.], *Teatr* [*Theatre* – J.L.], no. 1, https://teatr-pismo.pl/6459-krajobraz-po-bitwie/, last accessed: 5/10/2023.

Korzeniowska-Bihun A., Moskwin A. (2015), *Nowy dramat ukraiński*, vol. 1: *W ocze-kiwaniu na Majdan* [*New Ukrainian Drama*, vol. 1: *Waiting for Maidan* – J.L.], Wydawnictwa Uniwersytetu Warszawskiego, Warszawa.

Kosiński D. (2017), 'Nie ma ucieczki' ['There's no escape' – J.L.], The *Tygodnik Powszechny* Weekly, no. 26.

Kruszyńska A. (2022), 'Mariusz Treliński: opera milknie w takich momentach' ['Mariusz Treliński: The opera falls silent in such moments' – J.L.], Dzieje.pl, posted: 2/03/2022, https://dzieje.pl/kultura-i-sztuka/mariusz-trelinski-opera-milknie-w--takich-momentach, last accessed: 18/09/2022.

Kuligowski W. (2019), 'Żeby się nie bać. Praktyki artystyczne na rzecz uchodźców w Polsce' ('So as not to be afraid: Artistic practices for refugees in Poland'), *Media, Kultura, Społeczeństwo* (*Media, Culture, Society* – J.L.), no. 14.

Kulturalny Cham (2023), 'Nasi-Wasi-Wasi-Nasi – *Mój Sztandar Zasikał Kotek. Kroniki z Donbasu* – TR Warszawa' ['Ours-Yours-Ours-Yours – "A Kitten Peed on My Banner: Chronicles of Donbas" – TR Warszawa' – J.L.], posted: 14/05/2023, https://kulturalnycham.com.pl/aktualne/nasi-wasi-wasi-nasi-moj-sztandar-zasikal-kotek-kroniki-z-donbasu-tr-warszawa/, last accessed: 11/11/2023.

Łozińska O. (2022), 'Warszawa. Holland: jestem za bojkotem kultury rosyjskiej' ['Warsaw. Holland: I'm in favour of the Russian culture boycott' – J.L.], e-teatr. pl, posted: 8/04/2022, https://e-teatr.pl/warszawa-holland-jestem-za-bojkotem-kultury-rosyjskiej-24217, last accessed: 10/12/2022.

Majcherek W. (2022), *Laboratorium Dramatu* [conversation with Oksana Cherkashyna and Anna Korzeniowska-Bihun about Natalia Blok's 'Skin Deep', as part of the Theatre Lab series – J.L.], https://www.youtube.com/watch?v=7Ayt2y4mdhU, last accessed: 25/11/2022.

Majmurek J. (2017), 'Nie można dłużej dyskutować o kulturze z apolitycznych pozycji. Rozmowa z Pawłem Wodzińskim i Bartoszem Frąckowiakiem' ['It is no longer possible to discuss culture from apolitical positions: A conversation with Paweł Wodziński and Bartosz Frąckowiak' – J.L.], *Krytyka Polityczna*, posted: 23/10/2017, https://krytykapolityczna.pl/kultura/teatr/jakub-majmurek-pawel-wodzinski--bartosz-frackowiak-wywiad/, last accessed: 18/09/2023.

Mapy strachu (2016), [*Maps of Fear* project – J.L.], project information, https://instytutpolski.pl/kyiv/2016/07/13/проект-мапи-страху-мапи-ідентичності/, last accessed: 26/09/2023.

Marks P. (2023), 'Theater at the edge of war: Laughs, brutal truths and a Zelensky spoof', *The Washington Post*, posted: 6/01/2023, https://www.washingtonpost.com/theater-dance/2023/01/06/zelensky-play-festival-ukraine-poland/, last accessed: 12/01/2024.

Martiniello M. (2006), 'Towards a coherent approach to immigrant integration policy(ies) in the European Union. Intensive Programme', *Theories of International Migration*, Liège, Liège University, http://www.oecd.org/dev/38295165.pdf, last accessed: 26/11/2022.

Martiniello M. (2019), 'Introduction to the special issue "Arts and Refugees: Multidisciplinary Perspectives"', *Arts and Refugees Multidisciplinary Perspectives*, no. 8(3).

Miłkowski T. (2022), '*Nastia*, czyli uczta okrucieństwa' ['"Nastya" – a cruelty feast' – J.L.], *Przegląd* [*Review* – J.L.], no. 21, posted: 16/05/2022.

Miłkowski T. (2023), 'Ukraiński wariograf' ['Ukrainian polygraph' – J.L.], *Trybuna*, posted: 11/05/2023, https://trybuna.info/kultura/ukrainski-wariograf/, last accessed: 12/05/2023.

Moczulski M. (2022), 'Post od rosyjskiej kultury. Ukraińska odradza się w wojnie' ['Abstention from Russian culture: Ukrainian culture is being reborn in war' – J.L.], *Gazeta Krakowska*, no. 70, posted: 25/03/2022.

moż (2022), 'TAK dla (s)POKOJU. Aktorzy łączą siły, wspierają Ukrainę i czytają *Matkę*' ['Yes for peace: Actors combine forces, support Ukraine and read Witkacy's "Mother"' – J.L.], *The Gazeta Wyborcza. Białystok*, posted: 28/03/2022, https://bialystok.wyborcza.pl/bialystok/7,35241,28272053,tak-dla-s-pokoju-aktorzy-lacza-sily-wspieraja-ukraine-i-czytaja.html, last accessed: 21/01/2023.

Mrozek W. (2021), 'TVP szkalowała, warszawski ratusz zlikwidował. Koniec instytucji kultury otwartej na migrantów' ('Polish National TV criticised, Warsaw City Hall dissolved: The end of a cultural institution open to migrants'), *Gazeta Wyborcza* [*The Gazeta Wyborcza Daily*], no. 331, posted: 19/11/2021.

Mrozek W. (2022a), 'Czy polskie teatry przyjmą Ukraińców? Artyści apelują: Podzielmy się pieniędzmi' ['Will Polish theatres take in Ukrainians? Artists appeal: Let's share the money' – J.L.], *Gazeta Wyborcza* [*The Gazeta Wyborcza Daily*], no. 47, posted: 26/02/2022.

Mrozek W. (2022), 'Ukraińska aktorka w Polsce: "Nie wiem co zrobię, jeśli wybuchnie wojna"' ['A Ukrainian actress in Poland: "I don't know what I'll do if the war breaks out"' – J.L.], *The Gazeta Wyborcza Daily*, https://wyborcza.pl/7,75410,27958590,nie-boje-sie-konfliktu-ukrainska-aktorka-o-pracy-w-polsce.html, last accessed: 6/12/2022.

Nestorowich J. (2016), 'Parada odważnych' ('Парад сміливців', 'Parade of the Brave' – J.L.), *Zbruč*, https://zbruc.eu/node/52562, 09/06/2016, last accessed: 12/09/2023.

Nowacka-Goik M. (2022), 'Ukraińskie aktorki krzyczą ze sceny. To też walka, głos Ukrainy. Artystyczna bitwa trwa' ['Ukrainian actresses scream from the stage. It is also a struggle, the voice of Ukraine: The artistic battle continues' – J.L.], *Dziennik Zachodni*, posted: 6/08/2022, https://dziennikzachodni.pl/ukrainskie-aktorki-krzycza-ze-sceny-to-tez-walka-glos-ukrainy-artystyczna-bitwa-trwa/ar/c6-16547919, last accessed: 12/01/2023.

Odziomek M. (2022), 'Co robią kobiety podczas wojny? Wkrótce premiera spektaklu ukraińskich artystek *5:00. UA* w Teatrze Śląskim' ['What do women do during war? Coming soon the premiere of the Ukrainian female artists' play "5.00 UA" at the Silesian Theatre" – J.L.], *The Gazeta Wyborcza. Katowice*, posted: 8/06/2022, https://katowice.wyborcza.pl/katowice/7,35018,28555808,co-robia-kobiety-podczas-wojny-wkrotce-premiera-spektaklu-ukrainskich.html, last accessed: 15/12/2022.

Orędzie Polskiego Ośrodka Międzynarodowego Instytutu Teatralnego ITI na Międzynarodowy Dzień Teatru [Message of the Polish Center of the ITI International Theatre Institute for International Theatre Day] (2022), https://www.instytut-teatralny.pl/2022/03/25/oredzie-polskiego-osrodka-miedzy-narodowego-instytutu-teatralnego-iti-na-miedzynarodowy-dzien-teatru/, last accessed: 14/08/2023.

Piotrowska A. (2022), 'Rosja przestała dla mnie istnieć' ['For me Russia ceased to exist' – J.L.], *ZAiKS. Teatr*, posted: 4/05/2022, https://zaiks.org.pl/artykuly/2022/maj/rosja-przestala-dla-mnie-istniec-rozmowa-z-sasza-denisowa, last accessed: 10/01/2023.

Polish Theatre in Bydgoszcz (2023), Press materials related to the play *Buka*, https://www.teatrpolski.pl/buka.html, last accessed: 28/12/2023.

Portiernia wersja druga (2022) [*The Porter's Lodge: Second Version* – J.L.], https://www.klamra.umk.pl/teatr-osmego-dnia-portiernia/, last accessed: 8/08/2023.

Premiere of *ЯК ВИ? Jak u Was?* (2022), e-teatr.pl, posted: 23/04/2022, https://e-teatr.pl/warszawa-premiera-b-jak-u-was-i-wystawa-fotografii-w-teatrze-druga-strefa-24675, last accessed: 3/07/2022.

Prykowska-Michalak K., Szymańska E. (2020), 'Teatr społeczny, interkulturowy, postmigrancki' ('Social, intercultural, post-migrant theatre'), *Pamiętnik Teatralny* (*Theatrical Memoir* – J.L.), no. 4.

Psychosis (2019), The show's website from the Polish Theatre in Poznan, https://teatr-polski.pl/wydarzenia/psychosis-%D0%BF%D1%81%D0%B8%D1%85%D0%BE%D0%B7/, last accessed: 24/08/2023.

Radio Mariia (2022), The performance's description from the Powszechny Theatre's website, https://www.powszechny.com/spektakle/radio-mariia,s1889.html, last accessed: 14/10/2023.

Restaurant Ukraine (*Ресторан Україна*) (2019), The show's website from the Polish Theatre in Poznan, https://teatr-polski.pl/wydarzenia/restauracja-ukraina-%D1%80%D0%B5%D1%81%D1%82%D0%BE%D1%80%D0%B0%D0%BD-%D1%83%D0%BA%D1%80%D0%B0%D1%97%D0%BD%D0%B0/, last accessed: 15/07/2023.

Rigamonti M. (2022a), 'Czerkaszyna: Mam prawo nienawidzić' [Rigamonti's interview with Oksana Cherkashyna: 'I have the right to hate' – J.L.], *Gazeta Prawna* Daily, posted: 4/03/2022.

Rigamonti M. (2022b), 'Switłana Oleszko: Rosyjska sztuka to ich broń, która zawsze szła przed czołgami' [Rigamonti's interview with Svitlana Oleshko: 'Russian art is their weapon, which always preceded the tanks' – J.L.], *Gazeta Prawna* Daily, posted: 13/05/2022.

sk (2022), 'Rezydencje rozszerzone dla Ukraińców' ['Artists in residence programmes extended to Ukrainians' – J.L.], *Gazeta Polska Daily*, no. 51, posted: 15/03/2022.

sk, mc (2015), 'Jarosław Kaczyński boi się, że uchodźcy sprowadzą zarazę? Tak mówił na wyborczym wiecu' ['Jaroslaw Kaczynski is afraid that refugees will bring the plague? That's what he said at an election rally' – J.L.], *The Gazeta Wyborcza*, no. 239, posted 13/10/2015.

Słojewska I. (2023), 'Monodram na dwa głosy' ['Monodrama for two voices' – J.L.], *Dziennik Teatralny* [*Theatre Journal* – J.L.], posted: 29/11/2023, http://www.dziennikteatralny.pl/artykuly/monodram-na-dwa-glosy.html, last accessed: 17/12/2023.

Sosnowska D. (2018), 'Teatr krytyczny, wojna i przypadłość' ['Critical theatre, war and affliction' – J.L.], *Didaskalia*, no. 143.

Soszyński P. (2017), 'Teatr za pięć hrywien. Rozmowa z Joanną Wichowską' ['Theatre for Five Hryvnias: A conversation with Joanna Wichowska' – J.L.], *Dwutygodnik. com*, https://www.dwutygodnik.com/artykul/7450-teatr-za-piec-hrywien.html, last accessed: 9/09/2023.

Stern A. (2020), *Teatr dla wszystkich* [*Theatre for everyone* – J.L.], http://miroslawwlekly. pl/lwow-nie-oddamy/, last accessed: 12/12/2023.

Sting W. (2010), 'Interkulturalität und Migration im Theater' [Interculturality and Migration in Theater], [in:] *Irritation und Vermittlung. Theater in einer interkulturellen und multireligiösen Gesellschaft [Irritation and mediation. Theater in an intercultural and multireligious society]*, ed. by W. Sting, N. Köhler, K. Hoffmann, W. Weiße, D. Grießbach, Lit Verlag, Berlin.

Strefa WolnoSłowa's Facebook profile, https://www.facebook.com/StrefaWolnoSlowa/, last accessed: 16/06/2022.

Strefa WolnoSłowa's Manifesto, https://strefawolnoslowa.pl/o-nas/, last accessed: 15/09/2023.

Tarasińska J. (2023), 'Wojna oczami Oleny Apczel' ['War through Olena Apchel's eyes' – J.L.], *Performer*, no. 25, posted: 10/07/2023, https://grotowski.net/performer/ wojna-oczami-oleny-apczel-0, last accessed: 26/08/2023.

Teatr Powszechny, teatr, który się wtrąca, O co się zabijać? Wojna. Pokój. Ukraina [*The Powszechny Theatre, a theatre that gets in the way: What are we killing each other for? War. Peace. Ukraine* – J.L.] (2023), https://e-teatr.pl/warszawa-o-co-sie-zabijac-wojna-pokoj-ukraina-w-powszechnym-a187134, last accessed: 9/09/2023.

Teatr wobec kryzysu konstytucji i praw człowieka w Polsce [*Theatre in the face of the crisis of the constitution and human rights in Poland*] (2022), https://nno.pl/teatr-wobec-kryzysu-konstytucji-i-praw-czlowieka-w-polsce/, last accessed: 13.12.2022.

The Ghent Manifesto (2018), https://www.ntgent.be/en/wie-zijn-we/the-ghent-manifesto----mission/manifest-missie, last accessed: 17/11/2023.

Tomasiewicz A. (2020), 'To nie o panu' ['It's not about you, Sir' – J.L.], *Teatr*, no. 1, https://teatr-pismo.pl/7501-to-nic-o-panu/, last accessed: 10/12/2023.

Totah R., Khoury K. (2019), 'Theatre Against Borders: "Miunikh–Damaskus" – A Case Study in Solidarity', [in:] *Arts and Refugees, Multidisciplinary Perspectives*, ed. by M. Martiniello, Multidisciplinary Digital Publishing Institute, Basel.

Umięcka A. (2019), 'Sztuka o tym, co "pomiędzy". Więzi Oleny Apchel w Teatrze Wybrzeże od 6 stycznia ['The play about what's "in-between": "Bonds" by Olena Apchel at the Wybrzeże Theatre from January 6th – J.L.], Oficjalny Portal Miasta Gdańska [official website of the city of Gdańsk – J.L.], posted: 5/01/2019, https:// www.gdansk.pl/wiadomosci/Sztuka-o-tym-co-pomiedzy-Wiezi-Oleny-Apczel-w-Teatrze-Wybrzeze-od-niedzieli-6-stycznia,a,135058, last accessed: 2/09/2023.

Website of the 27th International Shakespeare Festival, https://teatrszekspirowski. pl/event/27-miedzynarodowy-festiwal-szekspirowski/, last accessed: 5/10/2023.

Wichowska J. (2014), 'Dość bohaterów. Potrzebny jest człowiek"' ['Enough heroes, a man is needed' – J.L.], Dwutygodnik.com, https://www.dwutygodnik. com/artykul/5332-dosc-bohaterow-potrzebny-jest-czlowiek.html, last accessed: 28/08/2023.

Wichowska J. (2021), 'Kierunek Wschód' ['Direction: East' – J.L.], kulturapoznań.pl, https://kultura.poznan.pl/mim/kultura/news/spektakle,c,4/kierunek-wschod,169794. html, last accessed: 2/09/2023.

Wiśniewski M., Hansen K., Bilewicz M., Soral W., Świderska A., Bulska D. (2016), *Mowa nienawiści, mowa pogardy. Raport z badania przemocy werbalnej wobec grup mniejszościowych* (*Hate Speech, Speech of Contempt: Report on the Study of Verbal Violence Against Minority Groups* – J.L.), The Stefan Batory Foundation, Warsaw.

Wyszomirska A. (2022), 'Kulturalne sankcje' ['Cultural sanctions' – J.L.], *Idziemy* [*We're going* – J.L.], no. 12.

APPENDIX

Profiles of selected Ukrainian theatrical artists, directors and playwrights associated with Polish theatre after 2014

Apchel Olena (born 1986) has a Ph.D. in Philosophy. She's an artist, director, performer, teacher, curator, playwright, screenwriter, artistic manager and cultural studies scholar. She is also a member of the Union of Theatre Artists and of the non-governmental organisation SEMA Ukraine. Apchel has authored numerous academic papers dedicated to the study of contemporary theatre, especially documentary, performative, and critical art. Additionally, she delivers lectures on theatre and performance art, on top of conducting masterclasses in directing, acting skills, stage movement and performative stage presence. In her curatorial practice, she explores horizontal systems of existence and management within cultural institutions. In her directorial work, Apchel primarily delves into themes such as intergenerational heritage, personal and historical trauma and social violence. She does so through critical art as well as through post-documentary and post-dramatic art, which she uses as a tool to design alternative realities.

2008–2011 – Co-organised the non-state theatre festival *Kurbalesia* in Kharkiv.

2010–2015 – Taught at the Kharkiv State Academy of Culture, focusing on theatre arts and directing.

2014 – Founded the School of Acting and Performing Arts *TESTO* in Kharkiv.

2017 – Co-founded (with Artem Vusyk) the independent amateur professional theatre Teatr Bardzo Znany (Very Well-Known Theatre) in Kharkiv.

2017–2019 – Held the position of Chief Director at the Lesya Ukrainka Lviv Academic Drama Theatre.

2019–2020 – Co-authored the main exhibition concept of the First Barrack at the Museum of Memory of Totalitarian Regimes *Territory of Terror* in Lviv.

2019–2020 – Directed and curated at the Kyiv Academic Theatre Golden Gate.

2020–2021 – Lane Kirkland International Scholarship Programme Fellow. Completed a two-semester study and internship at the University of Warsaw and the Aleksander Zelwerowicz National Academy of Dramatic Art in Warsaw, defending her second doctoral dissertation, focused on social and accompanying programmes for critical and political theatres.
2021–2022 – Served as the Head of the Department of Social Projects at the International Culture Centre New Theatre (Nowy Teatr), located in Warsaw, Poland.
2022–2023 – Held the position of co-director of the Theatertreffen Festival at the Berliner Festspiele.

Arie Pavlo (born 1977) is a Ukrainian playwright, conceptual artist, theatre activist and one of the curators of the inaugural Ukrainian Festival of Contemporary Drama Drama.UA. He lives and works in Lviv and Berlin. Arie represents the new generation of Ukrainian playwrights who break away from Russian models of Ukrainian drama and traditional local folklore. In his plays, translated into Slovenian, Czech, German, English, Polish and French, he explores contemporary themes, such as the complexities of national identity within Ukrainian society.

Armianovsky Piotr (born 1985) is a performer and director who holds an MSc in Computer Science. He is also a co-founder of the Pic Pic group. His studies in theatre and performance art took him to Kyiv, Lviv and Moscow, where he engaged in programmes such as the *School of Performance* by Janusz Bałdyga and *Artist is Present* by Marina Abramović. With the onset of conflict in his hometown, Armianovsky shifted his focus to documentary work. Currently based in Kyiv, he actively participates in projects and exhibitions across Ukraine, Poland, Hungary, France and Spain.

Barbara Mykhailo (born 1971 – died 2021) was a Ukrainian artist with diverse talents, including singing, composing, poetry, acting and translation. Born in Lviv in 1971, he graduated from theatre studies and actively engaged in cultural activities. In 1989, he co-founded and served as the vocalist of the renowned Ukrainian rock band *Martwy Kogut* (*A Dead Rooster*), known for blending poetic lyrics with contemporary music. He performed concerts and advocated for the development of original native creativity, challenging the historical dominance of Russian culture. He learned Polish in his youth, mainly by listening to broadcasts on Programme III of the Polish Radio. In 2001, he relocated to Kharkiv, where he joined the experimental Arabesky Theatre ensemble as an actor. The theatre was founded in 1993 by Svitlana Oleshko, who later became Barbara's partner in both artistic and personal endeavours. Mykhailo Barbara tragically passed away on October 11th, 2021, at the age of 49. He was posthumously honoured with the prestigious S.I. Witkiewicz Award by the Polish Centre of the International Theatre Institute (ITI) on March 27th, 2022, World Theatre Day. This award recognises foreigners who have significantly contributed to promoting Polish theatre globally. The prize was awarded to Mykhailo Barbara by the jury, who were unaware of his death at the time of making their decision.

Belikova Daria (born in 1997) is both a contemporary ballet dancer and a modern dance teacher. She graduated from Dnipro Polytechnic University with a specialisation in auditing and taxation. She served as the head of the modern choreography and dance gymnastics workshop *Inspiration* from 2015 to 2018. Additionally, she performed as a prima ballerina at the Lesya Ukrainka Theatre in Kamianske in 2018 and worked as a classical dance teacher from 2020 to 2021. Currently, she leads the modern choreography studio *Dance Time*. Her expertise lies in modern dance, modern-jazz, pop dance, jazz funk, high heels, vogue dance and dancehall/reggaeton.

Brama Sashko (born in 1988) is an independent theatre actor, playwright and director from Lviv, known for his involvement in experimental and exploratory documentary theatre who collaborates with various theatres both in Ukraine and internationally. He is a playwright, director and performance activist who creates, as he describes it, experimental theatre based on documentary material. His projects delve into challenging and often controversial subjects. If independent theatre were of concern to any official Ukrainian decision-makers, his works would likely provoke significant scandals. Nonetheless, while there haven't been any scandals, there's certainly been a buzz within the artistic community. For instance, his documentary play *Diploma*, which sheds light on the pathological dynamics within Ukrainian universities, has stirred up considerable emotions. Sashko Brama based it on over two hundred interviews with students, graduates, and parents. Equally impactful, though less labour-intensive, was his play *Pork Liver*, recognised in Poland through its inclusion in the anthology *New Ukrainian Drama: Waiting for Maidan*. Brama's serendipitous encounter with an Afghanistan war veteran served as inspiration for his play. Consequently, well before the current Russo-Ukrainian conflict, *Pork Liver's* narrative unveiled a disturbing tale of military violence, humiliation, privacy infringements and moral quandaries.

Cherkashyna Oksana (born in 1988) is a Ukrainian theatre and film actress, a two-time winner of the *Kinocolo* award: in 2020 for her role in Natalia Vorozhbyt's film *Bad Roads*, which premiered at the Venice Film Festival in the Film Critics' Week section, and in 2022 for the lead role in Marina Er's film *Klondike*. As a theatre actress, she works at the Kyiv Theatre on the Left Bank of the Dnieper as well as at the National Theatre in Warsaw and (as a guest) TR Warszawa. Since 2013 she has also collaborated with the popular Kharkiv theatre Beautiful Flowers. She has participated in numerous European theatre residencies and co-productions in Poland, Germany, Italy and Greece. In 2019 she won the most important theatre awards in Poland, including the 2nd prize for Best Actress at the Divine Comedy Festival in Krakow and the Main Actor Award at the National Contest of Contemporary Art. She was also listed among the 50 bravest women in Poland, alongside Agnieszka Holland and Olga Tokarczuk.

Denisova Sasha (born 1974) is a Ukrainian playwright, director, novelist and screenwriter. She graduated from the Faculty of Philology at Kyiv Shevchenko University and the Moscow Art Theatre School and Meyerhold Centre. Additionally, she studied dramaturgy at the Royal Court Theatre's workshop. With over 25 performances to her credit, primarily in Moscow, Russia, she has also showcased her work in Germany (Schaubühne), Poland (TR Warszawa) and Mexico (Babel Theatre). From 2011 to 2014 Denisova served as Deputy Artistic Director of the Mayakovsky Theatre in Moscow, and since 2014, she has been the Chief Playwright at the Meyerhold Centre, also in Moscow. Denisova's involvement with documentary theatre dates back to 2009, during which she authored over 30 documentary plays. She completed internships at the British Theatre Royal Court and the Edinburgh Theatre Festival. Since 2010 Denisova has been a playwright and director at the renowned Teatr.doc in Moscow. Known for her experimental approach that blends documentary theatre with phantasmagoria and the grotesque, Denisova has created notable performances such as *Light My Fire*, winner of the Golden Mask (2012), which delved into the aspirations of Soviet children inspired by Jim Morrison. Among her other works is *Hotel California* (2016, at the Meyerhold Centre), exploring the 1967–1969 protests against the Vietnam War in the USA, and *Harry on Fire* (2020), where the aged heroes of the Potteriana navigate Putin's totalitarian state, aiming to change it with magic. Following the outbreak of the war in Ukraine on February 24th, 2022, Denisova fled from Russia to Warsaw. In Poland, she produced the documentary performance *Six Ribs of Anger* (*Шість ребер гніву/Sześć żeber gniewu*), a unique Polish-Ukrainian project depicting the war and refugee life through the experiences of five Ukrainian women from Mariupol, Bucha, Kyiv, Chernigov and Dnipro, featuring Ukrainian actors, including AR-ENSH Resident Aleksey Yudnikov.

Doliak Zhenia – Ukrainian actress, graduate of the I.K. Karpenko-Kary National University of Theatre, Film and Television in Kyiv. Since 2020, she has been an actress at the Vasyl S. Vasylka Ukrainian Academic Musical and Dramatic Theatre in Odesa. She has performed in, among others, the play *Demons* based on the play by Natalia Vorozhbyt (Lidka), the staging of Horace McCoy's novel *Doesn't Horses Get Whacked?* (Ruby), *Pippi Longstocking*, staged by Lena Lagushonkova (Pippi), and in *Sorochin Fair*, based on Nikolai Gogol, directed by Konstantin Pivovarov. In 2022 she became a resident of the Polish Theatre in Bydgoszcz. She was nominated in the 'best actress' category by the prestigious *Theater heute* magazine. German-speaking critics appreciated her for the role of Zhenya in Lena Lagushonkova's play *Gorky's Mother* on the stage of Schauspiel Stuttgart.

Duda Tamara (born 1976) is a Ukrainian journalist and translator, author of two novels published under the pseudonym Tamara Horicha Zernia. Between 2014 and 2016 she worked as a volunteer in the war zone in eastern Ukraine. Her debut *Daughter* earned Duda the prestigious award of the BBC's Ukrainian editorial office for the best fiction book of 2019. The novel was also among the thirty most important prose works of independent Ukraine, according to the Ukrainian Book Institute. In 2022 Duda received the most important Ukrainian cultural award named after Taras Shevchenko.

Dzhuhostranska Yelyzaveta is an actress and choreographer, a graduate of the Kharkiv Academy of Culture. She has played leading roles in films such as *The Circle* (2022), *Interview* (2021) and *For Her* (2021). Additionally, she has appeared in theatrical productions including *Madrigal* at the Kharkiv Theatre and *Love is...* at the Kiev ProEnglish Theatre.

Ilnytska Lubov is a theatre expert, curator and manager of theatre projects. She graduated from Ivan Franko National University of Lviv. Since 2019 she has been serving as the manager of the Harald Binder Cultural Enterprises' Grant Programme. Between 2013 and 2019 she was in charge of the literary-dramatic department of the Les Kurbas Lviv Academic Theatre. From 2016 to 2020, she served as a lecturer at the Department of Theatre Studies and Acting at Ivan Franko National University of Lviv. She was behind the Polish-Ukrainian performative project *Maps of Fear/Maps of Identity* and the play *My Grandfather Dug. My Father Dug. And I Won't Dig* by Dmytro Levytskyi, Joanna Wichowska, Agnieszka Błońska and Roza Sarkisian (2016). Additionally, she served as a co-curator of the socio-theatrical project *Voices of the Neighborhood: On Choice* in 2018, alongside Iryna Harets and Roza

Sarkisian. Her research focuses on contemporary critical theatre in Ukraine and performative practices in theatre.

Jasinska Maria is involved in theatre journalism, documentary work and theatrical projects. She has collaborated with the Ukrainian Dakh Theatre, the International Festival of Contemporary Art GOGOLFEST in Kyiv, the Les Kurbas National Centre for Theatre Arts in Kyiv, the Artistic and Educational Center 'Maisternia pisni' in Lviv and Wrocław as well as international festivals like the *Week of Contemporary Dramaturgy* and *Drama: UA*. She curates Polish-Ukrainian projects. Since 2020 she has been collaborating with director Sashko Brama on the *Autumn on Pluto 2.0* project, focusing on research and fieldwork.

Khyzhna Nina is an actress, performer, choreographer and participant in many independent performative projects. She is a graduate of the Acting Department of the I.P. Kotlyarevsky Kharkiv State University of Arts. She has worked in various theatres in Kharkiv, such as the Vinora Studio Theatre, the State Academic Shevchenko Drama Theatre, the State Theatre for Children and Youth, and the Neft Theatre (ТЕАТР НЕФТЬ). Additionally, she teaches at the *TECTO* School of Acting Art (Школа актерского мастерства *TECTO*). She has also collaborated with Polish theatres, including providing choreography for the play *Devils* directed by Agnieszka Błońska at the National Theatre in Warsaw.

Kurochkin Maxim (born 1970) is a playwright and historian specialising in the archaeology of Kievan Rus. He pursued external studies in the History Department of Taras Shevchenko Kyiv University before continuing his education at the Gorky Literary Institute in Moscow, focusing on drama from 1995 to 1999. From 1990 to 1993, he worked at the Institute of Archaeology at the National Academy of Sciences of Ukraine. Kurochkin has been actively involved in various theatrical projects, serving as a member of the organising committee of the Festival of Young Drama and the Documentary Theatre project. In 1995, his plays *Askoldov Dir* and *Fighter-class Medea* were presented at the Festival of Young Drama in Lyubimovka. Between 1996 and 1998 Kurochkin worked at the Debut Centre at the House of Actor in Moscow. His notable works include *Vodka. Fucking. TV*, staged by Georg Genoux at the Theatre of the Displaced in Kiev (2017); *Titus The Irreproachable*, directed by Vladimir Mirzoev at the Moscow State Academic Chamber Musical Theatre (2015); *Switch*, directed by Dmitry Brusnikin at Teatr.doc (2014); *Dulcey and Roxy at City Hall*, directed by Graham Schmidt at The Breaking String Theatre (2014); *The Schooling of Bento Bonchev*, directed by Mikhail

Ugarov at the Centre of Drama and Directing Moscow (2010); *Steel Will*, directed by Dmytro Bogomazov at the Kyiv Academic Young Theatre (2001); and *Kitchen*, directed by Oleg Menshikov at the 814 Theatrical Association in Moscow (2000).

Levytskyi Dmytro (born 1986) is a Ukrainian playwright, director and conceptual artist. He graduated from Khmelnytskyi National University and The School of Dramatic Art in Moscow. He is a co-founder of the Pic Pic group, known for producing interactive audio tours. Levytskyi's interests revolve around urban space, exploring its social, economic and historical aspects. He wrote the script for the acclaimed Ukrainian play *Restoran Ukraina* (*Restaurant Ukraine*) (2017), co-produced by the Goethe-Institut, tackling the theme of corruption.

Liahushonkova Lena (born 1984) hails from the town of Stanitsa Luhanska in Ukraine. She holds a degree from the History Department at Luhansk Taras Shevchenko National University. Even in her childhood, she made attempts at writing poetry and prose, although she later discarded all of her early work. Her debut as a playwright came in 2018 with the play *BAZA* (*The Base*), delving into themes of women and prostitution, premiered during the Week of Contemporary Art festival (Тиждень актуальной пьесы). Liahushonkova collaborates with various Ukrainian theatres, including the Young Theatre, PostPlay Theatre and the Playwrights' Theatre. Since 2022 she has served as a resident playwright at the Polish Theatre in Bydgoszcz. She has actively participated in workshops and laboratories organised by the National Association of Theatre Activists of Ukraine. Liahushonkova has been recognised as a winner in competitions such as the aforementioned Week of Contemporary Art (Тиждень актуальной пьесы) and Drama.UA. To date, she has authored 8 plays. Her work *Chapaev and Vasilisa*, exploring themes of decommunisation and teenage violence, was staged at the Berezil Theatre in Kharkiv. Additionally, Liahushonkova has undertaken adaptations of texts by Bjorges, Bulgakov, Shakespeare and Marquez for theatres in Kyiv and other Ukrainian cities. In Poland, her plays *Mother of Gorky*, *A Kitten Peed on My Banner*, and *The Order of Made Beds* have been successfully staged. Notably, she was awarded the prestigious European New Talent Drama Award by Schauspiel Stuttgart in 2022. Furthermore, in 2021, she received recognition at the Bydgoszcz Dramaturgy Festival *Aurora* for her play *Mother of Gorky*.

Lozova Maria (born 1996) is a dancer and choreographer from Kharkiv. A graduate of the Academy of Culture in Kharkiv, she collaborates with en Casa, Festival Les Nuits Blanches, ParadeFest, Festival of Young Ukrainian Artists and others.

Nezhdana Neda (born 1971) – poet, playwright and journalist. Head of the Ukrainian committee of the international network *Eurodrama* (France), patron of Ukraine at the New European Plays biennial in Wiesbaden (Germany). Since 2001, a researcher at the Center for Theatre Arts named after Les Kurbas, curator of drama projects, defended her doctoral dissertation on *The structural role of myth in contemporary Ukrainian drama*. She has more than 20 scientific publications and more than 70 analytical publications in journals and books of Ukraine and abroad (Poland, France, Germany, Great Britain). One of the co-founders of the independent theatre and the MIST theatre school. Author of 25 dramas. Her plays have been translated into English, French, German, Polish, Russian, Armenian, Georgian, Bulgarian, Macedonian, Estonian, Serbian, Portuguese, Turkish and Kurdish. They were performed in: Ukraine, USA, Australia, Sweden, Germany, France, Portugal, Poland, Belarus, Russia, Armenia, Georgia, Estonia, Lithuania, Serbia, Macedonia, Kosovo, Iraq, Turkey, Kyrgyzstan and South Africa.

Oleshko Svitlana (born 1973) is a theatre producer as well as the founder and director of the Arabesky Theatre. She delves into the transformative power of theatre, infusing her work with a distinct social dimension. Holding a degree in philology from V.N. Karazin Kharkiv National University, she furthered her studies at the Academy of Performing Arts in the Netherlands and a school specialising in strategic management in Slovakia. Oleshko also completed an internship at the Polish Theatre Institute. From 1993 to 2019 she contributed as a researcher at the Literary Museum in Kharkiv. A dedicated cultural activist, she spearheaded the establishment of the Theatre Institute in Kharkiv. Collaborating with her ensemble, she has led numerous projects with social and rehabilitative aims, including initiatives involving incarcerated individuals and those with mobility limitations. Among her notable productions are *Post-Truth*, *Red Elvis*, *Aeneid* and *Radioshanson: Eight Tales of Yuriy Zoifer* (written by Serhiy Zhadan).

Penkova Kateryna (born 1983) graduated from the Kyiv State Academy of Variety Arts and Circus Arts with a focus on classical acting. She was a finalist in the 'I, II, III Drama Laboratory' at NSTDU and a member of the theatrical laboratory Young Playwright at the Molodyi Theatre and the PostPlay Fast Theatre School. Penkova won first prize in the international literary competition *Coronation of the Word* (2012) and was among the six laureates of the theatre competition organised by the Ukrainian Institute as part of the *Transmission.UA – Drama in Motion* programme with her text *Pork* (2020). Additionally, she regularly appeared on the shortlists of the *Drama. UA* festival, *The Week of Contemporary Arts*, and the Young Theatre Festival *Lyubimovka* (2020). Penkova is also a member of the artistic committee of the Playwrights' Theatre.

Sarkisian Roza (born 1987) is a Ukrainian theatre director originally from Kharkiv. She graduated from the directing department of Kharkiv's I.P. Kotliarevsky State University of Arts and from political sociology at Kharkiv's Karazin State University. She was the initiator, artistic director and director of Kharkiv's De Facto Theatre, active from 2012 to 2017. Her performances were shown at festivals such as: GogolFest in Kyiv, Urban Exploration Lviv Fest, GogolFest Start UP in Mariupol 2017, Desant.UA 2017 in Warsaw, ParadeFest 2018 in Kharkiv. In 2017–2019 she worked as the main director at the First Academic Ukrainian Theatre for Children and Youth in Lviv. In 2020–2021, she was a full-time director of the National Academic Drama and Music Theatre in Ivano-Frankivsk. Her plays pay special attention to themes of memory, identity, political manipulation, non-normativity and social oppression. Sarkisian's works are considered groundbreaking for the new Ukrainian theatre.

Skliarska Olha (born 1993 lives and works in Poznań) is a visual artist, specialising in ceramic art, performance art, concrete poetry and drawing. She studied at the School of Arts KASK in Ghent. She is a member of two artistic collectives: Zapora (PL/UA) and Zabih (UA). In her work she explores themes of memory, psychology, particularly sensitive groups and issues concerning public space. She has presented solo exhibitions and projects in cities including Lviv, Drohobych, Lublin and Poznań. Her works have also been exhibited in Berlin, Wrocław, Toruń and Brno.

Vasiukova Kateryna is an actress and a graduate of the Iwan Kotlarevsky National University of Arts in Kharkiv, completing her studies in 2017. After graduation, she joined the V.A. Afanasyev Kharkiv State Academic Puppet Theatre, where she performed in productions by Oksana Dimitrieva (*The Imaginary Invalid, Hamlet, The Steadfast Tin Soldier*). Since 2016 she has also been associated with the Kharkiv Publicist Theatre, appearing in plays by Konstantin Vasiukov (*Moby Dick, Sailing, Pro.log, The Dying Woman*). From 2018 she has been with the Neft Theatre in Kharkiv, starring in *Suffering at Goncharivka*, directed by Artem Vusyk. In 2019 she participated in the *European Ritual Management: Peace* international project in Nuremberg. In February 2022, upon arriving in Poland, she became a resident artist at

the Zagłębie Theatre in Sosnowiec and later secured a permanent acting position at the Śląski (Silesian) Theatre in Katowice.

Velcheva Alina (born in Odesa) is a modern dancer with ten years of experience. Prior to the invasion, she founded and worked in the Vertex Dance
Group in Odesa. She teaches both children and adults at beginner and professional levels

Vorozhbyt Natalia (born 1975) is a writer, playwright, director and screenwriter. She is widely recognised as one of Ukraine's most prominent literary figures, known for her contributions to the 'new drama' movement. Vorozhbyt's
accolades include the Women in Arts Award in 2020 and the Shevchenko
Award in 2022. She gained international acclaim for her film *Bad Roads*, based
on her novel of the same name, winning the top prize at the Venice Film Festival. From 2000 to 2010 Vorozhbyt lived and worked in Moscow, collaborating with esteemed institutions such as Theatre.doc, known for its opposition
to Putin's regime. Upon returning to Ukraine, she co-founded the Immigrant
Theatre with German director Georg Geno. This venture aimed to challenge
stereotypes perpetuated by Russian propaganda, particularly the notion of
Ukraine as divided between two nations, with an unbridgeable gap between
the Russian-speaking East and the Ukrainian-speaking West. The Immigrant
Theatre embarked on this mission from scratch. Vorozhbyt's plays have been
staged not only in Ukraine but also in Russia, Great Britain, Poland, the USA
and Latvia.

Zabuzhko Oksana (born 1960) is a writer, poet and essayist. Her works
have been translated into numerous languages. She has been honoured with
various domestic and international awards, including the National Prize of
Ukraine named after Taras Shevchenko (2019), the Antonovich International
Foundation Award (2008), the Central and Eastern European Literary Award
Angelus (2013), the All-Ukrainian Award *Woman of the Third Millennium*
(2015) and the BBC News Ukraine Book of the Year (2020). Zabuzhko holds
a doctorate in philosophy and focuses her writing on Ukrainian self-identifi-
cation, issues of post-imperial societies and feminism. She arrived in Poland
on February 23th, 2022, to promote her book *Wormwood Planet*. She was
compelled to remain in Poland due to the outbreak of the Russian invasion
against Ukraine.

Zakharova Nina, a theatre and film actress and choreographer, had prior en-
gagements at the Neft Theatre. Concurrently, she collaborated with the Beautiful Flowers stage, an independent group founded in 2011 by Kharkiv Uni-

versity of Arts alumni. After relocating to Poland, she became a resident artist at the Zagłębie Theatre in Sosnowiec and later attained a permanent acting role at the Śląski Theatre in Katowice.

Zhadan Serhiy (born 1974) – Ukrainian writer, translator, public figure, frontman of the bands *Zhadan and The Dogs* and *Mannerheim's Line*. Author of novels and numerous volumes of poetry. Serhiy Zhadan's literary works have not only received numerous national and international awards, but have also been translated into over twenty languages, making Zhadan one of the most famous contemporary Ukrainian writers. Serhiy Zhadan is also an active organiser of Ukrainian literary life and a participant in multimedia art projects. In 2017, he founded the Serhiy Zhadan Charity Foundation. On December 18th, 2019, the American PEN-club gave Zhadan their award for his book of poems *What We Live For, What We Die For*, which had been translated by theatre director Virlyana Tkach and American poet Wanda Phipps. In June 2022 Zhadan received the Peace Prize of the German Booksellers (German Friedenspreis des Deutschen Buchhandels) 'for outstanding creativity and humanitarian attitude with which he takes care of people during the war and helps them at the risk of his own life'.

INDEX

Managing editor
Zofia Sajdek

Language editor
Anna Kędroń

Proofreader
Małgorzata Denys

Typesetting
Wojciech Wojewoda

Jagiellonian University Press
Editorial Offices: Michałowskiego 9/2, 31-126 Kraków, Poland
Phone: +48 12 663 23 80

GPSR Authorized Representative: Easy Access System Europe, Mustamäe tee
50, 10621 Tallinn, Estonia, gpsr.requests@easproject.com

www.ingramcontent.com/pod-product-compliance
Lightning Source LLC
Chambersburg PA
CBHW072001260326
41914CB00004B/884